UNVEILING

11 Relationship Styles

Secrets Nobody Told You

AHMAD ALJAZEERI

Historical Figures and Examples

The book includes real historical figures or examples of living beings. These are only used as examples and do not constitute a significant portion of the book.

Extensive Research and Effort

We are proud to offer an enjoyable and seamless reading experience. This book, rich in multidisciplinary research and theories, results from extensive consultation of hundreds of references and thousands of hours dedicated to its production. All references are in the bibliography section at the end of the book. (Bibliography)

Health Disclaimer

This book is not intended as a substitute for professional medical, psychological, or therapeutic advice. The content is not intended to replace consultation with a licensed therapist or physician. All matters regarding your health require medical supervision. Neither the authors nor the publisher shall be liable for any loss or damage allegedly arising from any information or suggestion in this book.

Fair Use

This book is published with respect to the Fair Use Doctrine, which is especially relevant for educational and research purposes.

International Distribution

This book is distributed globally, so readers and users must adhere to applicable international copyright laws.

Contact Information

For further information, permissions, or inquiries, please visit our website at www.territie.com or email us at info@territie.com.

First published in New Zealand in 2024

E-Book ISBN: 978-1-0670002-0-2
Paperback (Black & White) ISBN: 978-1-0670002-6-4
Paperback (Standard Colored) ISBN: 978-1-0670002-1-9
Paperback (Premium Colored) ISBN: 978-1-0670002-8-8
Hardcover (Standard Colored) ISBN: 978-1-0670002-2-6
Hardcover (Premium Colored) ISBN: 978-1-0670002-9-5
Hardcover (Black & White) ISBN: 978-1-0670002-7-1
Audiobook ISBN: 978-1-0670002-3-3
IngramSpark Paperback (Colored) ISBN: 978-1-0670002-4-0
IngramSpark Paperback (Black & White) ISBN: 978-1-0670002-5-7

To those who like to see themselves as part of the universe and value love and friendship.

To those who seek improvements in relationships. And to those who, on occasion, have extended their belief in me to 37.73% or more.

Contents

Chapter One

Unmasking the Layers of Relationships

INTRODUCTION:

Relationships are more enigmatic than we often perceive. When we observe a couple bonding over a hiking trip, best friends laughing in a pottery class, or a date blossoming in a cultural restaurant, it's tempting to attribute these connections to shared interests or mere coincidence. But what if I told you that these moments represent one layer of the complex nature of relationships? To the extent that if you know the secrets behind it, they will completely transform how you view human connections.

In this book, when I refer to 'relationships,' I am predominantly discussing romantic and platonic connections, unless specified otherwise. This broad approach allows us to explore a wide spectrum of human interactions between couples or friends.

This book uncovers insights, evolutionary secrets, and alluring scientific theories, distilling the cumulative work of thousands of scientists across centuries into an accessible format. A pivotal challenge in science is connecting the dots of various disciplines. We have merged disparate scientific elements from evolution, history, biology, and psychology, piecing together a pioneering and comprehensive picture that we now present to you. This book, a synthesis of extensive research and diverse disciplines, unveils 11 fundamental relationship styles within the innovative 'PICCK A SPICE' framework – Playful, Intellectual, Creative, Culinary, Kind, Adventurous, Spiritual, Physical, Inspirational, Caring, and Empathetic. Each chapter blends fascinating facts and theories with engaging anecdotal or figurative stories, bringing the 'PICCK A SPICE' framework to life and making complex concepts relatable.

Evolutionary biology, in the context of human relationships, has faced criticism for oversimplifying social behaviors and reinforcing gender stereotypes. Critics argue that the traditional evolutionary narrative—where men are primarily driven by power and financial capability and women by physical attractiveness—overlooks the vast complexity of human social evolution and personal dynamics. Historically, the male-dominated field of evolutionary biology may have skewed some theories, emphasizing traits and behaviors aligning with patriarchal values. Reexamining scientific and evolutionary theories with a comprehensive lens, we embrace the diverse attributes shaping human bonding and attraction and challenge the traditional views, aligning with contemporary society's varied experiences and values.

Individuals often resonate with multiple relationship styles within our framework, forming a unique blend that shifts over time. As life unfolds through various changes, our connection styles dynamically evolve alongside, displaying a flexible rhythm without a fixed sequence, ensuring no style is superior to another. It allows for a colorful spectrum of relationships, each varying in priority and intensity. This adaptive nature allows for richly varied, deeply personal relationships that are as unique as we are. We invite you on a journey of discovery to identify and understand your unique relationship styles.

Understanding our relationship styles begins with recognizing the impact of our early attachments. Early interactions with caregivers shape how we perceive ourselves and others in relationships. We theorize that relationship styles start alongside attachment styles and influence each other. These styles are fluid, changing throughout life as we seek secure attachment for better relationships. The PICCK a SPICE framework, the basis of this book, offers practical strategies that may hold the key to helping individuals reach secure attachment.

Join us on a journey into the heart of human connections, where modern events like a comedy show or a shared wilderness adventure unlock surprisingly profound insights into our relationship dynamics. Throughout this journey, our book evolves from a mere compilation of theories into a guiding companion. Whether forging new connections or deepening existing ones, the wisdom within these pages empowers and enlightens you, offering practical advice, tools, and strategies to create more fulfilling and authentic relationships. By the end of your journey, you'll possess new knowledge and actionable acuities for real-life scenarios.

Moreover, this book offers innovative solutions for the challenges posed by dating and friendship apps. We explore the psychological nuances of choice overload, authenticity in digital personas, and the emotional impacts of modern phenomena to address the limitations inherent in some social apps. We will elaborate on the best methods of implementing our philosophy of 'Pick a Place, then a Face' to build new, more fulfilling, authentic connections. From the broader landscape of human relationships to the complexities of modern dating and friendship apps, this book will be your best friend.

Welcome to the captivating world of human connections, where each bond tells a unique story. Join us on this insightful journey, exploring the intersection of science, technology, and human relationships.

It should be mentioned that while this book contains information from various historical and scientific sources, we wanted to keep the reading experience as seamless and enjoyable for you as possible. For this reason, we have included a comprehensive list of references that correspond to each chapter at the end of this book. The information's veracity and integrity are crucial to us. This structuring allows you to investigate the sources behind certain insights if your curiosity is piqued while allowing you to stay immersed in our story throughout reading.

Chapter Two

Starting and Maintaining Relationships: From Within and Habituation.

As we explore relationship styles, it's integral to understand the foundational concepts that will guide us through. This chapter is a prelude to our deep dive into the eleven unique relationship styles. We commence with the central theories underpinning 'Starting from Within' and understanding 'Habituation' in relationships, essential concepts for anyone seeking to form or sustain meaningful connections.

THE JOURNEY BEGINS:
A TALE OF SELF-DISCOVERY

Elara, known for her vibrant canvases, resided in the tranquil village of Selforia, cradled by the verdant Hills of Reflection. Yet, beneath the brilliance of her art, Elara grappled with an unshakable sense of unfulfillment. Her paintings, while pleasing to others, left her own heart yearning for more, mirroring a life molded more by societal expectations than by her own desires.

On a fateful day, Elara met an elderly sage whose profound words would forever shift her perspective: "True beauty, in art and life, emerges from within. Begin a journey of self-discovery. Listen to your inner voice, and observe as your art and life flourish together." Motivated by this wisdom, Elara set out on a path of introspection.

She ventured through the Hills of Hope, discovering buried aspirations beneath layers of conformity. In the Forests of Fear, she confronted doubts that had shackled her spirit. Along the Rivers of Dreams, she embraced her emotions, strengths, and vulnerabilities, each step drawing her nearer to her authentic self.

As Elara grew more self-aware, her art underwent a profound transformation, reflecting her inner exploration. It struck a chord with those who viewed it, inviting them to contemplate their inner journeys. Elara's art served as a compass, guiding not outwardly but inwardly, urging viewers to seek guidance from within.

This transformation sparked a wave of authenticity and connection across Selforia. Elara's story became a beacon of empowerment, showing that the most reliable direction in life and art is not set by external validation but by courageously embracing one's inner truth.

Her journey, now a part of Selforia's lore, stood as a testament to the power of internal guidance. It motivated the villagers to release the external forces steering their lives, urging them to discover the vast landscapes of their inner selves. Her tale became a rallying cry for self-discovery, inspiring others to let their true selves chart the course of their life's journey.

Foundations of "Starting from Within"

The principle of 'Starting from Within' in relationships is deeply rooted in psychological and scientific understanding. This approach emphasizes self-awareness, which Dr. Daniel Goleman, a renowned psychologist and author, identifies as the ability to understand one's own emotions, strengths and weaknesses, values and drivers, and their impact on others. Self-aware individuals tend to possess superior relationship skills, displaying empathy and attentiveness to others' needs. This self-understanding allows for forming connections that are in harmony with their personal and emotional requirements.

This principle aligns with Carl Rogers' theory of Self-Concept, a fundamental part of humanistic psychology. It revolves around three main components:

❖ Self-image (our perception of ourselves).

❖ Self-esteem (our sense of self-worth).

❖ The Ideal Self (our aspirational self).

Rogers highlights congruence, the alignment between Self-image and The Ideal Self, as vital for authenticity in behavior. Attaining congruence, crucial for self-actualization, requires an environment of acceptance and understanding, thereby promoting personal growth and healthier relationships.

Understanding how group affiliations shape our perceptions and interactions can be further examined by the Social Identity Theory, developed by Henri Tajfel and John Turner. According to this theory, a substantial portion of an individual's self-concept is derived from their affiliations with various social groups, such as clubs, sports teams, or communities, based on shared interests. These affiliations contribute to our sense of identity and self-esteem, influencing how we relate to others within and outside these groups.

However, to apply Social Identity Theory in pursuing meaningful relationships, it is essential to engage in self-exploration to identify the groups that truly represent our interests and values. This congruence between group affiliations and personal values fortifies our identity and steers us towards forming relationships that are in harmony with our authentic selves.

People-pleasing behaviors, deeply rooted in the need for acceptance and approval, can be insightfully examined through the Self-Determination Theory, developed by psychologists Edward L. Deci and Richard M. Ryan. This theory highlights the importance of fulfilling three intrinsic psychological needs: autonomy, competence, and relatedness. In the context of 'Starting from Within,' a critical look at autonomy – the sense of being in control of one's actions – reveals how people-pleasing undermines this essential need. When individuals consistently prioritize others' preferences over their authentic desires, they inadvertently diminish their sense of self-agency, leading to a reliance on external validation for self-esteem. This behavior can create an imbalance, overshadowing the need for relatedness – a genuine connection with others. By recognizing and addressing this tendency, individuals can embark on a journey of self-awareness, aligning their actions with their true values and needs.

Self-disclosure, sharing personal preferences and information with others, is focal in meaningful relationships. This process involves revealing one's thoughts, feelings, experiences, and values – an act that requires a substantial degree of self-awareness and introspection. Effective self-disclosure balances openness and timing and encourages intimacy and trust. When individuals share their passions, fears, hopes, and dreams, they offer a glimpse into their inner world and invite others to connect more profoundly. The depth and quality of the interactions are significantly enhanced when individuals feel safe and comfortable sharing their true selves. This sense of authenticity is directly tied to the principle of 'Starting from Within' – understanding and accepting oneself first, then sharing that self with others.

The journey of finding compatible friends and partners begins with a deep understanding of oneself. By embracing our true selves, we create opportunities for genuine relationships. Once we achieve autonomy and self-awareness, we are better positioned to authentically develop relatedness in our relationships. Adding to the 'Starting from Within' perspective is the Similarity-Attraction Hypothesis. This theory asserts that individuals are naturally drawn to others who resemble them in various aspects, such as beliefs, values, and interests. The root of this attraction lies in the comfort and affirmation we derive from shared experiences and perspectives. When two people discover common ground, whether in hobbies, ideologies, or life goals, it creates a sense of kinship and understanding, fundamental to building strong, lasting connections.

Positive Psychology, the scientific study of factors that make life fulfilling, concentrates on human happiness and well-being. This field aligns with the 'Starting from Within' principle by firstly emphasizing the importance of self-reflection, which involves understanding what personally brings joy and fulfillment, and secondly by 'capitalization', the act of sharing positive news or achievements with others. Positive psychology also encourages shared happiness derived from positive experiences. This approach nurtures closeness in our relationships, making them more supportive and enriching.

Flow Theory, proposed by psychologist Mihaly Csikszentmihalyi, describes a state of deep immersion in activities. This state of being 'in the zone' is characterized by a profound engagement and enjoyment where time seems to stand still. The link between Flow Theory and 'Starting from Within' lies in pursuing personally meaningful and intrinsically rewarding activities. Sharing these activities with others amplifies the joy and satisfaction received from the experience. Furthermore, activities that induce flow often require cooperation, communication, and mutual support, critical ingredients for healthy relationships.

After exploring these foundational theories, we now turn our attention to understanding Habituation in relationships.

Breaking the Chains of Habit: A Tale of Transformation

In the bustling city of Routineville, where each day was a carbon copy of the last, Williamson and Anastasia resided—a couple entrenched in a predictable pattern of life. Days melded into a repetitive cycle, dimming the once-sparkling magic of their relationship. One pleasant evening, in their attic, they stumbled upon a mysterious old map labeled 'Land of Novelty.' Intrigued, they followed it, leading them out of their comfort zone. The map took them through the Forest of New Experiences, over the Mountains of Challenges, and across the Plains of Playfulness. Each new adventure rekindled the excitement and joy that had once defined their relationship. Dancing under the stars in the Desert of Dreams or cooking a new recipe in the Valley of Flavors, every experience was a chance to learn and grow together. They came to understand that shattering the chains of Habituation was essential in revitalizing their bond. Williamson and Anastasia returned to Routineville with a treasure trove of memories and a renewed piquancy for life, transforming their relationship and inspiring their neighbors to seek new adventures.

Understanding Habituation

As we prepare to explore the eleven distinct relationship styles, it's essential first to grasp the concept of Habituation and its relevance in relationships. This understanding is key because knowing how to reignite the spark of your dominant styles, or how to experiment with new styles in your relationships, requires basic knowledge of this psychological phenomenon. Habituation, where repeated exposure to a stimulus leads to a decrease in response, plays a significant role in the dynamics of long-term relationships. Although a natural and adaptive process, Habituation can sometimes lead to predictability and monotony in relationships.

Classical psychological studies by Ivan Pavlov and E.L. Thorndike have demonstrated that Habituation leads to diminished emotional or behavioral responses over time. In relationships, this often translates into a sense of familiarity and routine, which can lessen excitement or engagement. Psychologists and relationship experts advocate introducing new experiences to counteract this. As per Dr. Arthur Aron's research on self-expansion in relationships, engaging in novel activities with a partner can rekindle passion and increase satisfaction.

Neuroscientific findings corroborate this, revealing that new experiences activate the brain's reward system, particularly the release of dopamine, a neurotransmitter associated with pleasure and learning. This activation, as evidenced in studies by neuroscientists like Dr. Bianca Acevedo and Dr. Lucy Brown, mirrors the brain activity seen in the early stages of favorable relationships.

As we explore relationship styles, it's important to note that a comprehensive point-based test will be presented at the end of the book. This valuable tool is specifically designed to help you identify your dominant relationship styles, serving as a crucial aid in understanding your unique way of connecting with others. The test will also guide you in expanding your understanding of them and exploring additional styles.

This test is a critical element of self-awareness to Start from Within, allowing you to explore a variety of interpersonal dynamics. Coupled with the actionable steps outlined in each upcoming chapter, it encourages you to engage in experimentation and discovery, embracing the versatility of each style. Whether within your predominant styles or exploring new ones, each one offers unique possibilities for growth and novelty, essential for keeping your relationships vibrant and resilient. This test is also accessible via our website: www.territie.com.

Our goal is to provide you with the necessary tools to effectively counteract the effects of Habituation in your relationships. Through understanding, exploration, and practical application, you can ensure that your relationships continue to evolve, remain fulfilling, and endure over the years.

CHARTING THE COURSE: UNVEILING THE 11 RELATIONSHIP STYLES

Having explored the fundamental concepts of 'Starting from Within' and 'Habituation,' we are now ready to traverse the eleven diverse relationship styles that are pivotal in shaping human connections.

Our chapters are meticulously structured to provide a comprehensive perspective on each style. These segments are crafted to bring to life the unique aspects of every relationship style, offering a blend of narrative and analytical insights.

Moments You'll Recognize: Each chapter opens with a relatable story, vividly illustrating how the relationship styles manifest in real-life scenarios. These engaging narratives set the stage for the themes and nuances that will be explored in detail.

Defining the Style: Here, we clearly explain each relationship style, focusing on its defining characteristics. We aim to establish a foundational understanding that lays the groundwork for deeper exploration.

Unveiling Historical and Scientific Treasures: In this section, we investigate the compelling evidence and background of each style, incorporating insights from various fields like evolution, history, biology, and psychology. Our in-depth analysis reveals the complex factors that shape each relationship style.

Benefits and Considerations: This section balances our explorations by highlighting well-researched the benefits and potential challenges of each style. It also provides an opportunity to address points crucial for inclusivity and diversity, whether mental, cultural, or physical.

Your Relationship Revival: Offering actionable advice and innovative ideas, this section is designed to break Habituation and rejuvenate your relationship.

Places to Pick: We suggest locations complementing each style. More insights on selecting the ideal places will be explored in a subsequent chapter titled 'More Practicalities: Pick a "Place, then a Face!' Plus, a Surprise!' following our discussion of the eleven relationship styles, where we bridge theoretical concepts with additional practical applications.

Literary Echoes: To add depth to your journey, we intersperse literary quotes that resonate with the themes of each relationship style, offering deeper insights and connections.

Reflect and Discuss: Concluding each chapter are prompts for personal reflection and community discussion, encouraging practical application and a deeper understanding of these styles in everyday life.

The first two-thirds of this book focus on enhancing and maintaining current relationships, a crucial foundation, before introducing tools for initiating new connections. This structure ensures that you are equipped with the necessary theoretical and practical applications for successful relationship management.

We will explore the relationship styles in the order of the 'PIC-CK A SPICE' acronym: Playful, Intellectual, Creative, Culinary, Kind, Adventurous, Spiritual, Physical, Inspirational, Caring, and Empathetic. This systematic approach allows for an in-depth exploration of each style.

For those eager to share and reflect on their journey, our social media channels provide a space for engaging with a community of like-minded individuals. Details for joining these discussions are at the end of the book, offering you the opportunity to be part of a vibrant, supportive community.

We are excited to accompany you on this journey, illuminating the path to more enriching and resilient relationships.

Chapter Three

1. PLAYFUL TEASING

Moments You'll Recognize:

Jake and Emma's relationship was a delightful blend of humor and affection, an ongoing exchange of Playful Teasing that brought joy and laughter to their everyday lives. They had a unique way of turning even the simplest tasks into naughty adventures. One sunny Saturday morning in their cozy kitchen, the couple decided to do something new – making blueberry muffins and pancakes. The kitchen was filled with the sweet aroma of baking and the sound of their laughter as they friskily navigated their way through the recipes with a comedy of errors and affectionate banter.

As Emma carefully measured the flour, Jake sneaked up behind her and gently flicked a bit of flour onto her nose. Startled, she turned around, her face a picture of mock indignation. "Oh, you're going to pay for that, Mr. Chef!" she exclaimed, her eyes twinkling with mischief. "Oh, revenge will be sweet, Mrs. Chef!" He responded with a playful chuckle. The flour flick soon escalated into a full-blown, gentle flour war. Their laughter echoed through the kitchen with each gentle sprinkle, filling the space with warmth and playfulness. "You look like a ghost with all that flour on you," Jake laughed as he admired Emma's now white-covered hair and flour-dusted beauty. Emma, quick to retort, grinned and said, "Well, that makes two of us, Casper!"

Amidst their laughter, they somehow managed to prepare the pancake batter. Emma, feeling adventurous, attempted to flip a pancake high into the air, only for it to land with a comical splat on the floor. Instead of frustration, their laughter filled the room, and Jake teased, "So, we're adding floor seasoning now?" Emma, undeterred and with a grin, replied, "Absolutely! It's my secret ingredient!"

Their playful banter continued as they filled the muffin tray. Jake pretended to misjudge the distance and gently bumped into Emma, causing her to spoon batter onto the counter. "Oops, butterfingers! My hand slipped!" he exclaimed with a mischievous smile. Emma rolled her eyes in mock exasperation, laughing, "Sure, Jake, and I'm the reigning Muffin Queen of England." When the muffins were done, they were far from perfect, but that didn't matter. They laughed at the oddly shaped muffins, joking about starting a 'unique muffin' bakery. "We could call it 'Muffins with a Twist'," suggested Emma, her eyes gleaming with humor. "Or 'Flour Fights and Muffin Delights,'" added Jake as they both erupted into laughter.

Finally, as the muffins were baked and the pancakes were (mostly) successfully flipped, they sat together, sipping coffee. They playfully debated who was the better chef. Emma teasingly claimed the title due to Jake's 'creative' batter-spilling technique. Jake defended himself, insisting his unique approach made their kitchen escapades memorable. Jake and Emma's bond grew stronger in their comfy apartment, filled with the fragrance of baked goods and the warmth of shared humor. It was a place where they could tease each other lovingly, sharing the joy and comfort of each other's company. Their Playful Teasing was a language of love that kept their relationship vibrant and strong. Their story is a glimpse of the Playful, Teasing Relationship Style, which we will explore how, when navigated with care and affection, it can become a pillar of a robust and enduring bond, infusing relationships with joy, laughter, and an ever-present sense of companionship.

DEFINING THE STYLE:

Playful Teasing, a delightful and humorous form of affection, breathes vitality into relationships, enriching private moments and casual social interactions alike. It often involves inside jokes, cute nicknames, or lighthearted ribbing that says, "I know you, and I cherish our bond." This interaction reinforces closeness and increases mutual understanding, showcasing an intimate knowledge of each other's personalities. Its non-serious, friendly, and amusing nature is effective across romantic and platonic relationships, enhancing rapport and deepening the bonds of connection. Playful Teasing manifests in various forms, such as creating a unique secret language or nicknames that cultivate an intimate world exclusive to the relationship. It also thrives in cheerful bets and challenges, where even a simple wager of kisses on small matters can spark joy. The charm extends to assuming playful roles or humorously imitating each other, enhancing the relationship's playful spirit, and transforming everyday actions into moments of affectionate exchange.

Unveiling Historical and Scientific Treasures:

The roots of Playful Teasing and humor in relationships stretch back to our evolutionary and biological origins, indicating its deep-seated role in social bonding. Behaviors akin to Playful Teasing, observed even in non-human primates and preverbal human infants, suggest an evolutionary origin. This teasing – a mix of offering and withdrawing, playful non-compliance, and disrupting activities – has always been a cornerstone of strengthening social bonds and enhancing group cohesion.

Teasing with Offer and Withdrawal, a dynamic where one playfully offers something desirable and then humorously withdraws it, adds an element of surprise and delight to interactions. It's a kind of teasing where one playfully entices with a promise or an offer and then pulls back as a joke, "Just Kidding!". For example, a partner might say, "How about we go to Paris this weekend?" and as excitement builds, cheekily add, "Or maybe just to the new French café downtown?". A friend might offer the last piece of cake, and when the other reaches for it, quickly snatch it away with a grin, saying, "Too slow! But don't worry, I'll bake you a whole cake next time." In a group of chimpanzees, an individual may pick up a desirable object (like a fruit or a toy) and show it to others, then quickly move it away as others approach, engaging in a playful 'keep-away' game. This type of teasing is meant to provoke a playful response. Still, it's essential to be sensitive to the other person's feelings and ensure it remains fun for both parties.

Provocative Non-Compliance refers to a playful defiance to comply with a request or expectation, not out of rebellion but as a form of teasing. It's about playfully challenging norms or expectations within the relationship. For instance, if one partner asks to pass the salt at the dinner table, the other might mischievously pass them pepper instead. It's a way of adding humor to everyday interactions, but like all forms of teasing, it requires mutual understanding and a sense of humor to be enjoyable and not frustrating. Young gorillas sometimes ignore or playfully defy the commands of their elders or caretakers. When signaled to come closer, a young gorilla might mischievously move in the opposite direction, eliciting laughter or playful responses from others. For Humans, during a waggish pillow fight, one partner says, "Truce?" and when the other agrees and lowers their pillow, the first partner takes the opportunity for a gentle, mischievous strike, followed by laughter and a real truce. When playing a board game, a friend might jokingly make an outrageous, obviously incorrect move, like placing a chess piece in a completely wrong spot, just to provoke a humorous reaction and add some levity to the game.

Disrupting Others' Activities, which entails, as the name suggests, playfully interrupting someone's tasks, introduces unexpected moments of humor and joy, turning routine activities into opportunities for active interaction. For example, playfully messing up someone's hairstyle when they're trying to style it or playfully interrupting someone's story with a silly comment or joke. While one partner is trying to read a book, the other might playfully steal their bookmark or close the book gently, prompting a mock chase around the house, adding a bit of fun and spontaneity to their quiet evening. Orangutans in the wild have been observed interrupting the activities of their peers for fun. For instance, one might be resting or foraging, and another orangutan could playfully disrupt this activity by swinging on a branch into the other's space, initiating a playful interaction. The aim is to inject a moment of surprise and humor into ordinary activities. However, it's crucial to gauge the other person's mood and the appropriateness of the situation, as not every moment is right for this kind of playfulness.

Interestingly, even before they begin to speak, infants engage in Playful Teasing, laying the groundwork for more complex social interactions later in life. When learning to feed themselves, infants might playfully refuse food by turning their head away or playfully throwing food. This behavior is not just about refusal but can be a playful interaction with their caregivers, as they often look for a reaction and may giggle or smile when the caregiver responds. Preverbal toddlers might engage in mock biting or gently grabbing someone's nose or ear, doing so playfully and watching for a reaction. This is a form of playful physical teasing, where the action is gentle and intended to provoke a lively interaction. Toddlers love to imitate the actions of adults or other children in a playful manner. This can be seen as a form of teasing, where they mimic others not to comply or conform, but as a way to engage and interact socially. Even without words, infants make playful gestures or sounds to entertain others. For instance, they might stick out their tongue or blow raspberries as a form of playful communication and teasing. In a more physical sense, toddlers often engage in a game of chase, where they run away, expecting to be pursued. This is a form of Playful Teasing, where the thrill is in the chase and the playful interaction that follows when caught. Infants may hide behind furniture or a curtain, peeking out to see if they are being sought. This hide-and-seek game is a form of teasing where they are testing the attention and response of their caregivers.

The history and evolutionary context of Playful Teasing and humor emphasize their significance in human social interactions. In tribal and early human societies, humor likely evolved as a mechanism for building bonds, attracting mates, and navigating complex social hierarchies. The ability to make others laugh signified intelligence, creativity, and desirable genetic fitness, making humor a valued trait in mate selection. Those skilled in humor were often seen as wise and intelligent, essential qualities for leadership and social cohesion. Laughter and jest served as mechanisms to ease tensions, solidify alliances, and resolve conflicts non-violently. Humor has been vital in mate selection, demonstrating cognitive flexibility and the ability to view situations from different perspectives.

Playfulness also served as a way to test social bonds, communication skills, and the resilience of relationships. The ability to engage in playful banter without causing harm or offense indicated a strong social bond and mutual understanding, traits valuable for long-term relational success. It was also a means to communicate indirectly, allowing the expression of sensitive or risky thoughts.

Over time, the nature and perception of teasing have evolved. Historically, it has been more direct and possibly harsh, but it has become a more subtle and socially acceptable form of interaction in modern contexts. This evolution reflects changes in social norms and the increasing complexity of human social structures. Today, Playful Teasing is often seen as a sign of intimacy and comfort in a relationship, indicating familiarity and trust where individuals can engage in lighthearted banter without offending or hurting each other.

It's worth noting that some recent studies have explored "prosocial teasing," which uses seemingly negative remarks playfully to express positive relational messages. Intended to be friendly and supportive, it is associated with various personality traits, such as narcissism and sensation-seeking, but also with positive relationship outcomes when understood and appreciated by both parties. Gently teasing a partner about a harmless quirk or habit they have, in a way that makes them laugh and feel loved, not embarrassed. Using funny nicknames that reference shared experiences or inside jokes that strengthen the bond through shared memories. In both wild and captivity, Chimpanzees and

Gorillas engage in Playful Teasing. For example, they might mock fights or use sign language to tease each other. Similar to prosocial teasing, this form of humor involves playful, seemingly negative interactions that strengthen social bonds.

Humor and fun play a significant role in the biochemistry of our emotions, mainly through their influence on our hormonal systems. Laughter and humorous moments trigger the release of hormones and neurotransmitters in our brains, enhancing happiness and relaxation. One of the primary hormones involved is dopamine, a 'feel-good hormone.' Dopamine is a neurotransmitter that plays a crucial role in our brain's reward system. When we experience something pleasurable, such as a good laugh, our brain releases dopamine, which creates feelings of pleasure and satisfaction. This rewarding sensation leads to immediate gratification and encourages us to repeat behaviors that lead to laughter and enjoyment, reinforcing social connections and positive interactions. Moreover, dopamine has been linked to motivation and attention, indicating that humor and entertainment can make us feel good and improve our focus and drive.

Endorphins are also significantly impacted by humor. Endorphins are neurotransmitters produced in the brain that act as natural painkillers. They are released in response to stress or discomfort but also during moments of joy and laughter. Laughter, in particular, increases endorphins' production, helping alleviate pain and induce euphoria. Social laughter heightens pleasurable sensations and triggers the release of endorphins, leading to increased pain thresholds and relaxation. These endorphins contribute to feelings of calmness and happiness, improving mood and reducing anxiety, significant for emotional and mental well-being. This endorphin release can explain why we often feel a sense of light-heartedness and well-being after a good laugh.

Also, laughter triggers the release of oxytocin, sometimes called the 'love hormone' or 'bonding hormone.' Oxytocin is released during activities that promote bonding, such as hugging, and it fosters a sense of connection and trust among individuals. Its presence during shared laughter accentuates humor's social bonding aspect. The combined effects of dopamine, endorphins, and oxytocin boost our mood and alleviate stress, enhancing our social connections and emphasizing the importance of humor and fun in strengthening our relationships and overall well-being.

Laughing increases our intake of oxygen-rich air, enhancing circulation and improving blood flow to the brain, bolstering brain health, and reducing risks associated with cognitive impairment. Studies have found that laughter, both individually and socially, is linked to a reduced risk of dementia, highlighting its role in maintaining cognitive health throughout life.

Humor serves a crucial psychological role, particularly in stress mitigation, with laughter reducing cortisol levels and fostering a sense of relaxation and well-being. Cortisol, often referred to as the 'stress hormone', is integral to our body's 'fight or flight' response. However, elevated levels over prolonged periods can lead to various health issues, including anxiety and depression. By reducing cortisol, humor helps alleviate these stress-induced symptoms, promoting well-being and relaxation. Humor makes coping with life's challenges more manageable.

The influence of humor on emotional well-being is notable within relationships. Two distinct forms of humor, affiliative humor, and self-enhancing humor play pivotal roles in nurturing healthier and more harmonious connections. Affiliative humor centers around the creation and reinforcement of social bonds. It involves sharing jokes, anecdotes, or light-hearted comments that bring people closer together. On the other hand, self-enhancing humor revolves around maintaining a positive outlook on life through humor. It involves using humor as a coping mechanism to deal with stress and adversity, allowing individuals to find the silver lining in challenging situations. In relationships, self-enhancing humor contributes to a more optimistic atmosphere. It enables partners to face life's ups and downs with resilience and a smile, which, in turn, enhances emotional well-being. When affiliative humor and self-enhancing humor coexist within a relationship, they work in tandem to create a nurturing and supportive dynamic.

฿ENEFITS AND ℂONSIDERATIONS:

In modern relationships, Playful Teasing emerges as a many-sided tool – it's not just about sparking joy or easing communication; it's a subtle way to shed light on a partner's idiosyncrasies without veering into criticism. It makes communication more effective and helps resolve conflicts amicably, allowing couples to discuss serious issues in a non-threatening manner. Research has shown that positive, outwardly-focused Playful Teasing — teasing that focuses on shared experiences and external subjects rather than personal characteristics — is linked to increased happiness and satisfaction in relationships, including sexual satisfaction in romantic contexts. It serves as an effective means to broach sensitive topics without causing offense, enhancing communication and conflict resolution. A well-timed joke or playful tease can transform a tense situation into a moment of laughter, aiding couples in navigating disagreements with less hostility. It softens feedback delivery, making it more palatable and encouraging partner receptivity and understanding. Moreover, Playful Teasing fortifies social bonds, reflecting deep trust and comfort, enhancing positive emotions during interactions while mitigating negative ones. Playful Teasing aids in managing stress and anxiety, promoting improved emotional health and unity. Beyond mere affection, Playful Teasing acts as a balm in stressful or conflicted situations, introducing ease and lightness that can diffuse tension, communicate affection, convey respect and commitment, and bring joy to daily life.

In the journey of relationship building, self-disclosure plays a pivotal role. As established in the early chapters of this book, Starting from Within is essential. But how does laughter fit into this narrative of self-disclosure and trust-building? Recent studies reveal a fascinating facet of human interaction: laughter's ability to enhance self-disclosure intimacy. One study focused on how different video clips - varying in humor and capacity to elicit laughter - influenced the depth of personal information participants were willing to share. The result was clear: those who laughed disclosed more intimate details than those who didn't, suggesting a direct correlation between laughter and the willingness to open up. When we laugh with someone, we implicitly signal our desire to open up and readiness to share more of ourselves. This act, possibly unbeknownst to us, can lay a foundation of trust - a crucial element in any relationship.

Teasing can express emotions and affection safely, engagingly, and lightheartedly, breaking daily monotony and injecting excitement into the relationship. This ability to lighten the mood is crucial for nurturing a dynamic of health and resilience within relationships. Couples who laugh together often find it easier to face challenges and recover from difficulties. Shared laughter creates a sense of unity and connection, strengthening individuals' bonds in romantic and platonic relationships.

Understanding the dynamics of humor in relationships is vital, as not all forms of humor positively contribute to relationship dynamics. Aggressive humor, which aims to manipulate or disparage through unwelcomed sarcasm, teasing, or jokes at another's expense, often masks criticism or contempt and can lead to feelings of resentment or hurt. On the other hand, self-defeating humor involves self-mockery or putting oneself down in an attempt to amuse others, can inadvertently reinforce negative self-perceptions and affect one's self-esteem. Both aggressive and self-defeating humor, when used excessively or inappropriately, can erode the foundations of trust and respect in a relationship. Playful Teasing, while a source of joy and connection, demands a thoughtful approach. Its charm lies in being lighthearted and affectionate, yet there's a thin line between playful jest and hurtful sarcasm. It's essential to maintain teasing as a source of joy and connection, avoiding any drift into hurtfulness or belittlement. For instance, teasing about personal insecurities or past traumas can be destructive. Understanding and respecting each other's boundaries is paramount.

It's also essential to consider the tone and delivery of Playful Teasing. The same words can be received differently depending on factors like voice pitch, tone and volume, facial expression, and body language. Teasing should always be done in a way that clearly communicates affection and playfulness, not disguised criticism or contempt. A partner's response should be attentively observed; if they seem uncomfortable or hurt, it's vital to apologize and adjust the approach. Mutual participation and enjoyment ensure that Playful Teasing contributes positively to a relationship. It should be a two-way street, with both partners feeling comfortable and willing to engage in this kind of banter. Suppose one partner is always the subject of teasing while the other always initiates. In that case, it can create an imbalance, leading to feelings of resentment or inadequacy.

Context is king in the teasing world; what delights in one scenario may distress in another. A humorous tease about a partner's cooking mishaps might be fun at home but could be embarrassing if mentioned in front of friends or family. Open communication about what's enjoyable and what's off-limits sets the stage for a healthy exchange of playful banter. Regular check-ins are essential, offering a space to recalibrate and ensure that the teasing remains fun and respectful. Acknowledging that teasing isn't universally enjoyed as a form of affection is also crucial. Recognizing and adapting to this preference is a testament to the depth of understanding between individuals. Playful Teasing requires a delicate balance to thrive. By navigating these nuances with care and empathy, teasing can continue to be a delightful and enriching element of relationships.

Tracing its roots from the jesters of yore to today's stand-up comedians, humor has always been a cherished aspect of culture. In both friendships and romantic bonds, the shared laughter and gentle jibes of Playful Teasing are instrumental in forging strong and adaptable connections. Incorporating Playful Teasing into daily life can be done through sharing jokes, enjoying comedy together, or finding humor in mundane situations. It can transform ordinary moments into opportunities for connection and joy.

Your Relationship Revival:

Revitalizing the joy of Playful Teasing involves adding unexpected twists and humorous challenges to your daily routine. It's a delightful way to turn ordinary moments into laughter-filled adventures. Here's a list of activities for you to consider:

1. **Lawn Ambush:** Surprise your partner with a water gun fight while they're mowing the lawn on a hot day. These impromptu skirmishes refresh and exhilarate.

2. **Costume Dinner Delight:** Organize a themed dress-up dinner. Pick out whimsical outfits for each other, strengthening your bond through laughter and shared stories.

3. **Homebound Treasure Hunt:** Invent a scavenger hunt inside your home with clues leading to shared memories or inside jokes, or create an animated competition with quirky rewards like granting a wish.

4. **Spontaneous Dance-Off:** Transform an ordinary evening into an unexpected dance party. Play your favorite song and dance spontaneously, bringing lightness and connection.

5. **Dessert Experimentation Challenge:** Have a dessert-making contest using unusual ingredients. Enjoy the surprise and laughter that come with tasting the results.

6. **First Laugh Reward:** Start a 'first laugh' ritual. In romantic contexts, the first to laugh might receive a foot massage, while in friendships, it could mean winning the last slice of pizza.

7. **Backwards Day Fun:** Dedicate a day to doing everything backwards, like eating breakfast for dinner and wearing pa-

jamas during the day, to add a playful twist to routine activities.

8. **Improvised Home Theater:** Stage an unrehearsed performance, like a lip-sync battle or improvised skit, creating an evening filled with laughter and shared enjoyment.

9. **Character Cuisine Night:** Turn dinner into a roleplaying adventure. Adopt different personas or accents, adding a theatrical flair to your mealtime.

Remember, these playful activities are more than just fun; they're about breaking routine and rediscovering joy in your relationships. While Playful Teasing has its charm, similar creative actions can be applied to other relationship styles outlined in this book. Each style offers opportunities to rejuvenate and deepen your romantic or platonic connections. So, go ahead and introduce these delightful twists into your life – your relationships will thank you for it!

PLACES TO PICK:

Amusement parks, comedy shows, humorous film screenings, cafes, casual dining spots, karaoke bars, beach outings, escape rooms, mini-golf courses, ice skating rinks, street fairs, theme parties, trampoline parks, art workshops, costume parties, arcade centers, social gatherings, game nights, improv classes, roller skating rinks.

LITERARY ECHOES:

"Among those whom I like or admire, I can find no common denominator, but among those whom I love, I can: all of them make me laugh." — W. H. Auden, English-American poet and essayist.

"I believe there is a direct correlation between love and laughter." — Yakov Smirnoff, Russian-American comedian.

"Sexiness wears thin after a while and beauty fades, but to be married to a man who makes you laugh every day, ah, now that's a real treat." — Joanne Woodward, American actress.

"Once upon a time there was a boy who loved a girl, and her laughter was a question he wanted to spend his whole life answering." — Nicole Krauss, American author.

"And so, with laughter and love, we lived happily ever after." — Gail Carson Levine, American author of young adult books.

"Love and laughter hold us together." — Ingrid Trobisch, author and family counselor.

"From here on after let's stay the way we are right now. And share all the love and laughter that a lifetime will allow." — George Strait, American country music singer.

"I love people who make me laugh. I honestly think it's the thing I like most, to laugh. It cures a multitude of ills. It's probably the most important thing in a person." — Audrey Hepburn, British actress and humanitarian.

"The most important thing in a relationship is that you have fun." — Jim Halpert, fictional character from "The Office."

"Life is short. Spend it with people who make you laugh and feel loved." — Unknown

"In the sweetness of friendship let there be laughter." — Khalil Gibran, Lebanese-American writer, poet, and visual artist.

REFLECT AND DISCUSS:

Enhancing Connections:

1. Think of a time when Playful Teasing enhanced your connection with someone. What specific elements (like inside jokes or nicknames) made it special?

   _____

   _____

   _____

2. Recall a moment when Playful Teasing made you feel cherished and understood in a relationship. What about that moment stood out to you?

   _____

   _____

   _____

Navigating Boundaries and Conflict:

3. Discuss strategies for ensuring that Playful Teasing remains healthy and respectful. How can couples or friends regularly check in with each other to maintain this balance?

   _____

   _____

   _____

4. Consider a time when Playful Teasing might have gone too far in your experience. What lessons did you learn about the

boundaries and sensitivities in your relationships? Discuss how context and individual differences play a role in this.

_____

_____

_____

5. Consider the role of Playful Teasing in conflict resolution. Can you think of a scenario where a well-timed joke or playful remark helped defuse a tense situation?

_____

_____

_____

Understanding and Utilizing Playful Teasing:

6. Share your thoughts on the evolutionary origins of Playful Teasing. Why do you think this behavior is prevalent in many forms of social bonding, even beyond human interactions?

_____

_____

_____

7. Brainstorm ways in which Playful Teasing can be used to navigate challenging conversations or disagreements. Can humor be a tool for more effective communication?

_____

_____

_____

Chapter Four

2. INTELLECTUAL CONNECTION

Moments You'll Recognize:

In the cozy ambiance of a quaint corner café, bathed in the soft glow of morning light, sits a couple deeply engrossed in a passionate debate. A well-thumbed copy of Steven Pinker's "The Better Angels of Our Nature" lies between them, its exploration of the decline of violence through psychology and history sparking their discussion. As they sip their artisan coffee, they animatedly dissect Pinker's theories, quoting passages and challenging each other's interpretations. The woman leans forward, her eyes sparkling with excitement, as she posits that the book's analysis of historical trends and human psychology offers a hopeful perspective on humanity's future. The man counters with a thoughtful furrow of his brow, pondering the complexities of human nature and the factors driving societal changes. Their conversation knits through examples from the book, touching upon the Enlightenment's role in reducing violence and the implications of empathy and reason in shaping human societies.

As the discussion deepens, their intellectual tango draws them closer, each argument and counter-argument acting as a testament to their shared love for knowledge and critical thinking. They reference other works that have shaped their understanding, from Jared Diamond's "Guns, Germs, and Steel" to Yuval Noah Harari's "Sapiens," each book adding depth and context to their discussion. The world around them fades into a background hum as they lose themselves in the intellectual fervor of their debate. It's not about proving a point or winning an argument; it's about the exhilarating journey of exploring complex ideas together, challenging and expanding each other's viewpoints. The discussion is a symphony of minds, a celebration of intellectual curiosity that binds them closer as lovers and intellectual companions.

In this chapter, we'll explore how Intellectual Connection can become the heart of a relationship, offering examples and strategies for nurturing this profound bond. You'll discover how to create spaces for such stimulating discussions and how to integrate intellectual pursuits into the fabric of your relationship. This journey is about embracing the beauty of the mind and finding joy in the shared quest for understanding and wisdom.

Defining the Style:

Intellectual Connection in relationships represents a profound bond nurtured through engaging discussions and exploring ideas. This connection is about advancing each other's knowledge, values, and intellectual pursuits. It transcends superficial interactions, focusing on exchanges that challenge and inspire both partners with new thoughts and ideas. It extends beyond mere physical attraction and offers a robust and enduring foundation for relationships rooted in mutual intellectual stimulation. Picture a couple absorbed in books, jointly attending thought-provoking lectures, or lost in discussions about the intricate nuances of philosophy. Engaging in challenging debates or discussions on complex subjects is a hallmark of couples with a strong Intellectual Connection. Participation in educational activities, such as attending classes or workshops, significantly enriches this Intellectual Connection, facilitating shared growth and understanding.

Unveiling Historical and Scientific Treasures:

The evolution of intelligence in primates, especially in its role in fostering social interactions and relationships, provides crucial insights. It illustrates how developing intellectual capacities have been instrumental in forming social bonds in primates and humans. Studies of primate behavior, such as those by Byrne, Whiten, and others, have revealed that primates, including chimpanzees and gorillas, exhibit sophisticated problem-solving abilities and tool use, reflecting significant cognitive abilities. This intellectual prowess has been linked to social advantages, such as enhanced bonding, improved group cohesion, and successful mate selection.

Within human evolution, the development of higher intelligence was pivotal for our ancestors' survival and reproductive success. The transmission and accumulation of knowledge across generations, a trait more distinctively exhibited by humans compared to other species, has been crucial for our survival and advancement as a species. This ability to share and build upon knowledge over time is facilitated by our innate tendency to form social bonds and cooperate with others, underpinned by biological mechanisms like hormonal responses. In fact, natural selection has continuously given an advantage to intellectual individuals by increasing their chances of survival and, therefore, breeding—intellectual abilities allowed for better problem-solving and adaptability to changing environments. These abilities facilitated more complex communication and deeper bonds in social contexts, which were necessary in early human societies.

The evolutionary expansion of the human brain, particularly the neocortex, marks a significant milestone in our species' development, setting us apart from other species. This part of the brain, notably larger in humans, is crucial for higher cognitive functions such as complex problem-solving, abstract thinking, and language. The growth of the neocortex allowed for enhanced perception and motor skills and the emergence of sophisticated social interactions and cultural complexities. It facilitated a leap in cognitive abilities, enabling early humans to respond to their environment and actively reshape it. This advancement was instrumental in the development of tools, strategies for survival, and the sharing of wisdom and traditions through time. Furthermore, the neocortex played a vital role in processing complex social cues, promoting cooperative behaviors, and forming larger social groups. These developments created a feedback loop, further driving the evolution of social and cognitive skills. Consequently, the neocortex underpins the faculties that define humanity, including our ability to think, learn, communicate, and connect at an unparalleled level, essential for individual survival and early human societies' progression.

Evolutionary psychologist Geoffrey Miller's Intellectual Selection theory suggests that the evolution of the human brain was driven not solely by survival needs but also by sexual selection. He argues that the development of the human brain into an organ capable of abstract thinking, creativity, and wit was partially fueled by the desire to attract mates, akin to how physical attributes like the peacock's tail evolved for mate attraction. Intellectual prowess, signaling good genes, health, and the ability to provide and protect, became a desirable trait. This is evident in our ancestors' 'courtship displays' of intellectual capabilities through storytelling, art, and demonstrations of social intelligence and good judgment. Miller's theory profoundly suggests that many facets of human culture, including art, literature, and humor, have origins in showcasing intelligence for romantic pursuits. This implies that these social and reproductive dynamics have significantly shaped learning, creativity, and emotional complexity in the human brain. Thus, Intellectual Selection provides a fascinating perspective on the development of the human mind and culture, highlighting the interplay between cognitive evolution and the fabric of human relationships and society.

The discovery of mirror neurons has revolutionized our understanding of human social learning and interaction. These neurons, first identified in the early 1990s by a group of Italian researchers led by Giacomo Rizzolatti, represent a fascinating neural mechanism that plays a pivotal role in understanding and relating to others. Mirror neurons, a unique brain cell type, react similarly when we perform an action and when we observe another person performing the same action. This mirroring effect bridges the gap between observation and action, creating a direct pathway for empathy, learning, and understanding social cues.

Located in the premotor cortex and the inferior parietal cortex, mirror neurons are thought to be essential for imitation –

a key component of human learning. Beyond imitation, mirror neurons are integral to understanding the intentions and emotions of others. When we see someone smiling or frowning, our mirror neurons fire in a way that allows us to simulate these expressions internally, providing insights into the other person's emotional state. This internal mirroring forms the basis of empathy, enabling us to feel what others feel and understand their perspectives. It is a fundamental process that underpins social bonding and cohesion. The influence of mirror neurons extends to our engagement with arts, literature, cinema, and theater, enhancing our empathetic response and appreciation, and in physical activities like sports and dance, where observing and mentally simulating movements can improve training and performance.

Behavioral Synchrony, a phenomenon highlighted by social neuroscience, is pivotal in Intellectual Connection and deepening relationships. Research conducted by Uri Hasson, a professor at Princeton University, utilizing neuroimaging techniques like functional MRI (fMRI), shows that individuals can exhibit similar brain activity patterns during deep, stimulating conversations or collaborative intellectual tasks. This neural mirroring facilitates a high level of cognitive alignment, enhancing mutual understanding and cooperation. Couples who partake in intellectual activities together, such as Drs. John and Julie Gottman's concept of Shared Meaning in their relationship research, find that their connection deepens beyond mere emotional or physical aspects. The Gottmans' work highlights how shared intellectual pursuits and meaningful conversations can enrich a relationship with a more resounding understanding and mutual respect for each other's intellectual capacities.

The intellectual skills that were favored in our evolutionary past continue to influence our modern relationships. Nowadays, Intellectual Connection remains a key aspect of human relationships, as we are naturally drawn to partners who stimulate us intellectually and with whom we can engage in meaningful and thought-provoking conversations. Intellectual Connections have evolved significantly over time, reflecting changes in societal norms, cultural values, and our comprehension of human psychology. At some parts of our history, the apparent emphasis on relationships often lay in aspects like social standing, financial stability, and familial alliances rather than intellectual compatibility. Intellectual Connections, particularly in romantic relationships, were not always prioritized or openly acknowledged, partly due to the historical undervaluing of intellectual pursuits, especially for women, in many societies.

With societal evolution and increased access to education, people's appreciation for the role of Intellectual Connection in relationships has intensified. This shift coincided with a broader recognition of the importance of personal fulfillment, mutual respect, and shared interests in successful relationships. The rise of Romanticism in the late 18th and early 19th centuries, originating from earlier philosophies like Enlightenment thought and Classical Art, also played a role in redefining relationship ideals, emphasizing emotional and intellectual compatibility over traditional matchmaking criteria. In contemporary times, intellectual compatibility is increasingly recognized as an imperative factor in the success and satisfaction of both romantic and platonic relationships. People often seek partners with whom they can share and explore ideas, interests, and worldviews, as well as those who are on the same educational level.

The foundations of Intellectual Connections in relationships are anchored deeply in our biological and neurological makeup. Deep thinking, engaging in philosophy, and participating in intellectual activities profoundly impact our brain chemistry, particularly influencing the production and regulation of certain hormones and neurotransmitters. One of the primary neurotransmitters involved in intellectual stimulation is acetylcholine. This neurotransmitter plays a crucial role in learning and memory. Acetylcholine levels in the brain rise when we immerse ourselves in deep thinking or complex intellectual tasks, particularly in areas associated with attention and memory formation, such as the hippocampus and prefrontal cortex. This increase aids in encoding new memories and the focus required for philosophical reasoning or complex problem-solving, which, if done with a friend or a partner, would strengthen the relationship accordingly. Additionally, acetylcholine is linked to neuroplasticity—the brain's ability to form new connections and pathways—which is essential for learning new concepts and thinking critically about challenging subjects.

Another significant player in intellectual engagement is the neurotransmitter serotonin. Often associated with mood regulation, serotonin also plays a crucial role in cognition and learning. Elevated serotonin levels have been linked to an increased ability to make decisions and process information, which is vital in philosophical reasoning and intellectual pursuits. Serotonin contributes to feelings of well-being and contentment, enhancing the overall experience of engaging in intellectual activities. It helps regulate mood swings and reduces impulsivity, thereby allowing for more sustained and focused intellectual engagement. Serotonin's role also extends to social cognition, influencing how we perceive and interact with others' ideas, an essential aspect of philosophical discussions and intellectual debates.

Moreover, participation in intellectually stimulating activities triggers the release of Brain-Derived Neurotrophic Factor (BDNF), a protein essential for brain health. BDNF supports the survival of existing neurons and encourages the growth and differentiation of new neurons and synapses. This is particularly relevant in learning and memory, as BDNF is vital for long-term memory formation and cognitive flexibility. Engaging in challenging mental activities like deep philosophical thinking or complex problem-solving stimulates the production of BDNF, promoting brain resilience and adaptability. This biological response enhances cognitive function and contributes to long-term brain health, potentially reducing the risk of cognitive decline in later life.

The brain's reward system is instrumental in fostering these connections, with dopamine, a key neurotransmitter in the brain's reward pathway, being released during intellectually stimulating activities or conversations that we find rewarding. This release creates feelings of pleasure and satisfaction and can be activated during various interactions, including intellectual discussions, deepening the connection between individuals.

Two primary hormones, oxytocin, and vasopressin, are also key players in forming and sustaining social bonds, including Intellectual Connections. Oxytocin, often called the 'cuddle hormone,' is associated with feelings of attachment and closeness and can be stimulated through social interactions, including intellectual engagement. Vasopressin is connected to social behavior and pair bonding, playing a role in long-term relationships. The interplay between the biochemicals released during intellectual activities illustrates a harmonious orchestration of biological processes that enrich our mental capabilities and overall brain health and empower our relationships.

Benefits and Considerations:

Intellectual compatibility is often pivotal for long-term relationship satisfaction. It fosters a deeper understanding and respect for each other's perspectives. Friends or partners who share intellectual interests often find their conversations more rewarding. This connection adds depth to the relationship, making it more than just companionship based on shared activities or experiences.

The benefits of an Intellectual Connection in relationships are manifold. Studies have found that intellectual compatibility can contribute to relationship satisfaction to various degrees. Intellectual compatibility does not necessarily mean the absence of conflicts. Rather, it can enhance the ability to grow together by reconciling differences over time. The ability to engage in open, respectful, and stimulating intellectual discourse can play a significant role in navigating challenges and conflicts within a relationship.

Partners with such a connection tend to enjoy high-quality communication, where they are more likely to understand and deeply analyze each other, leading to a more fulfilling and expansive exchange of ideas. This understanding goes beyond the surface level of simple agreement or disagreement, probing into the whys and hows of each partner's thinking. For example, a couple who regularly engages in discussions about literature may not only share their favorite books but also discuss the themes, character motivations, and philosophical underpinnings of those works. This systematic analysis into each other's intellects fosters a profound respect for each other's mental faculties and perspectives.

Respect for differing opinions and knowledge is a critical aspect of Intellectual Connections. Intellectual compatibility is not synonymous with identical thinking. Instead, it embraces the diversity of interests and varying depths of knowledge as avenues for mutual growth and learning. Intellectual Connection in relationships can often be a fertile ground for exploring social and cognitive psychology theories, particularly through the lens of Cognitive Dissonance. Cognitive Dissonance highlights the tension experienced when holding contradictory beliefs, a state that can ignite meaningful dialogue and exploration within a relationship. Consider, for example, a couple confronted with divergent views on a moral issue. This discrepancy doesn't merely challenge them; it invites an intellectually stimulating journey. They find themselves grappling with their beliefs in light of their partner's perspectives, the ensuing cognitive dissonance propelling them toward introspection and reassessment. By navigating these complexities, partners deepen their intimacy and foster cooperation and collective growth. Hearing new perspectives or opinions - that one might ordinarily strongly disagree with or dismiss outright - in the voice of someone they love can force them to rethink their own mindset or embedded ideas. This cognitive dissonance, created by someone they care about presenting an opposing viewpoint, challenges individuals to move beyond their comfort zones. Rather than remaining unyielding in their views and unquestioning of themselves, it creates space for change and personal development. In this way, partners in an intellectually connected relationship often use these moments not as points of contention but as opportunities for deeper understanding. They approach conflicts and differences not as insurmountable barriers but as puzzles to be solved together, each bringing their unique perspective and intellect to the table. Intellectual compatibility often leads to a level of understanding where silences are comfortable and intuitive knowledge exists between partners, eliminating the need for lengthy explanations.

Intellectual Connections ought to create an environment where each partner feels valued and respected for their unique thoughts and ideas. However, in some relationships, intellectual discussions can inadvertently evolve into a covert competition of intellects, shifting the focus from collaborative exploration to a contest of mental agility. Such dynamics can engender a sense of intimidation, where one partner might feel inferior or reluctant to share ideas due to fear of judgment. To nurture a healthier intellectual bond, it is crucial to approach discussions with the intent to learn from each other, not to compete. For instance, in discussions on subjects like philosophy or politics, the emphasis should be on understanding each other's perspectives with genuine interest, rather than on convincing each other. This method helps appreciate the diversity of thought and perspective each partner brings. By celebrating these differences, the relationship becomes a safe space for intellectual exploration, free from the pressures of having to be the 'smarter' one.

Being with someone who mentally stimulates you can be a catalyst for personal growth, pushing the boundaries of your comfort zone. For example, one partner's fascination with biotechnology might expose the other to intriguing concepts previously unexplored, stirring new thought patterns.

In relationships graced with an Intellectual Connection, partners reap the benefits of fostering individual and shared intellectual growth. This dual focus allows each person to develop their own interests and knowledge bases, which in turn enriches the shared intellectual life of the couple. For example, one partner might have a deep interest in astronomy and spend time attending stargazing events or reading about the latest space discoveries. Concurrently, the other partner might be fascinated by literature and frequently engage in book clubs or writing workshops. By supporting each other's pursuits, they bring new insights and experiences into their shared life, enhancing their conversations and deepening their connection. Participating in joint intellectual activities, such as attending a lecture series or collaborating on a research project, further solidifies this bond. These shared experiences foster mutual respect and admiration and create a shared intellectual heritage unique to their relationship.

Despite the growing emphasis on Intellectual Connection, modern relationships still face challenges in nurturing this aspect. Nonetheless, the pursuit of Intellectual Connection remains a vital component of many relationships, with people increasingly valuing the ability to engage in meaningful conversations and shared intellectual pursuits. Several barriers can hinder intellectual intimacy in relationships. Busy lifestyles, fear of judgment, communication challenges, and differences in interests can all impede the development of this deeper connection. Overcoming these barriers involves creating a supportive environment that embraces intellectual diversity, improving communication skills, and fostering equality in the relationship.

In relationships where Intellectual Connection is central, it's imperative to recognize that intelligence is not just about academic or cognitive prowess. It encompasses a spectrum of skills and aptitudes, each enriching the relationship's depth and harmony in unique ways. Think about Practical intelligence, often termed 'street smarts.' This intelligence type involves effectively managing daily tasks and challenges, essential for a partnership's day-to-day functioning. It ensures smooth operation, handling everything from financial planning to household organization, demonstrating quick thinking and adaptability. Then again, Existential intelligence, closely linked to pondering life questions and philosophical ideas, also aligns with Spiritual Bonding in relationships. This form of intelligence fosters meaningful discussions about existence, moral values, and spirituality, leading to profound mutual understanding and deepening the relationship's emotional and spiritual layers.

Bodily-kinesthetic intelligence, significant for physical coordination and skill, uniquely contributes to relationships. Shared physical activities, such as dancing, hiking, or yoga, forge a special bond through shared experiences, resonating with the Adventurous Bonding and Physical Presence styles. Creative intelligence, meanwhile, goes beyond traditional arts. It involves innovative problem-solving and thinking outside the box. Partners with high creative intelligence bring freshness and inventiveness to the relationship, inviting exploration and shared creativity through various mediums, whether painting, writing, or brainstorming new ideas for projects.

Emotional, social, and linguistic intelligences play significant yet varied roles. While not necessarily the central focus in every relationship, their presence and interplay contribute to the diversity and depth of human connections. Emotional intelligence revolves around understanding and managing personal and partner/friend emotions. It's interpreting and responding in a way that fosters mutual respect and empathy. For instance, a partner might not grasp complex scientific theories like quantum physics but could excel in reading and navigating emotions. This is vital for understanding subtle mood shifts and providing support during challenges. While intertwined with emotional intelligence, social intelligence focuses on the broader social sphere. It involves navigating and managing relationships within various social networks, such as family, friends, and professional circles. Linguistic intelligence, distinct yet complementary to emotional and social intelligence, is essential for clear and effective communication. It extends beyond having an expansive vocabulary and eloquence to the ability to express thoughts, feelings, and ideas in a way that resonates with a partner. This includes active listening, fully engaging with a partner's words, and understanding both the explicit and implicit messages conveyed. These three forms of intelligence – emotional, social, and linguistic – form a vital triad in relationships, particularly those centered around Intellectual Connection and Empathetic Conversations.

Partners and friends can fully appreciate each other's unique contributions to their shared life by embracing the diversity of intelligence types. Every human is unique, beautiful, and intelligent in their own way. This appreciation of diversity leads to a more dynamic, inclusive, and resilient relationship. Nurturing intellectual intimacy requires conscious effort and a prioritization of authenticity in the relationship. This involves being vulnerable, genuine, and open, creating a space where partners can genuinely be themselves. Engaging in activities that stimulate the mind and provide opportunities for intellectual growth, like discussions about movies, setting life goals together, playing thought-provoking games, and discussing concerns or hobbies, are all effective ways to build this intimacy in a relationship.

YOUR RELATIONSHIP REVIVAL:

Intellectual Connections are nurtured through continuous learning and the sharing of ideas. Here's a list of activities to enrich your intellectual bond:

1. **Bi-Weekly Mini-Lectures:** Establish a tradition where each of you presents a short lecture on an intriguing topic every two weeks, sparking discussions on everything from scientific breakthroughs to philosophical theories.

2. **Museum Exploration Days:** Plan regular visits to museums and exhibitions, immersing yourselves in different cultures and historical periods to stimulate conversation and learning.

3. **Diverse Public Lectures:** Attend lectures on subjects unfamiliar to both of you. This expands your knowledge base and offers fresh perspectives to discuss.

4. **Strategic Game Nights:** Engage in intellectual games like chess or strategy-based board games. These games challenge your minds and encourage strategic thinking together.

5. **Book Club for Two:** Start a personal book club where you read and discuss books outside your usual preferences. This not only broadens your literary horizons but also deepens your Intellectual Connection.

6. **Documentary Evenings:** Dedicate an evening to watching and discussing thought-provoking documentaries, covering topics from science to social issues.

7. **Philosophy Walks:** Take walks together where you discuss philosophical ideas or ethical dilemmas, encouraging deep conversation in a relaxed setting.

8. **Artistic Creation Session:** Spend a day creating something together, be it painting, writing, or crafting, followed by discussing your creative process and inspirations.

9. **Language Learning Challenge:** Take up learning a new language together, providing a challenging and rewarding way to enhance communication and cultural understanding.

10. **Science Experiment Fun:** Conduct simple science experiments at home, learning and having fun with practical applications of scientific principles.

Remember, the essence of Intellectual Connections lies in continuously challenging each other's minds and exploring new realms of knowledge. By introducing these activities, you're avoiding Habituation and cultivating a rich, evolving intellectual landscape in your relationship. As you cherish Intellectual Connection, remember that each style presents unique opportunities to deepen and revitalize your bond. Blending it with other relationship styles, from creative endeavors to thrilling adventures, can offer new perspectives and depths, so embrace these ideas and watch your connection grow stronger and more profound.

PLACES TO PICK:

Libraries, book clubs, academic conferences, lectures, board game cafés, debate clubs, museums, poetry readings, educational workshops, trivia nights, science cafes, language exchange meetups, public forums, historical tours, art galleries, documentary screenings, philosophy meetups, chess clubs, astronomy clubs, technology expos, university campuses.

LITERARY ECHOES:

"Sharing knowledge is the most fundamental act of friendship. Because it is a way you can give something without losing something." — Richard Stallman, American free software movement activist and programmer.

"But they never again passed up the opportunity to read a good book, together." — Renata Bowers, American children's book author and founder of Frieda B. Herself.

"We told each other what movies we were currently watching and what books we were reading." —Unknown.

"There can be no disparity in marriage like unsuitability of mind and purpose." — Charles Dickens, English novelist and social critic who created some of the world's best-known fictional characters.

"I generally read every night before I fall asleep; Brad does too. I find it comforting to lie beside my husband, each of us with a book in our hands." — Debbie Macomber, New York Times best-selling author.

"Together, we form a necessary paradox; not a senseless contradiction." — Criss Jami, author of several books, poetry and philosophy, and musician for the metal project Crymson Gryphon.

"If I have seen further, it is by standing on the shoulders of giants." – Isaac Newton, English mathematician, physicist, and astronomer.

"The next best thing to being wise oneself is to live in a circle of those who are." — C.S. Lewis, British writer and lay theologian.

"Your understanding and interpretation of [a novel] is undoubtedly unique ... and that is the real beauty of the relationship that joins readers, books and writers together in a literary trinity - a bookish triumvirate." — John Green, American author.

"Be less curious about people and more curious about ideas." — Marie Curie, Polish and naturalized French physicist and chemist.

"Love looks not with the eyes, but with the mind. And therefore is winged Cupid painted blind." — William Shakespeare, English playwright and poet.

"The good life is one inspired by love and guided by knowledge." — Bertrand Russell, British philosopher and Nobel laureate.

REFLECT AND DISCUSS:

Deepening Connections through Intellect:

1. Reflect on when an intellectual conversation or shared pursuit deepened your connection with someone. What was the topic, and why did it resonate so strongly with both of you?

2. Consider a moment when differing viewpoints in an intellectual discussion with a partner or friend led to a deeper understanding or respect for each other. How did you navigate this difference?

Evolution and Impact of Intellectual Connections:

3. Discuss how Intellectual Connections have evolved in relationships over time, considering societal changes and the role of education. How do these historical shifts impact modern relationships?

4. Historically, Intellectual Connections have been celebrated in various cultures. Share a favorite intellectual couple from

history, media, or literature that you both admire. What can you learn from their relationship?

_____

_____

_____

Overcoming Barriers and Embracing Diversity:

5. Discuss the concept of Cognitive Dissonance in relationships. How can encountering and resolving conflicting beliefs with a partner lead to growth and deeper connection?

_____

_____

_____

6. Think about a time when intellectual incompatibility was evident in a relationship. How did it affect the dynamics of your interaction, and what did you learn from it?

_____

_____

_____

7. Share your thoughts on the importance of respecting differing viewpoints in an intellectually connected relationship. How do such differences contribute to personal and relational growth?

_____

_____

_____

8. Discuss examples of how Intellectual Connections have en-riched your relationships. What activities or discussions brought you closer to your partner or friends?

_____

_____

_____

Chapter Five

3. CREATIVE EXPRESSION

Moments You'll Recognize:

Jenna and Diego, best friends since college, found their sanctuary in a cozy, sunlit studio brimming with canvases and a kaleidoscope of paints. Known among their friends for their shared passion for the arts, they spent countless hours together, immersed in their creative pursuits. Their friendship was a masterpiece, richly smeared with shared experiences and deeply intertwined inspiration. With her flair for abstract painting, Jenna often drew inspiration from the vibrant hues of nature. Diego, contrastingly, found his muse in music, his fingers dancing over guitar strings, composing melodies that often served as a backdrop to their creative sessions.

On one particular afternoon, as the soft strumming of Diego's guitar filled the room, Jenna worked on a large canvas, her brushstrokes echoing the rhythm of the music. Their friends, who occasionally dropped by to witness their creative synergy, were always mesmerized by the flawless fusion of visual art and music. It was as if each brushstroke Jenna made was guided by Diego's melody, a perfect harmony of sight and sound. Their latest project was a fusion of their talents – a series of paintings inspired by specific musical pieces. Each artwork was a visual representation of a song composed by Diego, capturing the essence of the melody in vibrant colors and textures.

Their studio, adorned with Jenna's paintings and filled with the melodies of Diego's compositions, became a haven for their friends. It was a place where creativity knew no bounds, where ideas flowed freely, and where their friendship, rooted in mutual respect and admiration for each other's art, blossomed. As they prepared for their first joint exhibition, their excitement was palpable. It was the culmination of years of shared dreams and a celebration of a friendship that had grown and deepened through their creative journey. The exhibition, a vibrant blend of visual art and live music, was an opportunity to showcase their talents and to share the story of their friendship – a bond strengthened and enriched by their love for creativity.

Defining the Style:

Creative Expression in relationships manifests through a myriad of activities where imagination and creativity serve as conduits for expressing emotions, experiences, and ideas. It is a way of exploring and understanding one's emotions and the world around them, often allowing for a deeper connection with oneself and others. In friendships and romantic relationships, Creative Expression leverages diverse creative mediums - be it art, music, or writing - to convey emotions and thoughts. It goes beyond verbal communication, offering distinctive and potent ways to connect and understand each other more deeply.

Unveiling Historical and Scientific Treasures:

From an evolutionary perspective, Creative Expression has been a linchpin in human development, serving as a unique and vital trait for survival and progression. Creativity propels the exploration of novel ideas and inventive solutions, fueling adaptation and advancement. The synergy between creativity and fluid intelligence - the capacity for problem-solving, logical reasoning, and pattern recognition - is profound. This relationship underscores the multifaceted nature of creative thinking, merging spontaneous ideation with intellectual and analytical abilities. Human history, from its dawn with rudimentary stone tools to the intricate weaponry of subsequent eras, is a testament to collaborative innovation. These early inventions, reflecting an advanced understanding of material properties and a capacity for forward planning, were often the product of communal effort. In prehistoric sites such as the flint mines of Spiennes in Belgium, we find evidence of complex social structures centered around tool production. The creation of these tools required technical skills and a form of social organization and cooperation, indicating that these activities were integral in cultivating solid communal ties.

Beyond the practicalities of tool-making, early human creativity found expression in more symbolic forms, most notably in cave paintings. The caves of Lascaux in France and Altamira in Spain showcase some of the most exquisite examples of Paleolithic art. These paintings, depicting animals and scenes from daily life, are believed to be more than mere representations; they are seen as mediums of shared experience and expression among early human communities. The act of creating these artworks had likely involved collective effort and ritual, suggesting that they played a role in strengthening communal bonds and possibly even in courtship and mate selection.

Tracing back through the annals of human history, music and song emerge as profound forces in shaping courtships, friendships, and relationships. One of the earliest examples of music's role in social and romantic dynamics can be found in the traditional songs and dances of indigenous cultures. In many tribal societies, music was, and still is, an integral part of courtship rituals. For instance, among the Indigenous Australians, specific songs, known as 'love songs' in the Walbiri tribe, were traditionally sung to woo potential mates. These songs, rich in symbolism and often linked to the tribe's mythology, were expressions of affection and demonstrations of a suitor's cultural knowledge and artistic skill. In the Americas, Native American tribes used music in various social contexts, including courtship. Songs and dances were often part of rituals and ceremonies, creating spaces for individuals to connect and express emotions in a culturally sanctioned manner.

In ancient Greece, music, regarded as a divine art, was deeply interwoven with themes of love and friendship, symbolizing music's romantic power. The Greek god Eros, associated with love, was often depicted with musical instruments, symbolizing the seductive power of music in romance. Sappho, the famed lyric poet of Lesbos, composed passionate songs expressing love and desire, which were likely performed in social gatherings, revealing the power of song as a medium of emotional expression and connection. Furthermore, music was a key element in the symposiums, or convivial gatherings of friends, where participants would enjoy music performances together, strengthening their bonds over shared artistic appreciation.

Shifting to East Asia, traditional Chinese courtship rituals were often embellished with musical elements. Instruments such as the guqin, a melodious seven-stringed zither, and the pipa, a resonant four-stringed lute, often set the stage for romantic serenades and poetic declarations of love. During the Qixi Festival, also known as the Chinese Valentine's Day, the exchange of heartfelt love songs between suitors and maidens was a common and cherished practice. Young men and women would sing traditional ballads and folk songs, sometimes accompanied by these instruments, to convey romantic interest and affection. This practice of exchanging songs during the festival served as a subtle and refined means of expressing feelings, often upstaging ancient Chinese society's typically rigid norms of social interaction.

In the medieval period, the tradition of troubadours in Europe further exemplifies the link between music and courtship. Troubadours were poet-musicians who wandered from court to court, performing chivalric love and devotion songs. Their compositions, often centered around themes of unrequited love and idyllic romance, played a pivotal role in shaping the contemporary notions of Romantic Love.

The African continent, a mosaic of diverse cultures, offers numerous instances of music as a social binder. Music and dance are central to communal life in many African societies, often used to mark significant life events, including courtship and marriage. The Zulu people, for instance, have a rich music and dance tradition, with specific songs and rhythms designated for courtship and weddings, facilitating both romantic connections and communal cohesion.

These historical examples demonstrate that across cultures and epochs, music and song have been powerful tools in the art of relationship-building. They have served as mediums for expressing emotions, showcasing artistic prowess, and adhering to cultural rituals, thus playing an indispensable role in forming and strengthening romantic and social bonds.

The concept of Creative Expression has evolved substantially throughout human history, reflecting changes in societal values, philosophical understandings, and cultural practices. In ancient Greece, the notion of art, or *techne*, was closely tied to adherence to rules, except in poetry, which was seen as a domain of creativity due to its reliance on imagination and inspiration. The Roman era, with figures like Horace, began advocating for artistic liberty beyond poetry. During the Christian period, the concept of *creatio* became associated with God's act of creation, differentiating it from human functions. The Renaissance marked a significant shift, emphasizing the artist's ability to conceive and realize visions beyond mere imitation of nature, recognizing artists as creative individuals shaping 'a new world' through their art. The Enlightenment period in France resisted the idea of human creativity, associating creation strictly with divine action. By the 19th century, art was increasingly seen as a uniquely human domain of creativity.

The 20th century initiated the scientific study of creativity, with J.P. Guilford's address to the American Psychological Association in 1950 marking the start of its popularization as a subject of psychological and scientific inquiry. Contemporary society recognizes creativity as a universal human trait, fundamental to our evolution and essential to social and technological advancements. Creative individuals like Leonardo Di Vinci, Marie Curie, Mozart, and Victor Hugo are celebrated for their contributions.

Alongside human creativity, technology has evolved, providing new avenues for Creative Expression, with innovations like 3D printing, virtual reality, and Artificial Intelligence (AI) demonstrating the interplay between creativity and technological advancement. Historically, creativity has been a driving force behind social change, evolution, and revolution, shaping societies, fostering cultural development, and driving human progress across various domains.

Creative Expression, a vital aspect of human relationships, is deeply entwined with our biological framework, especially in how our brains function and the role of various hormones. One critical brain region involved in this process is the hippocampus, which is known for its role in memory and spatial navigation. The hippocampus is also key in synthesizing experiences and visualizing future scenarios. This ability to mentally traverse past and future, reality and possibility, is crucial in creative thinking and expression, especially within relationships. It allows individuals to use past experiences and future aspirations to forge deeper emotional connections and share more profound, imaginative experiences with their partners or friends.

The brain's default network, active during periods of rest and introspection, also plays an important role in the creative process. This network is associated with daydreaming, imagination, and self-referential thought—processes that are integral to developing new ideas and insights. In the context of relationships, this network can be instrumental in understanding a partner's perspective, empathizing with their emotions, and imagining shared future possibilities. The collaborative dealings between the hippocampus and the default network thus foster creativity that augments relational dynamics, allowing for a deeper exploration of shared experiences and dreams.

The roles of hormones like oxytocin and dopamine are also pivotal within Creative Expression as a relationship style. Oxytocin, often dubbed the 'love hormone,' is renowned for its role in social bonding and intimacy. In the context of Creative Expression, oxytocin extends its influence to encompass the domain of creative thought. It enhances the sense of connection with people, ideas, and imaginative processes, enriching the depth and quality of creative output within relationships. For instance, when couples engage in joint artistic endeavors, such as painting or writing, the surge in oxytocin fosters a deeper emotional bond. This hormone facilitates a space for openness and emotional vulnerability, which is essential for heartfelt and authentic artistic expression.

Dopamine, central to the brain's reward system, plays a crucial role in creativity and pleasure. Dopamine is released during enjoyable activities and is intricately linked to the process of Creative Expression. When individuals engage in creative tasks, whether it's composing music, crafting a fervent poem, or collaborating on a joint artistic project, the release of dopamine provides a sense of pleasure and fulfillment. This release enhances the immediate joy of the creative act and reinforces the desire to continue engaging in such endeavors. In a relationship, this dopamine-driven reinforcement of creativity strengthens the bond between partners, as they associate their shared creative pursuits with feelings of joy and satisfaction. This biological feedback loop encourages partners to continually explore and engage in creative activities, enriching their relationship with each new artistic venture.

These scientific insights into the role of the hippocampus, the brain's default network, and hormones like oxytocin and dopamine, reveal the deep biological and evolutionary underpinnings of Creative Expression in human relationships. By understanding how our brains and hormones influence our creative impulses and expressions, we can appreciate how our biological makeup supports and enhances our connections with others. This knowledge deepens our understanding of the science behind creativity. It highlights the importance of nurturing Creative Expression in building and sustaining meaningful and fulfilling relationships.

Benefits and Considerations:

Shared creative hobbies allow friends or couples to experience new aspects of each other's personalities and build memories together. Relationships thrive on shared experiences and interactions, with Creative Expression providing a unique avenue for these experiences. Engaging in creative activities allows individuals to explore and express their emotions nonverbally, improving self-awareness and self-esteem. This can be particularly helpful in expressing complex feelings that are hard to articulate with words.

Participating in creative activities together can enhance the bond between partners, providing a shared experience that is enjoyable and stress-reducing. Creative Expression also offers significant mental health benefits by reducing symptoms of conditions like anxiety, depression, and Post-Traumatic Stress Disorder (PTSD), providing a valuable therapeutic outlet for processing emotions.

Anxiety, a condition often characterized by excessive worry and stress, can be mitigated through Creative Expression. When couples or friends engage in creative activities like painting or music, they enter a Flow State. In this immersive experience, the outside world and its worries momentarily fade away. This State of Flow, akin to mindfulness, allows individuals to focus solely on the task at hand, reducing anxious thoughts. For example, a couple might engage in a collaborative art project, finding that their anxiety lessens as they concentrate on painting or sculpting. Creating something together, be it a piece of artwork or a musical composition, becomes a shared journey, offering relief and a sense of accomplishment.

In the context of depression, Creative Expression can act as a powerful mood enhancer. Creating art or music releases dopamine, the 'feel-good hormone.' This release can provide a natural boost to mood, counteracting feelings of sadness or hopelessness commonly associated with depression. For individuals struggling with depression, engaging in creative tasks with a friend or partner can be uplifting. As they create, they experience the joy of artistic expression and the warmth of connection and understanding from their companion. For instance, writing and performing a song together can be a liberating experience, allowing them to express emotions that might be difficult to articulate in words.

PTSD, a condition that can occur after experiencing or witnessing traumatic events, can also benefit from Creative Expression. Art therapy, in particular, has been recognized as an effective tool for those with PTSD. It provides a safe and controlled environment to explore traumatic memories without the need for direct verbal confrontation. By drawing, painting, or sculpting, individuals can externalize and process their traumatic experiences, often leading to significant therapeutic outcomes. A friend or partner can play a supportive role in this process by engaging in the creative activity alongside them or providing a supportive presence. This shared creative journey fosters a deep understanding and empathy, essential for healing.

Moreover, Creative Expression facilitates communication about difficult emotions in a less confrontational and more abstract way. For someone with anxiety, depression, or PTSD, articulating feelings through art or music can feel safer and more manageable than lingual communication. A couple of partners or friends might create a joint art piece that symbolizes their struggles, hopes, and fears. This symbolic representation becomes a conversation starter, allowing them to delve into deeper emotional discussions.

In addition, the shared experience of Creative Expression in a relationship builds a strong foundation of mutual support and understanding. It encourages vulnerability and openness, which are essential for emotional intimacy. Creating together or appreciating each other's creative output fosters a unique bond. These activities become a conduit for emotional support and understanding, whether through collaborative writing, joint musical sessions, or shared art projects.

Engaging in creative activities has been linked to increased positive emotion and a sense of flourishing. People report feeling happy and energized when involved in everyday creative endeavors, suggesting a strong link between positive emotion and creativity. It can be particularly beneficial in managing and expressing complex emotions and experiences in healthy and safe ways. Examples in daily life include engaging in painting, drawing, or sculpture to express and process emotions, using expressive writing such as journaling, poetry, or storytelling to articulate thoughts and feelings, learning an instrument, singing, or composing music as a form of emotional expression, and using dance or other forms of movement to express feelings and experiences.

Research suggests that creativity can sustain romantic passion, attraction, and desire in long-term relationships. Creative individuals tend to see their partners more favorably and maintain a sense of attraction and contentment within the relationship. This enduring attraction is often metaphorically described as seeing each other through 'rose-colored glasses,' a phrase that encapsulates a positive, idealized perception of one's partner.

The concept of 'rose-colored glasses' in relationships is interlaced with creativity. It refers to a state where partners view each other in a consistently positive light, focusing on strengths and virtues while downplaying flaws and shortcomings. In a healthy relationship, this optimistic outlook is not about ignoring reality but rather about choosing to appreciate and cherish what makes each partner unique. For example, when a couple collaborates on a creative project, such as writing a novel or painting a mural, they witness each other's imagination, problem-solving skills, and innovative thinking. This process can deepen their admiration and respect for each other, reinforcing a positive perception that often transcends the ordinary.

Creative activities also infuse wonder and excitement into relationships, combatting the monotony that can sometimes creep into long-term partnerships. By regularly engaging in creative pursuits, exploring new genres of music, trying out different art forms, or even cooking an exotic cuisine together, couples introduce fresh experiences and challenges into their relationship. This ongoing exploration keeps the relationship dynamic and engaging, continuously renewing the partners' interest in and passion for each other.

Moreover, creativity in relationships often leads to a deeper understanding and appreciation of each other's inner worlds. When partners express themselves creatively, they reveal parts of their personality that might not surface in everyday interactions. Observing and engaging with these expressions allows each partner or friend to see and appreciate the depths of the other's character and intellect, reinforcing the romantic and emotional connection.

Furthermore, the 'rose-colored glasses' effect, fueled by Creative Expression, can contribute to a more resilient relationship. When faced with challenges or conflicts, partners who maintain this positive outlook are more likely to approach issues constructively, focusing on solutions and growth opportunities rather than dwelling on problems. This approach fosters a supportive environment where both individuals feel valued and understood, crucial for maintaining a strong and healthy relationship.

While Creative Expression can significantly supplement a relationship, it comes with its own considerations to ensure that it remains a positive and fulfilling aspect of the partnership. Creative Expression is deeply personal, and what resonates with one person might not hold the same meaning for another. For instance, one partner may find solace and expression in painting landscapes, while the other might prefer the written word to convey their inner thoughts. Respecting these differences without imposing one's preferences on the other promotes a supportive and harmonious environment for creativity to flourish. Appreciating and engaging in each other's creative pursuits, even if they differ, helps build respect and understanding for each other's unique perspectives and expressions.

Creative Expression can be an emotional journey, and it's essential to be sensitive to the emotional states accompanying the creative process. A partner deeply immersed in a creative project might experience a range of emotions, from frustration and self-doubt to exhilaration and pride. Understanding these emotional nuances and providing support through the highs and lows is vital. For example, being there to offer encouragement during moments of creative block or celebrating together when a project is successfully completed can significantly strengthen the bond.

Open and honest communication about each other's creative work is vital. This includes offering constructive feedback, sharing thoughts and feelings about the work, and expressing appreciation for each other's efforts. It's important to strike a balance between being supportive and offering honest feedback. For example, suppose one partner writes a piece of poetry. In that case, the other should feel comfortable providing genuine feedback while also being mindful of delivering it in a constructive and supportive manner.

In cases where one or both partners' creative work gains external recognition or success, it's crucial to navigate this carefully within the relationship. Success can bring about its own set of challenges, such as jealousy or imbalance in the relationship. Celebrating each other's successes, maintaining open communication, and ensuring that the relationship remains grounded and balanced are crucial steps in handling these situations.

Another important consideration is balancing time spent on individual creative pursuits with time spent together. While each partner might need the space and freedom to pursue their creative interests, it's equally important to ensure that this doesn't come at the expense of quality time together. Setting aside dedicated time for joint activities and ensuring that the relationship remains a priority is crucial. This could involve scheduling regular date nights or participating in shared creative projects that allow both partners to express themselves while also spending time together.

YOUR RELATIONSHIP REVIVAL:

Keeping creativity alive in your relationship means regularly exploring new artistic avenues together. Here's a list of activities to enrich your Creative Expression style:

1. **Artistic Exploration Dates**: Set up 'creative dates' where you explore different art forms. This could be a pottery workshop, a painting class, or a DIY furniture-building project.

2. **Collaborative Art Project**: Create a shared art piece, like painting a mural in your home or embarking on a joint photography project centered around themes you both enjoy.

3. **Musical Creation Journey**: If music is your shared passion, consider writing a song together or learning a new instrument simultaneously, sharing the musical and emotional harmony of this adventure.

4. **Creative Digital Footprint**: Start a joint blog or YouTube channel to document and share your creative projects and insights with a broader audience.

5. **New Medium Experimentation**: Break your routine by trying art forms outside your usual repertoire. If you're painters, try sculpting or writing poetry together.

6. **Community Art Involvement**: Get involved in a community art project. This sparks creativity and connects you with like-minded individuals and groups.

7. **Theatre Night Out**: Attend a play or an improvisational theatre performance. Discuss the themes and performances afterward to inspire your own Creative Expressions.

8. **Creative Cooking Challenge**: Turn cooking into a creative art form by experimenting with new recipes or ingredients, making each meal a culinary adventure.

9. **Nature-Inspired Art**: Spend a day in nature, using natural elements to create art, like leaf collages or sand sculptures, fostering a deep connection with each other and the environment.

10. **Urban Sketching Excursion**: Explore your city with sketchbooks in hand. Find interesting spots to sit and sketch together, capturing moments and scenes that resonate with you.

Remember, Creative Expression in a relationship thrives on diversity and exploration. These activities foster your artistic skills and deepen your bond through shared creative endeavors. Embrace this journey of artistic discovery together, and watch as it adds a rich, colorful dimension to your relationship. Consider intertwining it with other relationship styles to enrich your connections, as each style offers a unique canvas for expression.

PLACES TO PICK:

Art studios, pottery classes, dance studios, music jam sessions, painting workshops, craft fairs, photography walks, open mic nights, DIY crafting centers, film festivals, theater productions, sculpture gardens, art supply stores, community murals, cultural centers, fabric workshops, literary events, music festivals, acting classes, creative writing groups, art exhibitions.

LITERARY ECHOES:

"Art must be an expression of love, or it is nothing." — Marc Chagall, Russian-French artist.

"Art and love are the same thing: It's the process of seeing yourself in things that are not you." — Chuck Klosterman, American author and essayist.

"The great difference between the two feelings is that love is always creative, and fear is always destructive." — Emmet Fox, Irish New Thought spiritual leader of the early 20th century.

"Love is a canvas furnished by nature and embroidered by imagination." — Voltaire, French Enlightenment writer, historian, and philosopher.

"There is nothing more truly artistic than to love people." — Vincent van Gogh, Dutch post-impressionist painter.

"Art and love are the same thing: they enrich the soul." — Nora Roberts, American author of over 225 romance novels.

"To write a good love letter, you ought to begin without knowing what you mean to say, and to finish without knowing what you have written." — Jean-Jacques Rousseau, Genevan philosopher.

"If music be the food of love, play on." — William Shakespeare's Twelfth Night, English playwright and poet.

"Love is the poetry of the senses." — Honoré de Balzac, French novelist and playwright.

"Music is the divine way to tell beautiful, poetic things to the heart." — Pablo Casals, Spanish cellist and conductor.

"Every heart sings a song, incomplete, until another heart whispers back. Those who wish to sing always find a song. At the touch of a lover, everyone becomes a poet." — Plato, ancient Greek philosopher.

"Music expresses that which cannot be put into words and that which cannot remain silent." — Victor Hugo, French poet, novelist, and dramatist.

Reflect and Discuss:

Creativity and Mutual Growth:

1. Discuss when you and your partner or friend inspired each other creatively. How did this mutual inspiration affect your relationship?

   _____

   _____

   _____

2. Share an experience where collaborating on a creative project led to learning new aspects about each other.

   _____

   _____

   _____

Balancing and Compromising in Creativity:

3. How do you balance your Creative Expression with that of your partner or friend in a joint project?

   _____

   _____

   _____

4. Describe a situation where you had to compromise creatively in a relationship. What did you learn from this experience about balance and respect for different ideas?

   _____

   _____

   _____

5. Can you recall when a creative disagreement led to a deeper understanding or a stronger bond? How was this achieved?

_____

_____

_____

Communication and Feedback in Creative Collaboration:

6. How do you provide constructive feedback to each other on creative projects while maintaining a supportive environment?

_____

_____

_____

Creative Expression as a Form of Communication:

7. Share an instance where a Creative Expression (like art, music, writing) helped convey feelings or thoughts you struggled to communicate verbally.

_____

_____

_____

History of Creative Expression:

8. Artistic expression has evolved significantly throughout history. Reflect on an art movement or style you both appreciate. How does this shared interest influence your relationship? Who were your favorite creative couple/friends?

_____

_____

_____

Chapter Six

4. CULINARY SHARING

Moments You'll Recognize:

Emily and Liam's shared haven was an old, fragrant kitchen, a sanctuary for their culinary adventures that seasoned their relationship with a passion for diverse flavors and global cuisine exploration. Their journey began on their first date at a small Italian trattoria, where they discovered their mutual love for gastronomy. From then on, their dates turned into culinary voyages. Whether experimenting with exotic recipes at home or exploring hidden gourmet gems in the city, each meal was a chapter in their love story.

Their beloved tradition, the 'Sunday Culinary Challenge,' brought a weekly dash of excitement. They would choose a theme – a cuisine, an ingredient, or a cooking technique – and each would craft a dish around it. These evenings brimmed with laughter and friendly rivalry, as they playfully vied to surpass each other's culinary creations. Friends invited to these dinners would often marvel at the couple's harmony in the kitchen and their ability to turn simple ingredients into extraordinary experiences.

Emily, a wizard at baking, delighted Liam with her exquisitely adorned cakes and pastries, masterpieces of flavor and artistry. Conversely, Liam excelled in grilling, devoting hours to marinating and honing his barbecue skills, anticipating Emily's reaction to each new dish. Their kitchen was a treasure trove of cookbooks from every corner of the globe, and their pantry was a testament to their culinary curiosity. Together, they embarked on a project to cook a dish from every country, documenting their journey through a blog that soon garnered a following of fellow food enthusiasts.

As they planned their wedding, they knew food had to play a central role. Their reception was an epicure tour, with each course representing a significant moment in their relationship – from the pasta dish reminiscent of their first date to the decadent dessert that mirrored their sweet journey together. This was a journey of discovery, an exploration of cultures and traditions that brought them even closer.

Defining the Style:

Culinary Sharing is a fundamental aspect of human social interaction, comprising cooking and dining experiences. This includes a variety of settings, from the warmth of home cooking to the exploration of diverse dining establishments. This style of connection brings forth the joy of selecting the perfect dining spot and the adventure of savoring miscellaneous flavors in restaurants. Moreover, Culinary Sharing extends to the collaborative and intimate meal preparation process at home. The anticipation of trying a recommended dish and the exhilaration of sampling diverse cuisines add to the richness of this shared journey. Cooking and dining together strengthen communication, enhance coordination, and deepen intimacy, setting the stage for creating special moments and physical closeness. Culinary Sharing is linked with increased satisfaction, the establishment of new traditions, and the forging of enduring memories. Additionally, Culinary Sharing promotes trust, a sense of community, belonging, and emotional closeness, making it a multisensory and bonding experience. Diverse activities, such as experimenting with new recipes, organizing themed culinary evenings to explore international cuisines, and participating in cooking classes, offer enjoyable ways for individuals to deepen their relationships through the universal language of food.

Unveiling Historical and Scientific Treasures:

Food sharing is a practice observed in many animals, particularly primates, which extends to humans and holds deep evolutionary significance. It is an essential aspect of social bonding and cooperation, contributing significantly to the human subsistence niche. The phrase "subsistence niche" refers to the specific strategies and behaviors that humans employ to obtain resources necessary for survival. This encompasses hunting, gathering, farming, cooking, and sharing food, which are all integral to human social interactions and cooperative living. Among primates, food sharing, often a luxury monopolized by dominant individuals, is exchanged for services like grooming or forming coalitions, playing a pivotal role in cementing social relationships and handling risks such as disruptions due to injury or sickness. In evolutionary biology, theories of reciprocal sharing propose that food-sharing behaviors are shaped by the availability of resources. Individuals often share food that others cannot readily access themselves. This behavior can be linked to the reproductive value of individuals, with older individuals in some societies tending to share food and care for younger, non-related individuals, becoming more structured and stringent as food becomes scarcer, favoring close relatives or those who reciprocate.

Culinary Sharing is closely linked to Costly Signaling and group cooperation dynamics in our evolutionary past, illustrating how food sharing has historically been a means to demonstrate individual value as prospective mates. Costly Signaling, a theory originating from evolutionary biology, posits that food sharing was, and still is, a way for individuals to demonstrate their value as potential mates. By sharing food, often acquired through considerable effort, individuals could showcase their abilities to provide, a desirable trait in a mate. This act of sharing highlighted an individual's resourcefulness, social status, and understanding of reciprocal relationships.

Culinary Sharing merges Altruism and Mutualism, playing a crucial role in relationship development, where selfless meal sharing builds trust and strengthens communal cohesion. Altruism in culinary contexts manifests when individuals prepare and share meals without expecting immediate reciprocation. These feats nurture social bonds and build trust within a group. This type of selfless sharing is more than a mere provision of sustenance; it acts as a signal of generosity and commitment to the well-being of others, thereby strengthening communal cohesion. Moreover, this cooperative strategy aligns with the concept of Mutualism, where all parties involved benefit from the joint effort. By working together, early humans could increase their food yields significantly compared to what they could achieve individually. This mutualistic approach to food acquisition and distribution played a vital role in developing early human societies, fostering a sense of community and interdependence.

Culinary Sharing, also known as commensality, has been integral to human social interaction across different cultures and historical periods, often central to communal hunting, gathering, and feasting practices. Historically, humans have engaged in collective hunting and gathering, targeting food sources that were beyond the reach of solitary efforts. These cooperative endeavors often focused on resources that demanded a coordinated approach, such as large preys or seasonally abundant forage. Among hunter-gatherer ancestors, feasts following successful hunts were celebrations of skill, cooperation, and survival, crucial in fostering community bonds and ensuring the collective well-being of the group. With the advent of agriculture and the development of larger societies, communal meals began to serve additional purposes, with feasts becoming a means for leaders and rulers to demonstrate status and power. Across different cultures, food and eating practices have been integral to shaping social identities, with traditional dishes often reflecting the history and geography of a particular region.

Family meals, where members come together to share food, have been a universal practice, fostering familial bonds and allowing for shared experiences and discussions. Communal meals are indispensable in various rituals and ceremonies, symbolizing unity and serving as a platform for collective bonding. Different cultures have unique practices and etiquette surrounding communal meals, reflecting diverse values and beliefs around food sharing and social interaction.

The Culinary Sharing relationship style, ingrained in our biology, encompasses a complex interplay of sensory experiences, communication, and hormonal responses, collectively enhancing our relationships.

Biologically, culinary activities stimulate a complex interplay of hormones like ghrelin and leptin, which influence our social interactions and bonding during shared meals in ways we didn't know before modern research. Ghrelin, often termed the 'hunger hormone,' is crucial in meal initiation. This fast-acting hormone increases appetite and is intricately involved in the anticipatory aspects of eating, such as the excitement and preparation for a meal. Meanwhile, leptin, a mediator of long-term energy balance, suppresses food intake and induces weight loss. It functions as a satiety signal, helping to regulate food intake over extended periods. The interplay between ghrelin and leptin in relationships is particularly noteworthy. Studies like "The Metabolic Mind: A Role for Leptin and Ghrelin in Affect and Social Cognition" provide a comprehensive view. These studies suggest that leptin and ghrelin may be sensitive to *social affective signals* and contexts, like *social status* and *support versus threat*, and contribute to psychological processes such as affection and social cognition. Social affective signals refer to the emotional cues and expressions communicated within social interactions, such as gestures, facial expressions, and vocal tones, which are crucial in understanding and responding to others' emotional states. Social status relates to one's position or rank within a social hierarchy, impacting individual experiences of inclusion, respect, and influence within a group. The term' support vs threat' encompasses the perceived nature of social interactions, where 'support' indicates a sense of safety, belonging, and positive reinforcement from others, while 'threat' denotes feelings of risk, hostility, or social rejection—understanding these concepts aids in appreciating how leptin and ghrelin, beyond their roles in physical appetite, may also be influenced by and influence these complex social and emotional dynamics. These hormones are implicated in how we respond to social situations, potentially influencing behaviors like emotion and risk-taking, all motivated by our allostatic needs - the brain's way of regulating physiology based on situational expectations. Shared culinary experiences, ranging from selecting ingredients to cooking and eating together, stimulate these hormonal responses quite differently than if we are eating separately, influencing our feelings of hunger and fullness. This biological mechanism affects our social interactions, enhancing the communal enjoyment of food and reinforcing a sense of contentment and connection.

In addition to ghrelin and leptin, serotonin, a neurotransmitter often associated with feelings of well-being and happiness, is paramount in the Culinary Sharing relationship style. A significant portion, approximately 90% of our serotonin production, originates in the digestive tract. The gut sends more signals to the brain than the other way around, emphasizing the gut's influence on brain activity. These facts underline the profound connection between our gut health and emotional state. The gut-brain axis, a bidirectional communication pathway between the gastrointestinal tract and the central nervous system, plays a crucial role in our overall well-being. This connection implies that gut health can influence brain function and emotional state. Consequently, shared dining experience impacts this dynamic, affecting our physical and emotional health. Serotonin in the digestive tract links eating with emotional responses, accentuating how shared culinary experiences can enhance emotional regulation and relational harmony.

Culinary Sharing, a relationship style characterized by the communal experience of cooking and dining, extends its influence beyond the mere act of eating together. This practice shapes our microbiome, the community of microorganisms living in our bodies, particularly in the gut, playing a pivotal role in our overall health, emotional well-being, and social relationships.

The influence of Culinary Sharing on relationships extends beyond healthy dietary choices to encompass the subtle yet profound ways close physical interactions shape our microbiome.

When couples or friends engage in physical contact, such as hugging, kissing, or even sharing living spaces, they inadvertently exchange microbial communities. This exchange can lead to the development of a shared microbiome profile unique to each relationship.

Research in microbiology has revealed that individuals who live together, especially couples, tend to have more similar gut and skin microbiomes compared to the general population. This similarity arises from the frequent physical contact and the shared environment, which facilitates the transfer of microbial species between individuals. Every hug, kiss, or shared meal is a potential moment of microbial exchange, subtly aligning the microbiomes of the people involved.

A diverse microbiome, often resulting from these shared microbial environments, is linked to improved health. It enhances immune system function and promotes overall vitality, which is crucial for the longevity of any relationship. Additionally, the gut-brain axis, a communication pathway between the gastrointestinal tract and the central nervous system, suggests that a balanced microbiome positively influences mood and emotional health. Couples with similar microbiomes may experience more aligned emotional states and responses, fostering deeper emotional connections and understanding. This alignment also extends to friends who share significant time together, enhancing their sense of connectedness and belonging. A healthy microbiome impacts cognitive functions such as memory and focus, which are integral for engaging conversations and interactions and a cornerstone of solid relationships.

Healthy dietary choices further amplify the benefits of a shared microbiome. Meals rich in fiber and diverse nutrients influence the production of short-chain fatty acids (SCFAs) like butyrate, propionate, and acetate. These compounds have anti-inflammatory properties, enhance gut barrier function, and, importantly, influence neurotransmitter production, including serotonin. This 'feel-good' hormone plays a significant role in mood regulation and contributes to a positive outlook and increased happiness. By sharing meals rich in fiber and diverse nutrients, couples and friends can indirectly influence the production of these beneficial compounds, thereby enhancing their overall mood and emotional well-being. This biochemical interplay can lead to a more positive outlook on life, increased happiness, and a strengthened emotional connection with each other.

Smell and taste, fundamental sensory experiences in culinary activities, not only trigger neurological and hormonal responses but also enhance the pleasure of eating, enriching both the emotional and social dimensions of shared dining experiences. The aromas and flavors of food can evoke memories, stimulate conversation, and create a multisensory experience deeply interwoven with our social behaviors and relationship building. Food's olfactory and gustatory stimuli engage more than just our primary senses. When we smell and taste food, it activates specific areas of the brain, particularly the limbic system, which is closely involved in emotion and memory processing. For instance, the aroma of a certain spice or the flavor of a particular dish can transport us back to cherished moments, triggering a cascade of fond or nostalgic feelings. This connection between smell, taste, and memory is not just a fleeting experience but a powerful neurological event that can strengthen social bonds.

Discussing food preferences and recipes or serving food to one another fosters a sense of companionship and mutual care. These interactions stimulate the release of oxytocin, the 'bonding hormone,' which enhances feelings of social connectedness and trust. Eating together, involving the sensations of taste and smell, engages our reward system. Tasting delicious food triggers the release of dopamine, a neurotransmitter associated with pleasure and satisfaction. This reward response is a powerful biological mechanism that reinforces social interactions and positive experiences related to Culinary Sharing.

BENEFITS AND CONSIDERATIONS:

Culinary Sharing as a relationship style is a delightful and enriching experience beyond consuming food. This inclusive activity brings people together, breaking down barriers and adopting a sense of belonging and community. Whether it's a family gathering, a dinner party with friends, or a romantic meal for two, sharing food is universally seen as an act of hospitality and care. It means saying, "You are welcome in my space, and I want to share this experience with you." For couples, Culinary Sharing can blossom into a romantic and intimate affair, where hands-on cooking, creating tantalizing dishes, and relishing the process all occur in a cozy, intimate ambiance. It also requires partners to work together, divide tasks, and support each other, strengthening their ability to collaborate effectively. This shared culinary space creates a relaxed environment for couples to learn about each other's preferences, backgrounds, and childhood memories, deepening their emotional bond.

Culinary Sharing plays a significant role in facilitating Empathetic Emotional Regulation (EER) and reinforcing bonds. EER represents a dynamic process of managing and responding to emotions in interpersonal interactions. In this empathetic exchange, it's not just about controlling one's own emotions but also affecting the emotional state of the other individual in the interaction. Scholars like Hamburg, Finkenauer, and Schuengel have explored the concept that the act of offering food is often motivated by the emotional state of both the giver and the receiver. It serves to increase positive affect and interpersonal closeness, demonstrating a profound link between food sharing and emotional well-being. In the intimate setting of a shared meal, individuals are more attuned to the subtle emotional cues of their dining partners. Gestures like passing a dish, serving a portion to another, or even selecting a meal can be imbued with emotional significance, signaling care, understanding, and connection. These seemingly minor acts of culinary generosity become powerful expressions of empathy, enhancing the emotional bond between the participants. Furthermore, the shared experience of enjoying a meal often leads to synchronized emotional states, a phenomenon supported by emotional contagion. As individuals share food, they often mirror each other's emotions, whether the joy of tasting a delicious dish or the warmth of a comforting meal. This synchronization deepens the emotional connection and reinforces the sense of unity and belonging. Culinary Sharing also offers a unique opportunity for individuals to express and receive love and care through food choices and preparation. For instance, preparing a partner's favorite dish as a surprise or choosing a restaurant with special memories demonstrates deep personal understanding and emotional attentiveness. These actions enrich the emotional quality of the relationship, building a stronger, more empathetic bond.

Culinary Sharing offers a plethora of benefits that strengthen bonds and create lasting memories. Preparing and enjoying meals is an opportunity to share the day's experiences, discuss future plans, or enjoy each other's company in a relaxed setting. Shared meals become a space for laughter, storytelling, and camaraderie, forging deeper connections through shared tastes and dining experiences.

The culinary eating experience often opens avenues for rich, organic conversations. Discussions about food preferences, cooking techniques, or the origins of different cuisines can lead to extended discussions about personal histories, preferences, and values. A simple conversation about a traditional dish can lead to sharing childhood memories or cultural backgrounds, providing a more profound understanding of each other. In this way, food catalyzes meaningful conversations, enhancing communication and mutual understanding.

Culinary eating encourages exploration and adventure. Trying new restaurants, cuisines, or recipes is an adventure in itself. For a couple or group of friends, this can mean embarking on culinary tours, attending food festivals, or even traveling to different countries to experience their cuisines firsthand. Each new flavor or dish tried together is an exploration of the unknown. It's about discovering new likes and dislikes, adapting to each other's tastes, and celebrating the diversity of the culinary world.

Eating can be a significant stress reliever, particularly in a relaxed and enjoyable setting. For couples and friends, sharing a meal can be a time to unwind, put aside the stresses of daily life, and enjoy the pleasures of good food and good company. The sensory experience of tasting, smelling, and savoring food can be incredibly therapeutic and relaxing, providing a much-needed break from the hustle and bustle of everyday life.

Sharing meals can also lead to better nutritional habits, as partners or friends often influence each other's food choices. Cooking and eating together encourage trying healthier options, portion control, and a more balanced diet. For couples, planning and preparing meals together can become an opportunity to focus on health goals and support each other in making better food choices.

Accommodating different tastes and styles in Culinary Sharing presents an opportunity to learn from each other and broaden culinary horizons. Cooking together can lead to disagreements or mistakes, and it's crucial to handle these situations calmly and respectfully, focusing on communication and compromise. Not all partners may have the time or interest in cooking together frequently, so finding a balance that suits both partners' lifestyles and preferences is essential.

Culinary Sharing carries a set of considerations to ensure that it remains a source of joy and connection rather than a point of contention. One of the first considerations in a Culinary Sharing relationship is acknowledging and respecting each other's dietary preferences and restrictions. This could range from allergies and health-related restrictions to personal or ethical dietary choices like keto or vegetarianism. For instance, if one partner is gluten-intolerant, the other partner should be supportive by either adapting recipes to be gluten-free or ensuring that there is always a gluten-free option available. This respect for each other's dietary needs is foundational in creating a mutually enjoyable culinary experience.

In any partnership, it's important to balance roles and responsibilities in the kitchen. This balance doesn't necessarily mean an equal division of labor, but rather an arrangement that works best for both partners. For some, this might mean one partner does the cooking while the other takes on the cleaning. In other cases, both partners might enjoy cooking together. For example, one partner might excel in preparing entrees while the other loves baking desserts. The key is to find a rhythm that feels equitable and satisfying for both individuals.

Differences in taste, culinary skills, and interest in cooking can be a significant consideration. One partner may have a more adventurous palate, eager to try exotic cuisines, while the other may prefer more traditional, comfort food. Compromise and experimentation can help bridge these differences. Planning meals that incorporate elements appealing to both tastes or dedicating certain days to experiment with different cuisines can turn these differences into opportunities for culinary exploration and fun.

Effective communication and planning are essential in a Culinary Sharing relationship. This could involve discussing meal plans, grocery shopping responsibilities, or even budgeting for food expenses. It's about making joint decisions that take into account each other's preferences, schedules, and nutritional needs. For instance, a couple might set a weekly "experiment night" where they try a new recipe or cuisine together, making it an anticipated and enjoyable event.

Culinary Sharing often becomes a medium for emotional expression. It can be a way to care for and nurture each other, to celebrate successes, or to provide comfort. Understanding the emotional significance of food in the relationship is important. A partner might prepare a family recipe to provide comfort on a tough day, or they might recreate a dish from a memorable date as an anniversary surprise.

Besides, lifestyle changes, such as changes in work schedules, health considerations, or even the addition of family members, can impact culinary dynamics. Being adaptable and willing to adjust culinary routines in the face of these changes is crucial. For example, the birth of a child might necessitate quicker, more nutritious meal options, or a shift in work hours might lead to experimenting with meal prep or slow cooker recipes.

YOUR RELATIONSHIP REVIVAL:

Culinary Sharing transforms everyday meals into exciting and bonding experiences. Here's a list of activities to enrich your culinary connection:

1. **Mystery Ingredient Challenge:** Have a cook-off where each of you prepares a dish with a surprise ingredient chosen by the other. It's a fun way to test culinary creativity and enjoy unexpected flavors.

2. **Global Cuisine Nights:** Host a 'round-the-world' dinner week. Dedicate each night to cuisine from a different country, complete with themed decorations and music, to explore global flavors together.

3. **Picnic Creations:** Plan a homemade picnic where you both contribute dishes. Enjoy your culinary creations in the great outdoors, adding a dash of romance and adventure to your meal.

4. **Shared Recipe Book:** Create a 'recipe book' together, compiling your favorite recipes and the memories associated with them. This personal cookbook will be a testament to your shared culinary journey.

5. **Culinary Class Adventure:** Enroll in a cooking class focusing on a cuisine you're both unfamiliar with, like Ethiopian or Peruvian. This is a great way to explore new flavors and cooking techniques together.

6. **Ingredient Limit Challenge:** Challenge each other to create a dish using a set of random or limited ingredients. This test of culinary skill and imagination can lead to surprising and delightful creations.

7. **Farmers' Market Exploration:** Visit a local farmers' market and pick fresh, seasonal ingredients. Then, cook a meal together using your market finds, celebrating fresh and local produce.

8. **Themed Cooking Marathon:** Choose a culinary theme, like vegan or dessert-only dishes, and spend a day cooking and tasting various recipes within that theme.

9. **Culinary Time Travel:** Pick a historical period and cook a meal using recipes and techniques from that era, immersing yourselves in the culinary traditions of the past.

10. **Fusion Food Experiment:** Experiment with fusion cooking by combining elements from your favorite cuisines to create new, unique dishes that represent both of your tastes.

Culinary Sharing is more than just cooking and eating; it's about exploring new tastes, learning together, and creating lasting memories. Yet, spicing up this style with elements from other relationship dynamics, like Playfulness or Spirituality, can make every meal a richer experience. Each shared culinary adventure strengthens your bond and adds flavor to your relationship. Embrace these activities to make your kitchen a haven of creativity and connection.

Places to Pick:

Cooking schools, gourmet food markets, wine tasting events, ethnic restaurants, food festivals, culinary tours, farmers' markets, home cooking classes, bake-offs, cheese tasting sessions, brewery tours, rooftop dining spots, pop-up restaurants, local cafes, sushi making workshops, coffee tasting experiences, chocolatier shops, specialty food stores, food truck rallies, picnic parks.

LITERARY ECHOES:

"Food brings people together on many different levels. It's nourishment of the soul and body; it's truly love." — Giada De Laurentiis, Italian-American chef and television personality.

"The people who give you their food give you their heart." — Cesar Chavez, American labor leader and civil rights activist.

"Cooking is love made visible." — Jep Robertson, American television personality.

"We should look for someone to eat and drink with before looking for something to eat and drink." — Epicurus, ancient Greek philosopher.

"The heart of the home is the kitchen, and the heart of the kitchen is the dining table." — Rachel Khoo, British cook, writer, and broadcaster.

"A shared meal is the activity most closely tied to the reality of love – it is an act of communion and connection." — Christine Pohl, Christian theologian.

"Sharing food with another human being is an intimate act that should not be indulged in lightly." — M.F.K. Fisher, American food writer.

"Cooking is one of the great gifts you can give to those you love." — Ina Garten, American author and host of the Food Network program "Barefoot Contessa."

"Food is symbolic of love when words are inadequate." — Alan D. Wolfelt, American author and grief counselor.

"Breaking bread together is a powerful way to open our hearts and build connections." — Attributed to many authors with slightly different variations.

"Eating together at a restaurant allows the family to savor not only the food but also the shared experience of being served and cared for." — Michael Pollan, American author, journalist, and activist.

"The table is a meeting place, a gathering ground, the source of sustenance and nourishment, festivity, and friendship." — Laurie Colwin, American author and columnist.

Reflect and Discuss:

Culinary Experiences and Connections:

1. Discuss a time when cooking together led to an unexpected but meaningful conversation. What was discussed, and how did it impact your relationship?

    _____

    _____

    _____

2. Share a story about trying a new cuisine with your partner or friend. How did this experience broaden your culinary horizons and affect your bond?

    _____

    _____

    _____

3. Share an experience where food became a medium for cultural exchange or understanding in your relationship.

    _____

    _____

    _____

Traditions, Celebrations, and Adaptations in Culinary Sharing:

4. Recall a fond memory of a family recipe you shared with your partner or friend. What traditions or stories are associated with this recipe?

    _____

    _____

    _____

5. Can you think of a time when food played a crucial role in celebrating a success or comforting in a time of distress in your relationship?

_____

_____

_____

6. Discuss the role of dietary preferences and choices (like veganism or allergies) in your culinary relationship. How do you accommodate and respect these preferences?

_____

_____

_____

7. Culinary tastes and habits are often shaped by cultural evolution. Discuss a traditional dish from your or your partner's culture and how sharing this meal has brought you closer.

_____

_____

_____

Learning and Growing Through Culinary Adventures:

8. Share a story of a cooking disaster you experienced with your partner or friend. How did you handle the situation, and what did you learn from it?

_____

_____

_____

Chapter Seven

5. KIND
CONTRIBUTIONS

Moments You'll Recognize:

Jasmine and Alex met during their college years, brought together by a shared passion for social activism and a drive to make a meaningful difference. What started as a partnership in a community service project soon blossomed into an inseparable friendship, with their Kind Contributions at its core. Their first endeavor was a small initiative to help the local homeless shelter. With her warm, empathetic nature, Jasmine would spend hours talking to the shelter residents, understanding their needs. Alex, practical and resourceful, organized donation drives and fundraisers. Together, they provided immediate aid and worked on long-term solutions for the shelter's challenges.

Recognizing the power of education in driving change, they co-founded a weekend tutoring program for underprivileged children in their neighborhood. Jasmine's creativity brought fun and innovative teaching methods to the sessions, making learning an adventure for the kids. Alex's organizational skills ensured the program ran smoothly, gaining support and resources from local businesses and volunteers. Watching the children's progress and their joy in learning was a source of immense satisfaction and deepened their bond.

Their friendship was a dynamic blend of Jasmine's compassionate outlook and Alex's pragmatic approach. They complemented each other perfectly, whether planning a community clean-up drive or advocating environmental conservation. Their shared vision for a better world was the thread that wove together their activities and friendship. One of their most impactful projects was the 'Green Spaces' initiative. They transformed neglected city areas into spirited community gardens, involving locals in the process. These gardens were symbols of hope and unity, fostering a sense of community and belonging.

They celebrated each victory, no matter how small, and supported each other through challenges. Their bond was forged in the fires of shared purpose and mutual respect for each other's ideals and strengths. Over the years, as their initiatives expanded, so did their friendship. They became known in their community as the duo who could always be counted on to lend a helping hand or spearhead a new project. Their Kind Contributions had created a ripple effect of positivity, touching countless lives.

DEFINING THE STYLE:

Kind Contributions is the shared passion for philanthropy and positive change. It involves individuals driven by a common goal to do good in the world, engaging in acts that benefit others and contribute to societal improvement. Engaging in philanthropic activities offers a resounding sense of purpose and fulfillment. Sharing a commitment to positive change can strengthen bonds between individuals as they work towards a common goal. Contributing to the welfare of others can enhance one's emotional and mental well-being. Participating in community service projects or volunteering for charitable organizations, organizing or contributing to fundraising events for causes or non-profit organizations, and engaging in advocacy work for social, environmental, or humanitarian causes are all examples of Kind Contributions.

UNVEILING HISTORICAL AND SCIENTIFIC TREASURES:

The practice of Kind Contributions in human relationships is deeply embedded in human evolutionary history and social behavior, underlining the significance of Altruism and kindness. Anthropological studies of hunter-gatherer societies, like those conducted by Richard Lee and Irven DeVore, reveal that sharing and cooperative behavior were essential for survival. This deep-rooted practice of Altruism in early human societies laid the foundation for more complex forms of social cooperation and community building. Research in evolutionary biology and psychology has long emphasized the significant role of Altruism and kindness in human societies. In a notable shift from traditional perspectives, recent studies suggest that Altruism evolved primarily for community benefit, challenging the earlier belief that it was mainly driven by Kin Selection, which focuses on benefiting genetically related individuals. These insights point to altruistic behavior as crucial not just for individual genetic advantage but for the survival and prosperity of broader social groups beyond immediate family ties. This evolution of Altruism highlights the critical role of cooperation and altruistic behavior in the survival and thriving of human groups.

Further supporting this perspective are the contributions of evolutionary biologists like E.O. Wilson, who revised his Kin Selection theory to emphasize the importance of Altruism and cooperation for group success. This view aligns with the Kind Contributions style, which focuses on acts of kindness and community service. Research from the Max Planck Institute for Evolutionary Anthropology reinforces this, suggesting that human cooperative skills developed out of mutual interest and necessity for survival. Additionally, the theory of Survival of the Friendliest, proposed by Brian Hare, posits that human social skills evolved as natural selection began favoring prosociality over aggression. This shift played a key role in the development of social bonding, prosocial behavior, and spiritual connections, further solidifying the importance of kindness and Altruism in strengthening community ties and ensuring collective well-being.

Altruism can be divided into three forms: kin-based, reciprocity-based, and care-based. Kin-based Altruism benefits biological relatives and ultimately benefits the altruist from a genetic standpoint. Reciprocity-based Altruism is performed with the expectation of future rewards, supported by dopaminergic cortico-striatal networks. Care-based Altruism is linked to empathic concern and relies on subcortical neural systems that support parental care, involving structures with receptors for oxytocin and vasopressin.

Altruism often takes the form of Kind Contributions, uniting people under the shared mission of driving positive change. Such actions are deeply rooted in the evolutionary drive towards mutual support within groups. When we explore the Kind Contribution relationship style, an overlap emerges between evolutionary tactics and neurological development aimed at societal betterment. Through philanthropy and community involvement, individuals embody evolutionary concepts of kinship and reciprocal altruism, while also tapping in their natural empathetic and caregiving capacities.

The history of philanthropy, from ancient to modern times, illustrates the evolution of Altruism from religious and ethical duties in ancient societies to more diverse forms in contemporary times. The idea that couples or friends should cooperate in acts of giving and helping others is supported by various historical, religious, and social traditions, and these teachings and practices align with the concept of the Kind Contribution relationship style.

In ancient Greek culture, *philanthropia* was not just an individual virtue but a societal ideal that extended to the public life of couples and groups. It was seen as a moral duty and a sign of good character to contribute to the welfare of one's community. This practice encouraged cooperation among all members of society, including couples and friends, fostering a shared commitment to the common good.

In Jewish tradition, *tzedakah* is more than charity; it's considered an act of justice and righteousness. The Torah and later Jewish teachings encourage communal responsibility, where helping others is a collective obligation. This idea is evident in many Jewish communities where families and friends come together to practice *tzedakah*, emphasizing shared participation in acts of giving and kindness. The New Testament of the Bible contains numerous references to joint acts of charity and support. For instance, in the Book of Acts, early Christians are described as sharing their possessions and providing for each other's needs (Acts 2:44-45). This communal approach to helping others suggests that couples and groups are encouraged to work together in their philanthropic efforts. In Islam, *zakat* is one of the Five Pillars and is obligatory for all Muslims. It is an individual obligation and a communal one, emphasizing the importance of shared social responsibility. This principle is often seen in action during Ramadan, when families and friends come together to give *zakat*, thereby reinforcing the concept of cooperative giving and support within the community. These practices were often tied to religious and ethical duties.

Integrating charitable acts into wedding ceremonies is a tradition that spans various cultures and countries, each with its unique expressions. These acts of kindness are seen as a way to share joy with others and as a means to start the marriage on a foundation of generosity and communal responsibility. In Western cultures, particularly in the United States and parts of Europe, it's becoming increasingly popular for couples to request that guests donate to a specific charity or cause close to the couple's heart instead of traditional wedding gifts. Websites and wedding invitations often include information on how to contribute to these chosen charities. This practice reflects the couple's commitment to social causes and desire to share their blessings. In countries like India, some couples volunteer for part of their wedding day. This might involve preparing and serving meals at a local homeless shelter or visiting an orphanage to spend time with children. Such acts are seen as good deeds that bring blessings to the marriage and demonstrate the couple's dedication to serving their community together. Community service is often a significant part of the wedding process in South Africa and in some other African cultures. Couples might engage in projects like building homes for the less fortunate or participating in environmental clean-ups. This communal involvement is not only a way to give back but also acts as a bond-strengthening activity, showing the couple's commitment to working together for the betterment of others. In Jewish weddings, it's common to incorporate *tzedakah*. Couples might donate a portion of their wedding budget to a charity or encourage guests to do the same. Similarly, in Islamic weddings, giving to *sadaqah*, charity, and helping the needy are actions greatly emphasized and often integrated into wedding celebrations.

The research of historians like Robert Bremner provides insights into how philanthropy evolved through different historical epochs, reflecting the values and social structures of the times. E.E. Evans-Pritchard's studies of the Nuer people and Bronislaw Malinowski's work on the Trobriand Islanders illustrate how altruistic practices were integral to maintaining social harmony and ensuring the survival of the community. The relationship between Altruism and social stratification, as studied by historians and anthropologists, sheds light on how acts of kindness have been influenced by and have influenced social hierarchies. This includes the role of philanthropy in reinforcing or challenging social inequalities, a topic explored by authors like Oscar Lewis in his studies of poverty and Altruism.

The practice of Kind Contributions has a rich history, evolving from traditional philanthropy to modern, dynamic social practices that address a range of societal issues. Historically, philanthropy worldwide encompassed giving time and moral concern to benefit others. This tradition, explored by scholars and curators at the Smithsonian's Philanthropy Initiative, illuminates how philanthropic acts have addressed issues like prejudice, racism, and economic disparities. The history of philanthropy reveals its capacity to empower and reinforce the fight against societal inequities. Significant philanthropic funds and organizations have played pivotal roles in shaping our human society. Philanthropy evolved to include more diverse and dynamic social practices, reflecting increased societal visibility and systematic scrutiny.

Historically, women's involvement in philanthropy was often viewed through a lens of domesticity or limited to 'soft' causes. However, over the years, women have broken through these stereotypes, asserting their influence in a wide range of causes, from educational reforms and healthcare initiatives to environmental conservation and social justice movements. Women philanthropists have contributed financially and brought unique perspectives and strategies to philanthropy, contributing to the shift towards community-centric approaches and long-term solutions. In the modern world, the input of women towards altruistic causes is essential, with many projects and movements led or uplifted by women and their aid adding strength, numbers, and innovation to waves of positive action.

In the modern era, philanthropy is often associated with large financial donations, but its essence as "recognizing and supporting the humanity of others" remains. Contemporary philanthropic efforts continue to address a wide array of social issues, reflecting societies' ongoing aspiration to care for one another. The modern understanding of philanthropy emphasizes its potential for social empowerment while being mindful of its historical complexities and diverse perspectives. Understanding philanthropy's historical and modern context can enrich our appreciation of Kind Contributions in relationships. Couples or friends engaging in philanthropic activities together not only contribute to societal welfare but also reinforce their shared values and commitment to positive change, deepening their bond and enhancing their sense of collective purpose.

Exploring the neurobiological basis of Altruism reveals how it is ingrained in our brain's evolution and mechanisms, with areas like the ventral tegmental area and nucleus accumbens playing pivotal roles. Altruism activates the same neural reward circuitry stimulated by tangible rewards or pleasurable experiences. This circuit includes key areas like the ventral tegmental area (VTA) and the nucleus accumbens. Performing acts of kindness triggers the release of serotonin and dopamine, leading to feelings of satisfaction and well-being for both the giver and receiver. Endorphins, known as natural painkillers, are also released, contributing to a "helper's high." Research by neuroscientists such as Jordan Grafman has shown that the mesolimbic system, responsible for processing rewards, is significantly activated during acts of Altruism.

The anterior insula and the anterior cingulate cortex are brain regions associated with empathy and emotional processing. When we empathize with others, these areas become active, and this activation can prompt altruistic behavior. This means that loving relationships can encourage you to take selfless actions. Tania Singer's studies in the field of social neuroscience provide insights into how empathy and Altruism are intertwined in the brain. Her research demonstrates that experiencing empathy towards others can lead to charitable actions mediated by these neural regions.

Research also indicates that performing acts of kindness can significantly boost the happiness of the person performing the act. This increase in happiness is true for acts directed toward friends, family members, strangers, or oneself. Stephen G. Post's work in 'Altruism and Health' suggests that altruistic behavior provides immediate emotional rewards and can have lasting positive effects on overall brain health, potentially reducing the risk of cognitive decline. Simple, consistent acts of kindness often have the most potent effects on relationship quality over time. Kindness can lead to viewing a partner more favorably, which has been linked to more positive relationship outcomes. This perspective involves overlooking a partner's shortcomings, making them feel more attractive and content in the relationship. Engaging in acts of kindness releases serotonin and dopamine, feel-good hormones contributing to happiness and stress reduction. Kindness has also been found to lower blood pressure and stress hormone levels, benefiting physical and mental health. Observing acts of kindness positively underscores the ripple effect of kind actions. Sharing the same pursuit of Kind Contribution within relationships can multiply these positive effects.

Benefits and Considerations:

The Kind Contribution relationship style epitomizes shared values of empathy, generosity, and community service, manifesting through philanthropy, charity, and volunteering. This concept, eloquently encapsulated in Charles Glassman's quote, "Kindness begins with the understanding that we all struggle," highlights that kindness in romantic or platonic relationships lays a foundation of trust, mutual respect, and emotional connection. These contributions go beyond mere acts of generosity; they are essential in building and sustaining healthy, satisfying relationships.

Participating in Kind Contributions, whether as a couple or in friendships, enriches these bonds by aligning mutual goals towards positive societal change. This shared passion for philanthropy and societal improvement fosters a deeper understanding and respect, creating a stronger emotional bond. Participating in philanthropic activities together provides substantial emotional support, allowing both individuals to experience the joys and challenges of their endeavors in a supportive environment. This kind of emotional backing is crucial for maintaining healthy, long-lasting relationships. Engaging in Kind Contributions together reinforces trust and shows commitment to shared values and goals. Such activities demonstrate a willingness to invest time and effort into the relationship and the wider community, enhancing the sense of security within the relationship.

Joint acts of kindness and charity deepen the bond between individuals through a shared sense of purpose. For example, a couple volunteering at a local shelter contributes to a worthy cause while experiencing a shared sense of accomplishment and fulfillment. This shared purpose reinforces their bond as they witness each other's compassion and empathy in action, deepening their respect and admiration for one another.

Kind Contribution activities often require effective communication, coordination, and teamwork. Whether organizing a community event or working on a fundraising campaign, partners must collaborate closely, enhancing their communication skills and ability to work as a team. This improved collaboration and understanding translate into other aspects of their relationship, making them more adept at handling personal challenges and conflicts.

For families, philanthropic activities are a powerful tool for instilling values of empathy, generosity, and community service in children. When children see their parents or family members actively involved in charitable work, they learn the importance of giving back to society. For instance, a family that regularly participates in beach clean-up activities teaches the children the value of environmental stewardship while contributing to environmental conservation. The Kind Contribution relationship style has a ripple effect, spreading positivity and a sense of community. Friends and family members who observe these acts of kindness are often inspired to engage in charitable activities, creating a network of goodwill.

Couples or friends deeply involved in philanthropy often build a legacy that transcends their relationship. Their collective efforts in various causes leave a lasting impact that continues to benefit others for years. This legacy of giving can become a central pillar of their relationship, a story that defines them and continues to inspire others even after their direct involvement.

Additionally, engaging in charitable activities provides a deep sense of personal satisfaction and growth. Individuals often discover new skills, develop a deeper understanding of societal issues, and gain a broader perspective on life. For instance, a couple that mentors young adults in underserved communities might find that the experience enriches their understanding of societal dynamics, making them more empathetic and knowledgeable.

Sharing a common goal in philanthropy can also help mitigate potential relationship conflicts. When both parties are focused on a larger purpose, it encourages a collaborative approach to problem-solving and reduces the likelihood of petty disagreements. Kind Contributions offer a unique opportunity for personal growth and self-expression within a relationship by aligning their mutual goals towards societal betterment. It allows individuals to explore their passions and interests in a supportive environment, contributing to personal development and relationship satisfaction. It is well known that kindness snowballs. Couples who perform acts of kindness together towards society tend to be kind to each other. The research underscores that kindness is foundational to happy relationships, with happy couples often prioritizing kindness through small, consistent, thoughtful acts that profoundly impact their bond.

While this style enriches relationships with a sense of purpose and shared goals, it also requires careful consideration to ensure it remains a fulfilling and positive aspect of the relationship. Kind Contribution demands mutual understanding and alignment of values. Both partners or friends should have a genuine interest and commitment to acts of kindness and service. This doesn't necessarily mean having identical interests in charitable causes, but a shared underlying value of wanting to contribute positively to society. For instance, one may be passionate about environmental conservation while the other is more inclined towards educational initiatives. Recognizing and respecting each other's areas of passion is crucial, and finding common ground or ways to support each other's interests is vital.

While engaging in philanthropic activities can be deeply rewarding, balancing these with personal time and relationship-building activities is essential. There is a risk of these endeavors consuming too much time and energy, potentially leading to burnout or neglect of the relationship. Striking a balance between contributing to causes and nurturing the personal connection is essential. For example, a couple might volunteer at a local charity event but also set aside time for regular date nights or personal activities that they enjoy together.

Differences in the level of commitment or approach to philanthropy can be a significant consideration. One partner might prefer hands-on volunteering, while the other might favor fundraising or advocacy work. Additionally, one might be more invested or able to dedicate more time than the other. Communicating openly about these differences and finding a harmonious way to contribute, which respects both partners' time and energy levels, is vital.

Engaging in acts of kindness and charity can positively impact relationship dynamics, fostering a sense of teamwork and shared purpose. However, it's important to ensure that these activities don't inadvertently create a power imbalance or a sense of competition within the relationship. For example, if one partner donates a significant sum to a cause, the other should not feel pressured to match this contribution if it's not feasible for them. The focus should always be on the collective impact and the joy of giving, rather than on who contributes more. Additionally, couples or friends involved in philanthropic activities might find themselves in the public eye or within certain social circles. Carefully navigating these external perceptions and interactions is necessary. It might be worthwhile to reflect on the balance and principles that link the allure of social status or recognition with the sincerity of the desire to serve and contribute.

Sustaining enthusiasm for long-term philanthropic involvement without experiencing burnout is another critical consideration. It's integral to regularly assess and discuss each other's feelings towards the activities. Kind Contributions might involve working overtime, traveling overseas, attending conferences, or being immersed in the sense of urgency of some endeavors. Taking breaks when needed, and diversifying the types of charitable activities can keep the experience fresh and rewarding.

Finally, cultivating a culture of gratitude and reflection within the relationship can enhance the giving experience. Regularly reflecting on the impact of philanthropic work and expressing gratitude for the opportunity to contribute and for each other's efforts can deepen the connection and add a meaningful dimension to the relationship.

Kind Contribution relationship style offers a unique and meaningful way to connect with a partner or friend, built around the shared values of empathy and generosity. By carefully considering and navigating the aspects of shared values, balancing personal time, respecting different approaches, managing dynamics and perceptions, sustaining enthusiasm, and cultivating gratitude, this style can enrich a relationship, making it not just a union of two individuals but a partnership that extends kindness and positivity into the wider community.

YOUR RELATIONSHIP REVIVAL:

Kind Contribution is about reinforcing your bond through acts of kindness towards each other and your community. Here's a list of activities to enrich this compassionate aspect of your relationship:

1. **Community Service Together**: Participate in community service projects, from volunteering at a local shelter to organizing a neighborhood clean-up. These shared experiences in giving back can strengthen your connection.

2. **Kindness Calendar**: Create a calendar where you plan a surprise act of kindness each week, either for each other or someone in your community. This could be anything from leaving a loving note to planning an unexpected day out.

3. **Charity Projects**: Embark on projects that benefit others, like knitting scarves for the homeless or building birdhouses for a local park. Collaborating on these projects can deepen your sense of shared purpose.

4. **Volunteer for a Cause**: Regularly volunteer for different causes that resonate with both of you. This shared commitment to helping others can bring you closer together.

5. **Community Garden Initiative**: Start a joint project like a community garden. It's a wonderful way to contribute to your neighborhood while spending quality time together.

6. **Charity from Scratch**: If you have the resources and passion, consider starting a new charity. Sometimes, the impact you can make takes less than you expect and can be deeply fulfilling.

7. **Random Acts of Kindness Adventure**: Spend a day performing random acts of kindness for strangers. This could be anything from paying for someone's coffee to helping someone with their groceries.

8. **Eco-Friendly Projects**: Engage in environmental conservation activities like tree planting or beach clean-ups, nurturing your bond over shared ecological concerns.

9. **Skill-Sharing for Good**: Use your skills to benefit others, such as offering free classes or workshops in areas you're both knowledgeable about.

10. **Donation Day**: Organize a day where you both gather items to donate to a local charity or shelter, turning decluttering into a meaningful and shared experience.

Kind Contribution is not just about the acts themselves but about growing together through compassion and empathy. These activities are designed to evolve with your relationship, meeting new needs and exploring new opportunities to make a positive impact. Embrace these acts of kindness to enrich your bond and find fulfillment in helping others. Kindness in relationships is a beautiful trait. When combined with other styles like Empathetic Conversations or Physical Presence, it nurtures a deeper and more varied connection.

Places to Pick:

Community service centers, charity events, social advocacy groups, animal shelters, senior centers, environmental clean-ups, food banks, non-profit organization events, community gardens, local libraries for literacy programs, habitat restoration projects, soup kitchens, youth mentoring programs, community art projects, hospital volunteer programs, clothing donation centers, homeless shelters, neighborhood watch groups, disaster relief organizations, community health fairs.

Literary Echoes:

Mike Schaefer and Ric Weiland: "Philanthropy was more than just a shared interest for Mike Schaefer and Ric Weiland, it was 'a core value that brought us together'... 'Why wait until you're old and senile—or dead—to give to the causes you believe in?'" Mike Schaefer and Ric Weiland were partners, with Ric being an early Microsoft employee and philanthropist.

Herb and Marion Sadler: "We are among the converted having committed to give all our net worth to philanthropy... Passing down fortunes from generation to generation can do irreparable harm... When you think about it, no other approach seems to make sense." Herb and Marion Sadler are philanthropists known for their commitment to donating their entire net worth to charitable causes.

Bill & Melinda Gates: "Both of us were fortunate to grow up with parents who taught us some tremendously important values... We feel very lucky to have the chance to work together in giving back the resources we are stewards of." Bill & Melinda Gates are co-founders of the Bill & Melinda Gates Foundation, one of the world's largest private charitable foundations.

"The more we love, the more love we have to offer." Mary C. Neal, an American orthopedic spine surgeon and author known for her books on near-death experiences.

"Love is the doorway through which the human soul passes from selfishness to service." Jack Hyles, leading figure in the Independent Baptist movement.

"Many hands make light work." John Heywood, 16th-century English playwright known for his epigrams and plays.

"When we strive to become better than we are, everything around us becomes better, too." Paulo Coelho, Brazilian lyricist and novelist, best known for his book "The Alchemist."

"Kindness in giving creates love." Lao Tzu, ancient Chinese philosopher and writer, known as the reputed author of the Tao Te Ching.

"Remember that the happiest people are not those getting more, but those giving more." H. Jackson Brown Jr., American author best known for his inspirational book, "Life's Little Instruction Book."

"Charity begins at home, but should not end there." Thomas Fuller, English churchman and historian.

"People working together in a strong community with a shared goal and a common purpose can make the impossible possible." Tom Vilsack, American politician who served as the United States Secretary of Agriculture.

"I don't want to live in the kind of world where we don't look out for each other..." Charles de Lint, Canadian fantasy author.

"Coming together is a beginning, staying together is progress, and working together is success." Henry Ford, American industrialist and the founder of the Ford Motor Company.

"Alone, we can do so little; together, we can do so much." Helen Keller, American author, political activist, and lecturer, and the first deaf-blind person to earn a Bachelor of Arts degree.

"None of us, including me, ever do great things. But we can all do small things, with great love, and together we can do something wonderful." Mother Teresa, Albanian-Indian Roman Catholic nun and missionary.

Reflect and Discuss:

Kind Contributions and New Perspectives:

1. Discuss a moment when engaging in humanitarian/volunteering work together brought a new understanding or perspective to your relationship.

_____

_____

_____

2. Can you recall a particularly impactful or emotional moment experienced during a humanitarian mission with your partner or friend?

_____

_____

_____

3. Research in evolutionary biology suggests that Altruism has survival benefits. Discuss how engaging in charitable activities together has strengthened your relationship and sense of partnership.

_____

_____

_____

Navigating Differences and Challenges:

4. Share an experience where you and your partner or friend had to navigate differences in opinion on a charitable cause. How did you reach common ground?

_____

_____

_____

5. What challenges have you faced when engaging in philanthropic activities together, and how have you overcome them?

_____

_____

_____

6. Share insights from any cultural or societal differences encountered while working on philanthropic projects together.

_____

_____

_____

Balancing Personal and Mutual Goals:

7. How do you balance personal goals and desires with the mutual goal of contributing positively to the world?

_____

_____

_____

8. Discuss the role of volunteer work in your relationship. How has volunteering together affected your bond?

_____

_____

_____

Chapter Eight

6. Adventurous Bonding

Moments You'll Recognize:

Elena and Marco's love story began in the lush rainforests of Costa Rica on a zip-lining adventure that neither had planned to join. Elena, a photographer, was there to capture the vibrant wildlife, while Marco, an avid traveler, was ticking off another item from his adventure bucket list. Their paths crossed at the highest platform, where amidst breathtaking views and the zip-line's exhilarating rush, a connection sparked, exceeding the moment's thrill.

Post their chance meeting, they found themselves drawn together by a shared thirst for adventure. Their next escapade was a hiking expedition in the Andes. As they traversed challenging trails and camped under the stars, their shared wanderlust revealed a profound compatibility. Each trek and climb deepened their bond as they found solace in each other's strength and companionship. Their adventures took them from the Sahara sand dunes to Antarctica's icy landscapes. Elena's photography captured the beauty of the world and the essence of their journey together. Marco's love for exploring the unknown complemented Elena's artistic eye, making each trip an odyssey of discovery and creativity.

Their shared passion soon became a profession with the launch of their own adventure travel company. Their business was built on the foundation of their experiences - offering off-the-beaten-path expeditions and immersive cultural experiences. They led groups on treks through hidden mountain paths, kayaking expeditions in remote rivers, and cultural tours in lesser-known local communities. Their enthusiasm and expertise attracted fellow adventure-seekers, and their company quickly gained a reputation for its unique and authentic tours.

Elena and Marco's relationship was the heartbeat of their business. Their love for each other and adventure was evident on every trip they organized. Clients were signing up for a tour

led by two people who lived and breathed the spirit of exploration. Years passed, and their relationship, like their adventures,
grew and evolved. They married in a curious ceremony atop a
serene mountain they had once climbed, surrounded by a close-
knit group of fellow adventurers who had become like family.
Their wedding truly reflected their journey - simple, beautiful,
and amidst nature.

DEFINING THE STYLE:

Adventurous Bonding in relationships is about sharing experiences that are exciting, challenging, and growth-inducing. This connection style thrives on activities often involving novelty that pushes
individuals out of their comfort zones by fostering trust, mutual
support, and effective communication. It also allows individuals to
learn about new aspects of each other and themselves. Activities
like hiking, skydiving, rock climbing, and traveling to new places
are examples of how couples can explore and grow together. These
shared adventures create lasting memories, enhance emotional
intimacy, and foster a unique shared history, creating a sense of
nostalgia and camaraderie that brings individuals closer together.
Engaging in adventurous activities together can help individuals
overcome fears, develop new skills, build confidence, and gain a
sense of accomplishment. Engaging in such dynamic experiences
enhances mutual respect and admiration. It creates a greater understanding that is vital for a flourishing relationship.

UNVEILING HISTORICAL AND SCIENTIFIC TREASURES:

From an evolutionary standpoint, engaging in adventurous and
challenging activities has been crucial to human development
and social bonding. In societies like those at the 400,000-year-
old Terra Amata site in France, cooperation and social networks
were vital for survival and prosperity, as seen through the com-

munal effort in building extensive shelters. These early social groups provided protection and facilitated sharing resources and knowledge. The shelters found here, some as long as 49 feet, suggest a level of social organization and cooperation in building and maintaining these structures. The ability to construct such shelters would have required a significant degree of collaboration, problem-solving, and physical skill – attributes integral for survival and essential in modern adventurous activities. The presence of fossil human feces containing pollen from plants that blossom in late spring and early summer indicates a seasonal occupation of these shelters. This seasonal movement and occupation require a degree of adaptability and adventure-seeking behavior, as early humans had to navigate and survive in different environments and conditions. Though rooted in survival rather than leisure, these early forms of human adventure laid the foundation for the complex social interactions and bonding experiences that we associate with adventure today.

Bonding through adventurous activities has roots in our primate ancestors, where shared challenges and explorations were vital to survival and social cohesion. For instance, group hunting and foraging expeditions required significant cooperation, trust, and mutual support. These activities provided opportunities for individuals to demonstrate their skills, bravery, and reliability – traits desirable in a mate. The shared sense of accomplishment and the adrenaline rush from facing and overcoming challenges together would have fortified bonds within the group, setting the stage for deeper relationships.

Similarly, primate behavior offers parallels to human adventure-seeking tendencies. For example, in some primate species, exploration and play in young individuals serve as vital learning experiences, contributing to their social and cognitive development. These activities often involve risk-taking and navigating new environments, which can be seen as early forms of adventure that enhance the individual's adaptability and help establish social hierarchies and alliances – factors that could influence mate selection.

In gorillas, the formation of long-term social relationships and the high levels of paternity certainty provide a basis for strong parental investment, a trait shared with humans. Paternity certainty, the confidence a male has in being the genetic father of an offspring, significantly influences his willingness to engage in and contribute to the care and upbringing of that offspring. This suggests that our ancestors likely had a long evolutionary history of forming stable family units and relationships. Encounters between gorilla groups, which allow females to transfer from one group to another, involve physical competition and *mate-guarding* among males. Mate-guarding, one of the most prevalent defensive tactics seen in animals, is the physical defense of a female to prevent competitor males from having the chance to mate with her. This aspect of competition and the need for protection in the wild can be compared to the human experience of facing challenges and overcoming obstacles together in adventurous activities. The bonding in these scenarios, whether in gorillas or humans, is rooted in mutual support, teamwork, and sharing a common goal or challenge.

In human evolutionary history, adventurous activities played a significant role in relationship formation. The ability to navigate challenging environments and situations was likely a desirable trait in a partner, as it indicated good health, resourcefulness, and the ability to provide protection and support. This preference for traits conducive to survival and success in adventurous endeavors could have influenced mate selection processes. The development of these social bonds through shared adventurous experiences extended from familial relationships to friendships and larger social networks. As human societies evolved, the complexity of these networks increased, with evidence suggesting that groups living hundreds of kilometers apart engaged in resource exchange as early as 130,000 years ago. This expansion of social networks and the sharing of resources and information were vital for the survival and evolution of human societies.

Historically, adventure has been integral to human nature, driving humanity to attempt new things and explore further. The term *l'aventure* has been present in the French language since the 11th century, but its usage and representation varied greatly across time and space. Earlier adventure stories focused more on anecdotal accounts of travels and discoveries, with less emphasis on the traveler's personality and more on the objective knowledge gained. During the Renaissance, with the advent of Romanticism, the modern adventure novel emerged, popularizing geographical knowledge and communicating the values of bourgeois society.

Historical evidence shows that women have actively participated in adventurous activities, challenging the stereotype of adventure as a predominantly male domain. Research into women's experiences in outdoor adventures reveals that they place significant value on such activities, often associating them with feelings of rejuvenation, calm, and overcoming fear. These experiences emphasize the importance of physical challenges, shared experiences, and interpersonal relationships outdoors. For instance, Amelia Earhart, the pioneering aviator who became the first female pilot to fly solo across the Atlantic Ocean, exemplified the spirit of adventure and determination. Similarly, Junko Tabei, who led the first all-female expedition to summit Mount Everest, showcased extraordinary courage and the power of collective effort among women adventurers. Women's participation in adventurous activities has deep-seated motivations and impacts, influencing all aspects of their lives, including personal development and social connections. The emphasis on shared experiences aligns with the concept of Adventurous Bonding in relationships, where the collective overcoming of challenges and the mutual support required in such activities strengthen interpersonal bonds across genders.

Needless to say, there are numerous examples of brave women throughout history in various societies who sought adventure and played significant roles in their communities. Women have always been involved in gathering, hunting, and exploring, which are inherently adventurous activities. In many indigenous cultures, women were integral to exploration and resource gathering, often traversing challenging terrains. In various historical narratives and folklore, women are depicted as warriors, explorers, and leaders, undertaking perilous journeys and challenges.

Though sometimes mythologized, these stories reflect the active and adventurous roles women have played throughout history.

Among these narratives that offer insight into the ancient mythological roots of Adventurous Bonding as a relationship style are the legends of the Amazons. The Amazons, a tribe of fierce warrior women, are one of the most captivating legends of ancient Greece. Described as living in a society free from male influence, they represented the epitome of strength, independence, and bravery. Their stories tell of formidable women who embarked on grand adventures, engaged in battles and established a society where communal bonds among women were paramount. In the tales of their encounters with legendary heroes such as Hercules and Theseus, the Amazons are not simply adversaries but equals, challenging the norms of their time. The Amazonian way of life, centered around mutual support and shared adventure, exemplifies the essence of Adventurous Bonding. Their legacy teaches us the value of unity and collective strength in pursuing common goals, illustrating how deep, lasting relationships can be formed and sustained through shared challenges and achievements.

In contrast to the mortal Amazons, Artemis, the Greek goddess of the hunt, wilderness, and childbirth, offers a divine perspective on Adventurous Bonding. Accompanied by a band of nymphs, Artemis roamed the ancient world's forests, mountains, and wild spaces. Together, they ventured hunts, faced dangers, and explored the untamed corners of the earth. This fellowship, bound by their devotion to Artemis and their shared love for the wilderness, highlights the spiritual and emotional dimensions of Adventurous Bonding. Artemis and her hunters represent a celestial blueprint for the indelible relationships generated in the pursuit of adventure. Through their stories, we understand that Adventurous Bonding encompasses shared values, mutual respect, and an environmental connection. In weaving the ancient threads of the Amazons and Artemis's tales into the fabric of contemporary adventure, we find a timeless truth: Adventurous Bonding is a fundamental human experience.

When we turn our gaze toward the recent involvement of women in adventurous activities, we will find extensive evidence. The research article "The Meaning of Adventurous Activities for 'Women in the Outdoors'" by Maggie Boniface examines women's long-term participation in outdoor adventure activities. It explores narratives from life story interviews with women working in education, focusing on the significance, experiences of fear, and relationships in outdoor settings. Key findings highlight the benefits and values women place on adventurous activities, emphasizing the rejuvenation and calm they associate with time spent outdoors. Their narratives reflect high levels of fear encountered and the value placed on shared experiences, often overshadowing the physical challenge aspect.

A seminal moment in the history of women's adventure is the first all-female ascent of Annapurna I in 1978. This expedition was a mountaineering achievement and a profound demonstration of Adventurous Bonding. The team, facing the unpredictable wrath of nature and the daunting challenges of the Himalayas, relied on an unbreakable chain of trust, support, and shared determination.

Gertrude Bell, often remembered for her solitary travels, was a master of developing significant relationships throughout her journeys. The English writer, traveler, political officer, and archaeologist played an essential role in British imperial policy-making due to her extensive travels in Syria, Mesopotamia, Asia Minor, and Arabia. Often referred to as the 'Queen of the Desert,' Bell's work in mapping and archaeological expeditions, marked her as a formidable figure in the traditionally male-dominated domains of exploration and political diplomacy. Her collaborations with local communities, other explorers, and leaders in the Middle East were instrumental in her success, showcasing another facet of Adventurous Bonding. Gertrude Bell had a well-documented working relationship and friendship with T.E. Lawrence. Both were key figures in the Middle East during and after World War I, collaborating on political and intelligence missions. Bell also formed a friendly connection with Sheikh Majid Al-Sabah of

Kuwait based on mutual respect and understanding during her tribal negotiations.

In the recent context, women across the spectrum of sports are shattering barriers and fostering communities, exemplifying how pursuing physical challenges can unite us in collective triumph and understanding. For example, Mirna Valerio, also known as 'The Mirnavator,' displays Adventurous Bonding through her engagement with the ultramarathon community. Her story is a powerful narrative of how shared passions can unite individuals from diverse backgrounds, creating a community that thrives on encouragement, shared experiences, and mutual respect. Valerio's advocacy for inclusivity in adventure sports further amplifies the message that the heart of adventure lies in the connections we forge along the way.

In modern times, adventure is seen as a means of personal expression and self-discovery, acknowledged for virtues like fulfilling oneself in the moment, claiming one's destiny through voluntary confrontations with death, and unveiling the hidden meaning of the world. Adventure's role in personal growth is emphasized, extending beyond physical feats to mental and emotional boundary-pushing activities. The shared exhilaration in adventure activities contributes to lasting personal and relational growth.

Building on this, Adventurous Bonding in the contemporary landscape has revealed its broader impact, particularly during periods of societal stress. For example, the global upheaval brought on by the COVID-19 pandemic challenged our collective capacity to endure and adapt. It was observed that those who routinely participate in adventurous pursuits, accustomed to the unpredictability and inherent risks, exhibited a remarkable kind of resilience. Their inherent agility came to the fore amid sudden lockdowns and prolonged isolation. This skill set, fostered through Adventurous Bonding, proved to be a substantial support system, embodying swift decision-making, tranquility under duress, and innovative problem-solving.

Shared adventurous activities can significantly impact biological pathways and hormonal responses, enhancing emotional and behavioral bonding. Participating in adrenaline-inducing activities together can significantly strengthen relationships, owing to the biological and emotional responses such experiences trigger. Adrenaline, also known as epinephrine, is a hormone and a neurotransmitter that plays an integral role in the body's fight-or-flight response. It is released in response to stress or excitement, leading to increased heart rate, heightened senses, and a surge of energy. When couples or friends engage in activities that trigger this adrenaline release, such as bungee jumping, skydiving, or even intense competitive sports, they experience simultaneous physiological arousal, or a shared intense rush. This synchronized physiological state fosters a unique and powerful bond, accompanied by a sense of euphoria, partly driven by the concurrent release of dopamine and adrenaline. These biological pathways that interact during Adventurous Bonding can lead to a sense of accomplishment and mutual support, which builds trust and reliance on one another. Working together towards a common goal, particularly in a high-stakes situation, reinforces the importance of the bond and signals to both individuals that they can depend on each other in challenging situations, enhancing the perceived value of the relationship.

The release of adrenaline in these shared experiences can also create a phenomenon known as Misattribution of Arousal. This psychological concept suggests that the high arousal state and intense awareness caused by an exciting activity may be unconsciously attributed to an individual's feelings for a person accompanying them and heighten the emotional experience of the moment. In other words, the intense feelings roused by the activity can enhance the perceived attractiveness of an accompanying partner or the significance and strength of a bond between participants.

Additionally, engaging in these shared adrenaline-inducing activities can increase oxytocin levels, known for its role in social bonding and trust. This combination of adrenaline, dopamine, and oxytocin creates a potent mix that can deepen connections, enhance emotional intimacy, and reinforce the bond in a way that more mundane or routine activities might not. Endorphins also play a significant role in the context of adventurous activities. These neurotransmitters act as natural pain relievers and are released in response to stress or discomfort. Endorphin levels typically increase during reward-producing activities like exercise, often a component of adventurous experiences. The release of endorphins can lead to deeper feelings of well-being and improve mood, thereby enhancing the quality of the relationship.

Furthermore, adventurous activities can influence the balance of other hormones and neurotransmitters, such as serotonin, which regulates mood and sleep, and GABA (Gamma-aminobutyric acid), which acts as an inhibitory neurotransmitter, reducing feelings of stress and anxiety. By participating in adventurous activities together, couples can optimize these hormonal functions, contributing to a healthier and more balanced emotional state.

In Adventurous Bonding, our behaviors and emotions are deeply connected with the complex functions of our neuroendocrine system, highlighting the role of hormones in relationship dynamics. At the heart of this interplay are vital hormones and neurotransmitters, which, though often associated with reproductive behaviors, play a crucial role in fostering bonding and mating dynamics.

While testosterone and estradiol (estrogen) are often stereotypically associated with males and females, respectively, it's crucial to understand that both hormones are present in all individuals, regardless of gender, contributing to a wide range of behaviors and emotional responses that transcend traditional gender roles. These hormones, typically linked to reproductive functions, extend their influence beyond mere physiological readiness for mating. These hormones also significantly impact bonding and courtship behaviors, suggesting a complex dual function in human interactions. Testosterone, often associated with traits like assertiveness and risk-taking, can enhance the allure of adventurous activities, making individuals more inclined toward thrilling and challenging experiences. This inclination toward adventure can be attractive in a mate, signaling vitality, bravery, and a zest for life.

On the other hand, estradiol plays a vital role in modulating social behaviors and emotional responsiveness. Its presence can enhance the depth of emotional connections and responsiveness to a partner, making shared adventurous experiences more emotionally enriching and supporting bonding. When couples or friends engage in adventurous activities together, the shared adrenaline rush and subsequent emotional experiences can be amplified by the presence of these hormones, strengthening the bond between them.

In early human societies, hormonal responses to these activities could have strengthened social bonds and group cohesion, essential for our survival. In modern times, while survival challenges differ, the biological and hormonal responses to adventure still play a significant role in amplifying bonding experiences, improving mental and physical health, and contributing to overall well-being. The biology and hormones associated with Adventurous Bonding underscore the connection between our physical responses and the emotional and psychological benefits of shared adventurous experiences, enhancing the adventure and strengthening bonds between participants.

Benefits and Considerations:

Adventurous Bonding is characterized by shared experiences that are often exciting, challenging, and unexpected, offering a heap of benefits that enrich relationships in multiple ways. From building trust to creating unforgettable memories, enhancing communication skills, and promoting personal and relational growth, Adventurous Bonding is a dynamic and rewarding aspect of relationship dynamics. Partners forge a deeper, more re-silient bond by engaging in shared adventures.

Activities outside one's comfort zone, like rock climbing or white-water rafting, necessitate high trust. For instance, when a couple decides to go rock climbing, they literally put their safe-ty in each other's hands. This act of reliance and the successful navigation of the activity strengthens trust in each other's capa-bilities and judgment. The shared experiences that come with Adventurous Bonding become an integral part of the relation-ship's narrative, which are often extraordinary in nature, mak-ing them even more memorable. For example, friends who trav-el to a foreign country immerse themselves in a new culture and experience a unique adventure that becomes a defining moment in their relationship. These shared memories act as a bond, rein-forcing the relationship's strength and providing a source of joy and nostalgia for years to come.

Adventurous activities often require effective communication to be successful. When navigating a sailing trip, partners must communicate clearly and effectively to maneuver the boat. This enhanced communication, born out of necessity during adven-turous activities, often translates into better communication in other aspects of relationships. Adventurous Bonding often push-es individuals out of their comfort zones, promoting personal growth. Facing fears and overcoming challenges together fos-ters individual resilience and contributes to the relationship's growth. A couple interested in martial arts taking their first ka-rate classes learns a new self-defense style and unique aspects about patience, cooperation, and the joy of learning together.

Many adventurous activities involve physical exercise, which is beneficial for physical health. Moreover, these activities can also have positive mental health effects. Engaging in adventure sports like hiking or kayaking releases endorphins, increases happiness, and decreases stress levels. Sharing these physical activities with a partner amplifies these health benefits. Adven-turous Bonding allows partners to explore and develop shared interests. Friends discovering a new mutual interest in bird-watching can explore this passion by visiting different habitats and learning about various species. This shared interest adds another layer to the relationship, providing common ground and a sense of companionship in pursuit of a shared hobby.

However, like any voyage into uncharted territories, Adventurous Bonding requires thoughtful consideration, understanding, and adaptability. When partners face and overcome obstacles together, it reinforces their ability to work as a team. This could be as simple as solving problems during a camping trip or as complex as navigating cultural differences during international travel. Overcoming such challenges builds resilience and a sense of accomplishment in the relationship.

Understanding and respecting each other's physical and emotional limits is essential. Adventure means different things to different people. For some, it might be about physically demanding activities like hiking, skydiving, or scuba diving. For others, it could be exploring new cultural experiences, traveling to unknown places, or engaging in martial arts classes. It's essential to have an honest conversation about what each partner considers adventurous and is comfortable trying. When one or both partners have physical disabilities, Adventurous Bonding takes on an added layer of consideration. The key here is to find activities both partners can participate in and enjoy equally. This might involve seeking out adventure companies that specialize in accessible travel or activities, or simply being creative in how you define adventure. The focus should be on inclusivity and the shared experience, rather than on the limitations. Open and ongoing communication is vital in Adventurous Bonding. Regular check-ins about comfort levels, interests, and experiences help ensure both partners enjoy the journey. It's also essential to be open to feedback. Suppose one partner isn't enjoying an activity or is causing stress or discomfort. In that case, it's important to reassess and adjust plans accordingly.

Adventurous activities often come with an element of unpredictability. It's important to be prepared for changes in plans, unexpected challenges, and the need to make quick decisions. How partners handle these situations can either strengthen the relationship or lead to stress and conflict. Developing a mindset that embraces flexibility and a positive approach to problem-solving can be immensely beneficial. Safety should always be a priority. This means doing proper research, preparing adequately, and not taking unnecessary risks. It's important to remember that being adventurous doesn't mean being reckless. Ensuring both partners feel safe is essential for a positive and enjoyable experience.

Reflecting on and discussing the experiences post-adventure can provide additional value to them. Sharing thoughts and feelings about the adventures can deepen understanding and appreciation for each other. It's also a time to relish the memories created and to plan future experiences, keeping the flame of adventure alive in the relationship.

YOUR RELATIONSHIP REVIVAL:

Adventurous Bonding is about infusing your relationship with exciting experiences that challenge and invigorate you both. Here's a list of activities to enrich this thrilling aspect of your relationship:

1. **Surprise Adventure Trip**: Plan a spontaneous weekend camping in an unknown destination or a day trip to a nearby city without an itinerary. Embrace the thrill of exploring new places together without a set plan.

2. **Extreme Sports Duo**: Step out of your comfort zone and try adventurous sports together, like paragliding, scuba diving, or rock climbing. These activities not only bring adrenaline but also strengthen your trust and teamwork.

3. **Geocaching Exploration**: Engage in geocaching, which combines hiking with a treasure hunt element. It's a fun way to explore the outdoors and experience the excitement of discovery together.

4. **Adventure Race Challenge**: Participate in an adventure race or tackle a challenging outdoor obstacle course. These events test your endurance and collaborative skills, adding a competitive edge to your bonding.

5. **Night Under the Stars**: Go for an overnight stargazing trip. Find a remote location, set up a tent, and spend the night marveling at the stars, adding a touch of romance to your adventure.

6. **Kayaking or Canoeing Journey**: Embark on a kayaking or canoeing trip together. Navigating rivers or lakes offers serene and challenging moments, perfect for adventurous spirits.

7. **Urban Exploration**: Explore the hidden gems of your city – visit abandoned buildings, discover underground art scenes, or find the highest point in the town for a unique view.

8. **Hot Air Balloon Ride**: Experience the thrill of a hot air balloon ride, offering breathtaking views and a sense of freedom, perfect for adventurous couples.

9. **Backpacking Expedition**: Plan a multi-day backpacking trip. Trekking through nature and setting up camp in different locations offers a sense of adventure and deepens your connection.

10. **Cultural Adventure**: Immerse yourselves in a completely different culture. Visit a new country or region and discover local traditions, food, and lifestyle.

Remember, Adventurous Bonding is about sharing experiences that bring excitement and discovery, key elements for maintaining a dynamic and lively relationship. These activities are designed to challenge you both, build trust, and create unforgettable memories. Embrace the spirit of adventure and watch your relationship flourish with each new experience. An Adventurous spirit thrives on new experiences, but incorporating aspects of other styles, like the Intellectual or Caring, can elevate your adventures to new heights of enjoyment and bonding.

PLACES TO PICK:

Adventure sports centers, national parks, nature reserves, exotic travel destinations, kayaking routes, mountain biking trails, scuba diving spots, safari parks, zip-lining locations, backpacking trails, ski resorts, surfing beaches, off-road vehicle parks, spelunking caves, hot air balloon ride spots, white-water rafting rivers, paragliding launch sites, ice climbing venues, wilderness survival camps.

LITERARY ECHOES:

"We haven't been everywhere, but it's on our list." — Susan Sontag, American writer and filmmaker.

"I've fallen in love with adventures, so I begin to wonder, if that's why I've fallen for you." — E. Grin, author.

"Oh darling, let's be adventurers." — Anonymous.

"Actually, the best gift you could have given her was a lifetime of adventures." — Lewis Carroll's 'Alice in Wonderland', English writer and mathematician.

"Love is meant to be an adventure." — Gordon B. Hinckley, American religious leader and author.

"You are my greatest adventure, always and forever." — Gretka Milkovic, writer.

"Sharing adventures means enjoying them 100% more." — Unknown.

"Travelling in the company of those we love is home in motion."
— Leigh Hunt, English critic, essayist, poet, and writer.

"No road is long with good company." — Turkish Proverb.

"Travel brings power and love back to your life." — Rumi, 13th-century Persian poet and Sufi mystic.

"Never go on trips with anyone you do not love." — Ernest Hemingway, American journalist and novelist.

"A couple who travel together, grow together." — Ahmad Fuadi, Indonesian novelist.

"In life, it's not where you go. It's who you travel with." — Charles Schulz, American cartoonist.

"So, come with me, where dreams are born, and time is never planned." — J.M. Barrie, Scottish novelist and playwright.

"What we find in a soulmate is not something wild to tame, but something wild to run with." — Robert Brault, author.

"A journey is best measured in friends, rather than miles." — Tim Cahill, Australian footballer.

REFLECT AND DISCUSS:

Memorable Adventures and Bond Strengthening:

1. Reflect on your most memorable adventure with your partner or friend. What made it unforgettable, and how did it strengthen your bond?

    _____

    _____

    _____

2. Share an experience where an unexpected challenge during an adventure brought you and your partner or friend closer together.

    _____

    _____

    _____

3. Share a story of an adventure that didn't go as planned. How did you adapt, and what did you learn from the experience?

    _____

    _____

    _____

Growth and Learning through Adventure:

4. Can you recall when stepping out of your comfort zones together led to a significant growth in your relationship?

    _____

    _____

    _____

5. Can you imagine an adventure that significantly impacted your perspectives or life philosophies?

_____

_____

_____

6. From an evolutionary standpoint, shared adventures helped strengthen bonds in early human societies. Reflect on an adventure you had together that felt particularly bonding. What survival skills, if any, did you learn about each other?

_____

_____

_____

Planning and Balancing in Adventures:

7. How do you balance each other's risk tolerances and adventure preferences when planning activities?

_____

_____

_____

8. Discuss the role of spontaneity in your adventurous activities. How does being spontaneous affect your experiences and relationships?

_____

_____

_____

Chapter Nine

7. Spiritual Bonding

Moments You'll Recognize:

Maya and Lila's journey of Spiritual Bonding began in their college dorm room, amidst the clutter of textbooks and the chaos of youthful dreams. They were roommates with vastly different backgrounds: Maya, a grounded student of anthropology, and Lila, an aspiring artist with a free spirit. Yet, they found common ground in their search for deeper meaning in life. Their spiritual journey together started unexpectedly during a philosophy class, where discussions about Existentialism and the purpose of life left them both intrigued and restless. This restlessness soon turned into a quest, a yearning to understand the larger universe and their place within it.

Their first step was attending a meditation retreat in a serene ashram nestled in the Himalayas. Surrounded by the tranquility of the mountains and the wisdom of seasoned monks, Maya and Lila immersed themselves in mindfulness and meditation practices. They learned to quiet their minds and listen to the whispers of their inner selves. This retreat was the awakening of a new perspective on life. Back home, their friendship blossomed into a deep spiritual companionship. They started exploring various spiritual traditions and practices together, from the mystical Sufi poetry of Rumi to the ancient texts of the Bhagavad Gita. They attended spiritual workshops, practiced yoga, and participated in community service, seeking to apply their spiritual insights in the service of others.

Their bond grew stronger as they shared these experiences. They would spend hours discussing the nature of existence, the interconnectedness of all beings, and the pursuit of inner peace. Their conversations were no longer just exchanges of words; they were exchanges of soulful insights. As they journeyed together, their spiritual growth had a gentle touch on those around them. Their friends and families noticed a profound change in them – a sense of serenity, a deep well of empathy, and a steady positive outlook. Maya and Lila had become beacons of light and understanding in their community. They organized local meditation sessions and art therapy workshops, combining their passions to help others find peace and purpose.

Eventually, Maya and Lila decided to extend their journey of spiritual exploration by traveling to various sacred sites around the world. From the temples of Bali to the monasteries of Tibet, each destination brought new revelations and deepened their understanding of the world's spiritual embroidery. Their spiritual companionship transcended the ordinary bounds of friendship. It was a bond forged in the quest for existential truths, nurtured through shared experiences of self-discovery, and strengthened by their impact on the world around them. Maya and Lila's story is a testament to the transformative power of Spiritual Bonding – a journey that began with two individuals seeking purpose and culminated in a friendship that brought light and understanding to themselves and those around them.

DEFINING THE STYLE:

Spiritual Bonding encompasses deep, meaningful connections that transcend physical and emotional aspects, flying into a realm of shared understanding, mutual growth, and profound intimacy. It involves deep connections rooted in shared beliefs, values, and practices. It plays a crucial role in friendships and romantic relationships, sometimes even forming what can be called 'soul ties.' A Spiritual Bonding often feels like a profound sense of familiarity and comfort, surpassing boundaries such as race, gender, age, and appearance. Joint spiritual practices, like meditation, enhance creativity and problem-solving abilities while improving physical health by boosting the immune system and overall wellbeing. Spiritual Bonding fosters effective communication and empathy, enabling partners to approach conflicts collaboratively and deepen their intimacy and trust. It provides a safe space for expressing feelings, seeking comfort and guidance, and being vulnerable, leading to understanding and acceptance. Engaging in spiritual intimacy allows for deeper self-understanding and personal transformation, enhancing life satisfaction, allowing individuals to release the need for constant proof of affection, and reducing anxiety and insecurity in relationships.

Unveiling Historical and Scientific Treasures:

We, as people, possess an innate urge for human connection and belonging within a group. The early distinction between 'ingroup' and 'outgroup' in human societies underscored this need, emphasizing security, comfort, and psychological attachment as central to human motivation. Social bonding, including Spiritual Bonding, emerged as pivotal for physical and mental survival advantages. Living in cooperative groups not only boosted safety, resource access, and emotional security but also likely served as the catalyst for the development of spiritual practices. These practices, as expressions of community bonding and care for one another, fulfilled the inherent desire for belonging. The need for Spiritual Bonding can be seen as an extension of the basic human need for positive social connections, as well as a nourishment to the wellbeing of individuals within a community.

Spiritual practices have been pivotal in shaping human relationships throughout history. Spanning from the Middle to Upper Paleolithic era, these practices reflect the evolution of human culture, cognition, and social behavior. Archaeological evidence from the Middle Paleolithic era, around 200,000 to 45,000 years ago, reveals early indications of spiritual behavior. Among the key findings are intentional burials of the dead, often accompanied by grave goods—objects placed within graves, ranging from everyday items to precious artifacts, suggesting beliefs in an afterlife or a spiritual realm. Sites like the Qafzeh and Skhul caves, dating back approximately 100,000 years, provide some of the earliest examples of these burials. Moving into the Upper Paleolithic era, starting around 45,000 years ago, a significant increase in cave art marks a further development in spiritual expression. The sophisticated paintings and carvings found in European caves like Lascaux and Chauvet-Pont-d'Arc, dating from this period, are often interpreted as having spiritual or ritualistic significance. These artworks, through their vivid, symbolic illustrations, may have been integral to shamanistic practices—spiritual rituals led by shamans, who are believed to interact with the spiritual world through altered states of consciousness—or other ritual activities, illuminating the deepening complexity of spiritual life in early human societies.

In terms of Spiritual Bonding, these early forms of spirituality likely played a crucial role in strengthening communal ties and fostering a sense of unity and shared purpose among early humans. Rituals and shared beliefs would have been integral in creating a collective identity, serving as a social glue that held communities together. These practices may have also provided frameworks for understanding the world, coping with life's uncertainties, and establishing moral codes and social norms.

In ancient civilizations, spiritual practices and beliefs often dictated social norms and interactions, including those in romantic relationships and friendships. For instance, in ancient Greece and Rome, the gods and goddesses of love and friendship, such as Aphrodite, Philotes and Eros, were revered, and their myths and stories influenced how love and friendship were perceived and celebrated. Rituals and festivals dedicated to these deities were common, providing a spiritual framework for understanding and expressing romantic and platonic love.

In ancient Sumeria, around 4000 BCE, spirituality manifested in beliefs in spirits and the practice of divination. People performed rituals to communicate with and appease these spirits or gods, seeking their guidance and favors. This interaction with the spiritual realm fostered a sense of community and shared purpose, strengthening social bonds within these early societies.

Moving to ancient India, spirituality was closely linked with Hinduism, which emerged from the Vedas around 1500 BCE. These sacred texts guided Hindus in various spiritual practices, including meditation and yoga. Similarly, the teachings of Buddhism, originating around 500 BCE, emphasized spiritual liberation and enlightenment achievable through meditation and adherence to the Eightfold Path. These practices facilitated personal spiritual growth and fostered a sense of community among practitioners. Within these Eastern traditions, the spiritual concepts of Karma and Dharma also influenced romantic and platonic relationships. The idea that past actions influence future events led to a belief in the spiritual significance of relationships. Karma refers to the concept that every action has consequences that affect an individual's future. It's the idea that good actions lead to positive outcomes, while negative actions lead to unfavorable results. Karma is often understood as a law of moral causation, influencing an individual's future experiences based on their past actions, thoughts, and deeds. Dharma is a more complex concept with multiple meanings, depending on the religious or philosophical context. In general, it refers to a person's duty or righteousness, guided by the moral order of the universe. It's about living in a way that upholds cosmic law and order, which includes performing one's societal and moral duties. In the context of relationships, Dharma can imply the importance of acting in ways that are harmoniously aligned with one's personal ethics, societal roles, and spiritual responsibilities. These cultures emphasized the importance of spiritual compatibility and the pursuit of joint spiritual growth within relationships.

In ancient Egypt, spirituality was deeply embedded in the culture, with pharaohs considered responsible for the health of their subjects. Spiritual practices included religious rites and ceremonies that invoked deities' mysterious and miraculous powers for healing. The Egyptians believed that the body was divided into parts, each under the sway of a particular god. Thus, invoking these gods was integral to healing the diseases of the limbs. The practice of healing through spirituality was a means of physical wellness and reinforced the societal structure and the relationships within the community.

In the tapestry of medieval Europe, the concept of courtly love wove an intricate pattern, intertwining Romantic Love with spiritual and chivalric ideals. This concept, which emerged notably in regions like France and Italy, painted Romantic Love as an emotion and a noble, almost sacred journey. It was a transformative experience, suffused with spiritual aspirations and bound by the codes of chivalry. Courtly love was often portrayed as an unattainable, idealized form of love, where knights expressed devout admiration and love for a lady, who was typically of higher social standing and often married. This form of love was more about the pursuit and the courtship than physical union, meaning it was love for love's sake, more of a personal spiritual journey of the heart.

The troubadours, the wandering poets of the medieval period, were instrumental in popularizing and romanticizing this concept. They depicted love as a path to spiritual enlightenment, elevating the beloved to a near-divine status. For instance, in the works of poets like Guillaume de Machaut and Dante Alighieri, love was portrayed as a force that could elevate a man's moral, ethical, and spiritual standing. Dante's 'Divine Comedy', for instance, illustrates this notion beautifully, where his love for Beatrice catalyzes his spiritual journey and redemption.

Furthermore, courtly love celebrated the era's chivalric ideals, including valor, honor, and gallantry. Knights pursuing courtly love were expected to uphold these virtues, using their love as a motivation to achieve great deeds and maintain a noble character. The lady, often placed on a pedestal, became a symbol of moral and spiritual excellence, inspiring the knight to strive for the highest ideals of character and conduct. The concept of courtly love also influenced the structure and dynamics of relationships during medieval times. It introduced a more cerebral and spiritual component to love, where physicality was often secondary to emotional and spiritual connection. This idea resonates with the modern Spiritual Bonding relationship style, where the bond between individuals transcends physical aspects and finds its roots in deeper emotional and spiritual harmony.

With the advent of major world religions, spirituality continued to play a significant role in relationships. In Christianity, the concepts of *agape* (selfless, sacrificial love) and *philia* (deep friendship) were central to how relationships were understood and practiced. In Islam, the concept of *'Aṣ-ṣaḥābah'*, spiritual companionship, is emphasized, where marriage and friendship are seen as opportunities for spiritual growth and mutual support towards a righteous life.

Throughout history, various religious and spiritual groups have established guidelines and norms regarding personal relationships, particularly in the context of marriage and friendship. These rules, deeply rooted in each faith's doctrines and cultural practices, often dictated with whom individuals could form marital and social bonds. For instance, marriages were typically arranged within the same faith or spiritual community in many traditional societies to ensure the continuity of religious beliefs and practices. Such restrictions extended to friendships and social interactions, where forming close bonds with those outside the faith was often discouraged or outright prohibited. These norms served to maintain the purity of religious beliefs and practices, strengthen communal ties, and ensure that religious traditions were passed down through generations.

The contemporary era, shaped by globalization and cultural exchange, has seen a significant shift away from traditional norms in relationships and spirituality. Interfaith marriages and relationships are becoming more common, reflecting a broader acceptance of diverse spiritual and religious beliefs. Around one in five Americans were raised in interfaith households. This change is partly driven by global societies' greater mobility and interconnectedness, where individuals from different faiths and backgrounds interact more frequently and intimately. Additionally, the rise of Secularism and Individualism in spirituality has influenced this trend, promoting relationships based on personal compatibility over strict religious alignment. As a result, modern relationships often navigate a complex landscape of mixed beliefs and practices, leading to a richer, more diverse understanding of spirituality and religion.

This evolution in relationship dynamics represents a significant cultural shift, opening up opportunities for greater understanding and appreciation of different spiritual perspectives. It challenges traditional notions of religious homogeneity within relationships, paving the way for a more inclusive approach to spirituality. As individuals form bonds that transcend religious boundaries, they contribute to a global culture that values diversity and promotes a more holistic and multifaceted view of spiritual and religious life. This shift towards embracing interfaith relationships reflects a broader movement toward a more interconnected and tolerant world where spiritual and religious diversity is accepted and celebrated.

Today, spirituality in relationships encompasses a broader, more diverse range of meanings. The emergence of new-age spiritual movements has brought a focus on individual spiritual journeys and their intersection with relationships. Concepts like 'soulmates' and 'twin flames' have become popular, emphasizing the idea of spiritually predestined relationships that serve a higher purpose of personal growth and evolution. A soulmate is often described as a person with whom one has a deep and natural affinity, encompassing compatibility, love, intimacy, and friendship. The concept suggests a recondite, predestined connection that deeply enriches each individual's life and fosters personal growth. Twin flames are thought to be two halves of a single soul that have been split and placed into two different bodies. This concept represents an intense, soul-level connection that challenges and accelerates personal and spiritual growth, often described as both deeply challenging and profoundly transformative. Many people seek partners and friends who share their spiritual outlook, whether it is grounded in traditional religious beliefs or more personal, eclectic spiritual practices. Activities like yoga, meditation retreats, and mindfulness practices have become ways for individuals to connect with others on a spiritual level.

Spirituality, ranging from ancient traditions to contemporary practices, profoundly influences our biology, affecting biochemical and hormonal processes. This connection becomes particularly significant when considering how shared spiritual activities can strengthen family bonds, partnerships, and friendships. A key aspect of spirituality's biological influence is the awe and ecstasy experienced during transcendental moments, whether in nature or through practices like meditation and yoga. The concept of Transcendentalism, spearheaded by Ralph Waldo Emerson in the 19th century, emphasizes finding spirituality in one's personal connection to nature. This connection can evoke feelings of awe and transcendence, which are believed to be closely linked to our biology. For instance, individuals who engage in practices like meditation and spending time in nature report feelings of superfluidity, a state where the mind, body, and brain function harmoniously without friction, enhancing a sense of Spiritual Bonding.

These experiences are not just limited to organized religion but extend to personal, dogma-free spiritual experiences. For example, the music of John Denver and Cat Stevens in the 1970s, which often personified nature as a type of lover, resonated with many individuals, fostering a Spiritual Bonding with the environment. These experiences can trigger a psychological and emotional response deeply ingrained in human biology. Marghanita Laski's research in the mid-20th century highlighted that nature often catalyzes feelings of ecstatic transcendence. Together with modern research, Laski's findings point to a neurobiological underpinning for these experiences. Activities that promote spirituality, such as meditation or connection with nature, can enhance the release of oxytocin and other biochemicals, leading to a greater sense of connection and bonding with others.

The Default Mode Network (DMN) is a neural system within the brain associated with self-referential thought and mind-wandering. During experiences of spiritual transcendence, whether in nature or in other settings conducive to deep reflection, there is often a notable decrease in DMN activity. This reduction is associated with a sense of ego dissolution or a loss of the sense of self. In the context of Spiritual Bonding, this phenomenon is crucial. When individuals experience a diminished sense of self, it can lead to a feeling of unity and connectedness with others and the world around them. This sense of oneness is a critical element in many spiritual traditions and is central to forming deep, spiritual connections with others. Shared experiences that lead to this state of transcendence can significantly strengthen the bonds between individuals, fostering a shared spiritual journey and a deeper understanding of each other's inner worlds.

Furthermore, interactions that evoke a sense of spiritual transcendence, such as being in nature or engaging in meditative practices, can activate the parasympathetic nervous system. This part of the autonomic nervous system is responsible for the 'rest-and-digest' response, a state of relaxation and rejuvenation, in contrast to the 'fight-or-flight' response triggered by the sympathetic nervous system. This activation results in a state of relaxation and mental clarity, which is conducive to experiencing transcendental moments. In Spiritual Bonding, this physiological shift can be profoundly impactful. It allows individuals to step away from the stresses and distractions of everyday life and enter a space where deep, meaningful connections can flourish. This shift's calm and clarity provide an ideal environment for nurturing spiritual bonds, where individuals can engage in open and heartfelt communication, share profound insights, and develop a shared sense of purpose and understanding.

Benefits and Considerations:

Spiritual Bonding centers around shared spiritual beliefs, practices, or quests for meaning. This style can significantly enrich relationships, providing a powerful foundation of shared values and experiences. Spiritual Bonding allows partners or friends to explore the deeper aspects of life together, leading to heightened emotional intimacy. A couple who meditates together or attends spiritual retreats can experience a form of non-verbal communication and understanding that transcends ordinary interaction. This shared spiritual journey fosters a deeper empathy and understanding of each other's inner worlds, strengthening the emotional bonds.

Engaging in a shared spiritual path can imbue a relationship with a sense of purpose and direction. This could manifest in joint participation in religious activities, exploring philosophical questions, or engaging in practices like yoga, prayers, or mindfulness. Such shared experiences give couples or friends a common goal and outlook on life, uniting them profoundly. For example, a couple volunteering at their place of worship can deepen their bond through shared values and communal experiences.

Spiritual Bonding often involves principles like compassion, patience, and understanding, which can greatly enhance communication and conflict resolution in relationships. When partners share a spiritual bond, they are more likely to approach conflicts with a mindset of understanding and empathy, drawing on their shared spiritual principles. This can lead to more constructive and compassionate conflict resolution, strengthening rather than straining the relationship.

These are some examples that we can draw from various spiritual and religious teachings regarding the benefits of Spiritual Bonding:

❖ Buddhist lessons, particularly those revolving around compassion and loving-kindness, offer profound insights into conflict resolution. The concept of Metta, or loving-kindness meditation, encourages individuals to cultivate unconditional love and compassion towards themselves and others. For example, in a conflict situation, partners can practice Metta by first calming their minds, then consciously directing thoughts of love and understanding towards each other. This practice can help diffuse anger and foster a more compassionate approach to resolving disagreements.

- ❖ Christianity emphasizes the virtue of patience, often encapsulated in the biblical teaching of "Love is patient, love is kind" (1 Corinthians 13:4-5). This principle suggests that true love involves tolerating imperfections and enduring challenges without frustration or anger. In a relationship, this might mean giving your partner time to express their views without interruption or judgment, actively listening, and responding with kindness, even in moments of disagreement.

- ❖ In Islam, the concept of understanding and mutual consultation is emphasized in the Quran: "And whose affair is [determined by] consultation among themselves" (42:38). This encourages partners to engage in open dialogue and collaborative decision-making. During conflicts, couples can draw upon this teaching by ensuring both parties have the opportunity to express their perspectives and feelings, fostering a mutual understanding that can lead to more amicable resolutions.

- ❖ Jainism promotes non-violent communication with its core principle of Ahimsa (non-violence). This involves expressing one's needs and feelings without blame or criticism, and empathetically receiving the other person's needs and feelings. For instance, instead of accusing a partner of negligence, one might express the feeling of being overlooked and needing more attention. This approach reduces the likelihood of defensive reactions and opens the way for constructive dialogue.

❖ Hinduism teaches the importance of selflessness in relationships, as illustrated in the Bhagavad Gita's emphasis on performing one's duty with dedication but without attachment to the results. In a relationship, this can translate to addressing conflicts focusing on finding solutions that benefit the relationship rather than satisfying individual egos. Partners can strive to approach disagreements with a mindset of what is best for the relationship rather than what is best for the individual.

❖ Both Christianity and Islam place a strong emphasis on forgiveness. The Lord's Prayer in Christianity includes the plea, "Forgive us our trespasses, as we forgive those who trespass against us." Similarly, in Islam, forgiveness is considered a virtue and a sign of strength. Couples can draw on these teachings by making a conscious effort to forgive each other's mistakes, understanding that forgiveness is key to healing and moving forward in a relationship. These examples from various spiritual and religious teachings illustrate how principles like compassion, patience, understanding, non-violent communication, selflessness, and forgiveness can be applied to enhance communication and conflict resolution in relationships.

Political and religious beliefs are pivotal in shaping the dynamics of relationships. These beliefs guide how individuals interact and bond, influencing choices in spending time and resources, and aligning actions with shared values. This foundation is especially strong in relationships where partners or friends hold similar spiritual or philosophical views. Such common ground often leads to a deeper connection, as it affects key life aspects, including lifestyle choices, parenting approaches, and values imparted to children. Couples and friends find a deep connection in the shared experience of these beliefs, manifested in everyday life through communal activities, family traditions, and daily practices. This influences personal identities and contributes to the collective identity of a group or community. In romantic and platonic relationships, this shared spiritual or political understanding fosters unity and empathy, often leading to joint actions like participating in religious ceremonies, community service, or political events to solidify these bonds further.

A shared spiritual foundation can offer immense comfort and support in times of hardship or loss. Whether it's a shared belief in a higher power, a common understanding of life's cycles, or the support found in spiritual communities, this relationship can be a source of strength and resilience. For example, a couple that turns to their shared faith during challenging times may find solace and strength in their beliefs and practices.

Acknowledging the historical and cultural context in which many religious and spiritual teachings were developed is crucial. Often centuries old, these teachings were formulated in times vastly different from our own, reflecting the societal norms and understandings of those eras. As we evolve in our collective morality and knowledge of human rights, it becomes essential to approach these teachings with a blend of respect, critical thinking, and contemporary relevance.

Over the centuries, human society has undergone significant changes in terms of ethics, morality, and the understanding of human rights. Teachings that were once considered standard may now conflict with contemporary views on equality, justice, and personal freedom. For example, historical texts from various traditions may reflect gender roles or social hierarchies that are no longer applicable or acceptable in modern society. Recognizing this evolution is integral to understanding how to integrate spiritual teachings into our lives today.

Many spiritual and religious texts are rich with metaphorical and allegorical language, often open to interpretations. Scholars and theologians within every tradition have historically debated the meanings and applications of these teachings. This diversity of interpretation is a strength, allowing for flexibility and adaptation to new understandings and contexts. For instance, when interpreted metaphorically or within their historical context, certain parables or teachings in religious texts can offer valuable insights without being taken as literal directives for modern living.

In applying spiritual teachings to contemporary relationships, adopting interpretations that align with progressive values and an inclusive understanding of human rights is important. This means selectively embracing aspects of spiritual wisdom that promote equality, compassion, respect, and personal and communal growth. Partners should feel free to discuss their beliefs, express their doubts, and explore how spiritual teachings resonate with their personal values and the kind of relationship they aspire to build. For example, while some religious texts may have prescribed specific roles for men and women in historical contexts, many modern believers focus on overarching themes of mutual respect and partnership that align with contemporary values.

Integrating political and religious dimensions into Spiritual Bonding reflects the complex interplay between individual beliefs and societal structures in shaping human relationships. In romantic and platonic relationships, shared spiritual or political beliefs create a sense of unity and understanding and can lead to collective actions such as participating in religious activities, community service, or political events, further strengthening the bond.

Navigating a relationship where Spiritual Bonding plays a pivotal role requires thoughtful consideration, especially when it intersects with aspects like religious affiliation, political beliefs, or cultural backgrounds. While Spiritual Bonding can offer a profound connection, addressing certain considerations is essential to maintain a harmonious and respectful relationship.

One of the primary considerations in Spiritual Bonding is the respect for individual beliefs and practices. In a relationship where partners or friends come from different spiritual or religious backgrounds, it's crucial to acknowledge and respect these differences. For example, a couple where one partner follows a particular religious faith while the other identifies as spiritual but not religious must find a way to honor each other's beliefs without imposing their own. This respect forms the basis of a relationship where both individuals feel valued and understood.

In cases where spiritual beliefs are closely tied to cultural identities or political views, navigating these differences becomes a delicate task. A couple might share a spiritual connection but have differing opinions on cultural traditions or political matters. Open, honest communication and a willingness to understand and empathize with each other's perspectives are essential. Partners might need to find a balance that honors their spiritual practices and cultural traditions during religious holidays. Additionally, couples or friends involved in Spiritual Bonding may face external pressures or expectations from their religious communities, families, or social circles. These external influences can impact the relationship, particularly if there is a misalignment between the couple's beliefs and the expectations of others. Traversing this requires a united front, where both individuals support each other in the face of external pressure.

Spiritual journeys can be dynamic, with beliefs and practices evolving over time. This can challenge relationships where Spiritual Bonding is a core element. For example, if one partner undergoes a significant shift in their spiritual beliefs, this can affect the relationship dynamics. Navigating these changes requires flexibility, open-mindedness, and ongoing dialogue to ensure both partners feel supported and respected. For instance, deciding how to incorporate spiritual teachings in child-rearing requires mutual understanding and agreement.

While Spiritual Bonding can be deeply fulfilling, it's important to ensure that it's not the sole basis of the relationship. Maintaining an emotional connection beyond spiritual practices is vital for a well-rounded and healthy relationship. For example, engaging in non-spiritual activities together and cultivating shared interests outside of spirituality can help maintain a balanced relationship. Finally, while shared spiritual practices are enriching, it's also important to encourage individual spiritual growth.

Giving each other the space to explore personal spiritual paths allows for individual development, which in turn can enrich the shared spiritual experience.

Spiritual Bonding allows for greater empathy and a more intuitive understanding of each other's emotions and needs. It's crucial to respect differences in spiritual beliefs and practices within relationships, promote a mutually supportive environment, and encourage honest communication about spiritual beliefs and experiences to deepen spiritual intimacy. These connections often provide a strong sense of security and belonging, enhancing the overall quality of the relationship. Being sensitive to different cultural and spiritual backgrounds ensures inclusivity and understanding.

YOUR RELATIONSHIP REVIVAL:

Spiritual Bonding involves exploring both spirituality and religious practices together to deepen your connection. Here's a list of activities to enrich this meaningful aspect of your relationship:

1. **Diverse Workshops and Retreats**: Attend workshops or retreats from various spiritual traditions for shared growth and understanding.

2. **Meditation and Mindfulness Journey**: Explore new meditation or mindfulness practices together to deepen your sense of peace and connection.

3. **Yoga Exploration**: Try different styles of yoga, each offering unique insights and benefits for your spiritual and physical well-being.

4. **Spiritual Pilgrimage**: Visit places of worship or spiritual significance from different cultures or denominations to appreciate diverse spiritual perspectives.

5. **Nature-Based Spirituality**: Engage in activities like forest bathing or sunrise meditation sessions for a powerful connection with nature.

6. **Spiritual Texts Discussion**: Read and discuss spiritual texts or listen to spiritual podcasts together, reflecting on their meanings in your lives.

7. **Candlelit Gratitude Ritual**: Share what you're grateful for in a candlelit setting, deepening your spiritual bond.

8. **Community Service as Spiritual Practice**: Engage in community service with a spiritual mindset for fulfilling spiritual experiences.

9. **Guided Spiritual Journey**: Join a guided spiritual journey or pilgrimage, exploring sacred sites and their spiritual significance.

10. **Create a Sacred Space**: Designate a space in your home for spiritual practices, decorating it with items that hold spiritual significance for both of you.

11. **Religious Study Group**: Start a study group together focusing on religious texts, delving deeper into your faith and understanding.

12. **Religious Festivals and Rituals**: Participate in religious festivals or rituals from your own or different faiths. This exposure can deepen your respect and understanding of each other's beliefs.

13. **Volunteering at Religious Events**: Volunteer together at events organized by your place of worship, strengthening your bond through service.

14. **Interfaith Exploration**: If you belong to different faiths, take time to learn and participate in each other's religious practices, fostering a deeper understanding and respect.

Remember, Spiritual Bonding encompasses spiritual and religious practices, growing together in understanding and faith. These shared experiences foster a profound sense of connection, learning, and mutual growth. Embrace these activities to enrich and deepen your bond in a way that resonates with your shared spiritual and religious journey. Spiritual connections run deep, and weaving in elements from other relationship styles, such as Kind Contributions or Culinary Sharing, can illuminate new paths of spiritual growth and shared exploration.

PLACES TO PICK:

Spiritual retreats, meditation sessions, yoga classes, places of worship (churches, synagogues, temples, mosques), mindfulness workshops, tai chi or qigong classes, spiritual book clubs, religious study groups, pilgrimage sites, holistic health centers, new age festivals, chanting sessions, spiritual healing workshops, nature sanctuaries, religious holiday celebrations, interfaith dialogues, spiritual art exhibits, sacred dance workshops, religious history museums, community prayer groups.

LITERARY ECHOES:

"Spiritual partnership is the partnership between equals for the purpose of spiritual growth." — Gary Zukav, American spiritual teacher and the author of four consecutive New York Times Best Sellers.

"The best love is the kind that awakens the soul and makes us reach for more." — Nicholas Sparks, American novelist and screenwriter, best known for his romance novels.

"This fire that we call Loving is too strong for human minds. But just right for human souls." — Aberjhani, African American historian, columnist, novelist, and poet.

"Love is composed of a single soul inhabiting two bodies." — Aristotle, ancient Greek philosopher and polymath during the Classical period in Ancient Greece.

"In true love, it is the soul that envelops the body." — Friedrich Nietzsche, German philosopher, cultural critic, composer, poet, and philologist.

"The most important ingredient for a compatible relationship is having a shared set of values." — John Hernandez, Professor of Philosophy at Palo Alto College.

"A woman's heart should be so hidden in God that a man has to seek Him just to find her." — Maya Angelou, memoirist and actress, importantly figured in the civil rights movement.

"If we claim to love God, but don't love each other our love is nothing and meaningless." — David Alley, Christian minister and author.

"Don't build your marriage on your feelings that constantly change. Build your marriage on your faith in Allah." — Dr. Bilal Philips, contemporary Islamic scholar, teacher, speaker, and author.

Ramban on Genesis 24:67: "Yitzhak's love came from an appreciation of Rivka's righteousness." — Ramban, or Nahmanides, was a medieval Jewish scholar.

"To love another person is to see the peace of God." — Victor Hugo, French poet, novelist, and dramatist of the Romantic movement.

"The biblical concept of love says no to acts of selfishness within marital and other human relationships." — R. C. Sproul, American theologian and ordained pastor in the Presbyterian Church.

"I cannot love you as I love myself until I love God as I ought to love Him." — Jack Hyles, prominent figure in the Independent Baptist movement.

REFLECT AND DISCUSS:

Incorporating Spirituality and Religion into Daily Life:

1. How do you incorporate spiritual or religious practices into your daily life as a couple or with a friend? What impact does this have on your relationship?

_____

_____

_____

2. Discuss the role of prayer, meditation, or other spiritual rituals in your relationship. How do these practices strengthen your bond?

_____

_____

_____

3. Spiritual practices often evolve over time. Discuss how the historical evolution of a particular spiritual practice has influenced the way you and your partner experience spirituality together.

_____

_____

_____

Navigating Differences in Spirituality and Religion:

4. Discuss how you navigate differences in spiritual/religious beliefs or practices in your relationship. What strategies do you use to maintain harmony?

_____

_____

_____

5. Discuss the challenges and rewards of being in an interfaith relationship. How do you celebrate and respect your diverse beliefs?

_____

_____

_____

Growth and Support through Spiritual Journeys:

6. Can you share how supporting each other's spiritual journey led to mutual growth in your relationship?

_____

_____

_____

7. Reflect on a moment when a shared spiritual or religious value helped you overcome a challenge or conflict in your relationship.

_____

_____

_____

Community and Shared Spiritual Activities:

8. Share how participating in spiritual or religious community activities together has affected your relationship.

_____

_____

_____

Chapter Ten

8. PHYSICAL PRESENCE

Moments You'll Recognize:

*A*riana and Zain's relationship was a canvas painted with moments of Physical Presence, an unspoken language that communicated love and connection in a way words never could. Their story was marked by the subtle, everyday moments where their physical closeness spoke volumes. Their mornings began with a ritual as simple as it was meaningful. Before the rush of the day took over, they shared a quiet cup of coffee on their balcony, nestled in a small loveseat. As the city below them awakened, they sat shoulder to shoulder, sometimes in conversation, sometimes in comfortable silence, watching the sunrise paint the sky. This shared moment of tranquility, with the warmth of the morning sun and each other's company, was the perfect grounding start to their day.

Inside their home, their physical connection laced through their daily routines. Whether it was Zain enveloping Ariana in a spontaneous embrace while she cooked or Ariana reaching out to gently massage Zain's shoulders as he worked at his desk, these touches affirmed their love and presence. They had a language of gentle touches, soft kisses, and comforting hugs that filled their home with warmth and affection. Their physical bond extended beyond the four walls of their home. They shared a love for simple walks over the weekends. Hand in hand, they navigated walkways, their steps in sync. Amidst the beauty of nature, these moments reinforced their connection, serving as reminders of the strength and support they found in each other. During tough times, a reassuring squeeze of the hand or a supportive arm around the waist was all the encouragement needed to keep going.

Even in public spaces, their physical closeness was evident. At a crowded concert or a busy market, they maintained a subtle but constant physical connection – a hand at the small of the back, an arm looped through the other's, a head resting on a shoulder. It was their way of saying, "I'm here with you amidst it all." Their evenings often ended as they began – together. They'd curl up on the couch, Ariana's head resting on Zain's lap as they watched a movie or talked about their day. These quiet moments of physical closeness were their sanctuary, a time to reconnect and recharge in each other's presence.

Zain and Ariana's relationship was a testament to the power of Physical Presence. It wasn't about grand romantic gestures but about everyday touches, shared physical spaces, and comfort in each other's presence. Their story exemplified how physical closeness can be the silent yet powerful language of love, fortifying the beautiful structure of their relationship to create a tender and resilient bond.

Defining The Style:

Physical Presence in relationships entails being physically available and actively engaged with a partner or friend, encompassing support, affection, and proximity. It includes being there for someone in times of need or desire, offering support and strength through presence, and showing support and affection through physical touch and proximity, including non-sexual and sexual forms of touch. These broader categories encompass the key aspects of Physical Presence in relationships: the role and impact of being physically close, managing the balance between closeness and personal space, and the ways in which physical gestures express care and support. Physical closeness promotes feelings of security and comfort, and enhances non-verbal communication and understanding in a relationship. Examples include comforting a partner during difficult times by embracing them or just being with them, expressing affection through hugs or holding hands, and being physically present during important life events or milestones.

Unveiling Historical and Scientific Treasures:

Examining the role of Physical Presence in relationships from an evolutionary perspective reveals its fundamental importance across various species, particularly humans. Throughout the animal kingdom, physical touch is a crucial communication tool and a means of forming and maintaining social structures. In primates, including humans, the evolution of physical touch as a bonding mechanism is especially pronounced. They are vital for survival, ensuring group harmony, establishing social hierarchies, and facilitating reproductive success. Primatologists like Jane Goodall and Frans de Waal have documented extensive grooming behaviors among primates, which had extended purposes from cleanliness to maintenance of the social fabric of primate societies, reinforcing alliances and demonstrating care and trust among group members.

Anthropological evidence suggests that early hominins' survival depended on close-knit groups where cooperative care and mutual support were necessary to withstand harsh environmental conditions. This emphasis on Physical Presence and touch is supported by the work of evolutionary psychologists like Dr. Robin Dunbar, who theorized that the evolution of the human brain, particularly the neocortex, was driven by the need to maintain complex social networks. Physical touch was a key component of these social interactions, facilitating empathy, trust, and cooperation among early humans.

Historical studies on primates provide stark evidence of the importance of touch. Psychologist Harry Harlow's controversial experiments with rhesus monkeys in the 1950s demonstrated the psychological impact of touch deprivation. Monkeys raised with surrogate wire and cloth mothers exhibited severe behavioral problems, underscoring the necessity of physical contact for healthy psychological development. This finding parallels human experiences, where touch deprivation can lead to emotional and developmental issues.

One of the most significant bodies of research in this area comes from the work of John Bowlby, a British psychologist who developed Attachment Theory in the mid-20th century. Bowlby's work, initially inspired by his observations of children separated from their parents during World War II, was further informed by studies of children in orphanages. He found that children who lacked a consistent caregiver and did not receive adequate physical affection and emotional support exhibited severe developmental delays, emotional distress, and attachment disorders.

Developmental psychologists such as Charles Nelson have conducted more recent studies on children in orphanages, particularly those in Eastern Europe post-Cold War. These studies highlighted the detrimental effects of institutionalization on children's brain development and functioning. Children raised in deprived orphanage environments showed significant delays in cognitive and emotional development, smaller brain size, and altered brain activity compared to those raised in nurturing environments. In terms of physiological impacts, these children often exhibited dysregulated stress responses, a consequence of the lack of comforting physical touch and emotional care. The absence of a nurturing touch in early life was found to disrupt the normal development of the hypothalamic-pituitary-adrenal (HPA) axis, the body's central stress response system. This disruption can lead to long-term issues with stress regulation, anxiety, and emotional processing.

The significance of Physical Presence is profoundly evident right from infancy, where skin-to-skin contact, commonly known as 'kangaroo care,' plays a vital role. Such contact has been shown to be crucial for the development and stability of an infant's nervous system and overall growth. Dr. Ruth Feldman, a developmental psychologist, has highlighted in her research that premature infants who receive extended skin-to-skin contact with their parents exhibit significant improvements in cognitive and emotional development and more stable autonomic functioning than those who do not.

Moreover, the benefits of skin-to-skin contact in the care of premature babies extend to their very survival. Dr. John Bowlby's Attachment Theory supports this notion, emphasizing the importance of physical contact in forming secure attachments from an early age. This perspective is further corroborated by the work of Dr. Tiffany Field at the Touch Research Institute in Miami. Her studies have found that premature infants who receive regular tactile stimulation, including gentle massage and skin-to-skin contact, not only show better weight gain and more stable vital signs but also demonstrate overall better developmental outcomes compared to infants who lack such contact. This tactile stimulation plays an integral role in regulating the infants' physiological functions, enhancing their growth, and strengthening their immune systems.

Attachment Theory, developed by John Bowlby, plays a critical role in understanding relationship dynamics. Bowlby's theory, initially focused on the bonds between infants and their primary caregivers, has profound implications for adult relationships. It suggests that the quality of attachment experiences between children and their caregivers can significantly influence an individual's approach to relationships throughout their life. These experiences form the basis for different attachment styles, each reflecting varying comfort levels with intimacy and physical contact.

1. Secure Attachment: Individuals with this style typically had consistent and supportive care in childhood. They are comfortable with intimacy and are usually warm and loving in their relationships. They can maintain healthy boundaries and are adept at supporting their partners emotionally.

2. Anxious-Preoccupied Attachment: This style often develops in individuals who have experienced inconsistent caregiving. They may crave closeness and validation, constantly feeling

insecure about their partner's feelings towards them. This can lead to clinginess and a heightened sensitivity to their partner's actions.

3. Dismissive-Avoidant Attachment: Those with this style might have experienced neglect or emotional unavailability from caregivers. They tend to be independent to the point of pushing others away, often seeming aloof or uninterested in deep emotional connections.

4. Fearful-Avoidant Attachment (also known as disorganized): This style typically emerges in individuals who have experienced trauma or extreme inconsistency in caregiving. These individuals often have conflicting desires for closeness and distance, leading to turbulent relationships.

Each attachment style influences how individuals perceive and respond to physical touch and presence in relationships. For instance, securely attached individuals are generally comfortable with physical affection and can provide and receive comfort through touch. In contrast, those with avoidant attachment styles might find excessive physical closeness suffocating, preferring more space and independence. For those interested in delving deeper into Attachment Theory and its applications in adult relationships, numerous resources are available. Books such as "Attached" by Amir Levine and Rachel Heller offer insights into how attachment styles play out in romantic relationships. Another noteworthy resource is "Hold Me Tight" by Dr. Sue Johnson, which explores the concept of emotional attachment and provides guidance for cultivating deeper, more fulfilling connections with partners.

The vagus nerve, an extensive network of fibers that emerges from the brainstem and extends to various organs, is a necessary component of the parasympathetic nervous system, often referred to as the 'rest and digest' system. Its activation through touch has profound calming effects on the body. When the skin is gently touched or stroked, it triggers neural responses that stimulate the vagus nerve. This stimulation leads to a series of healthy physiological changes: a decrease in heart rate, a reduction in blood pressure, and a lowering of cortisol levels, the body's primary stress hormone. These changes foster a state of relaxation and wellbeing, counteracting the effects of stress and anxiety.

The impact of touch on the immune system is another critical area of research. Studies have demonstrated that positive physical interactions, such as hugging or holding hands, can enhance the immune response. For instance, research by Dr. Sheldon Cohen at Carnegie Mellon University found that individuals who experience frequent hugs and physical support show greater resistance to developing infections and display milder symptoms when they get sick. This immune-boosting effect is partly attributed to the reduction in stress-related hormones, which can compromise immune function, and the stimulation of the skin, which is closely linked to the immune system.

Physical Presence, involving being there for someone and offering support through physical closeness and touch, plays a significant role in friendships and romantic relationships. A study involving over 14,000 adults from 45 countries found that embracing, stroking, kissing, and hugging are common in relationships with partners and children across diverse cultures. However, the amount and type of physical touch vary widely between cultures, with more collectivistic cultures being more reserved and influenced by family and societal expectations, while individualistic cultures prioritize personal autonomy but still value physical attraction and passion in romantic relationships. Intercultural romantic relationships can face unique challenges regarding physical expression, requiring understanding and respecting each partner's cultural norms and finding a balance that satisfies both. Strategies for navigating physical expression in intercultural relationships include open communication, mutual respect, and finding common ground that aligns with both partners' comfort levels and cultural norms.

In contemporary society, the role of physical touch in relationships has become increasingly complex, with digital communication and virtual interactions changing the dynamics of Physical Presence. Despite this, studies have consistently shown that physical touch remains vital to close relationships, linked to increased relationship satisfaction, emotional bonding, and overall wellbeing. Research exploring the expression of affection through touch across cultures has revealed both universal patterns and notable variations. Various factors, including climate, conservatism, religiosity, and attitudes toward physical contact, can influence cultural differences in affectionate touch behaviors. Individual preferences for touch in relationships can be influenced by factors such as attachment styles, with different attachment patterns affecting comfort levels with intimacy and physical contact, and gender differences also influencing touch preferences.

The significance of sexual intimacy and physical touch – including cuddling and other forms of close physical connection – is deeply rooted in our evolutionary history, biology and psychology. This aspect of human interaction is not merely a source of pleasure but plays a crucial role in our survival and wellbeing, influenced by a complex interplay of hormones and evolutionary processes. The study of romantic love, as explored by Helen Fisher's team at Rutgers, reveals a fascinating hormonal journey that underscores the importance of Physical Presence in relationships. Fisher categorizes romantic love into three distinct stages: lust, attraction, and attachment, each governed by specific hormonal responses.

In the initial stage of lust, the hormones testosterone and estrogen play pivotal roles. These hormones drive sexual desire and arousal, laying the groundwork for romantic attraction. They are fundamental in the initial phase of romantic relationships, sparking the physical and sexual interest essential for developing deeper connections.

The second stage, attraction, is characterized by a potent cocktail of neurotransmitters: dopamine, norepinephrine, and serotonin. Dopamine, linked to the brain's reward pathway, heightens feelings of pleasure and elation and is released during enjoyable activities, including spending quality time with a loved one. Norepinephrine, akin to adrenaline, increases alertness and arousal, while serotonin contributes to feelings of happiness and well-being. This stage of attraction encapsulates the exhilarating and often euphoric sensations associated with the early phases of romantic love.

Finally, the attachment stage cements the long-term bond between partners, mediated by oxytocin and vasopressin. Oxytocin, the 'cuddle hormone,' is released during intimate activities such as sex, breastfeeding, and childbirth. It plays a crucial role in promoting bonding and attachment, fostering feelings of trust and security between partners. Vasopressin complements this by supporting long-term commitment and monogamous tendencies, reinforcing the relationship's stability.

These hormonal responses highlight the biological underpinnings of romantic love and the importance of Physical Presence. The act of sex, central to human reproduction and crucial for the continuation of our species, triggers a cascade of hormonal changes that deepen emotional connections, reinforce attachment, and contribute to relationship satisfaction and longevity.

Just like our non-human primate cousins, we humans have a powerful, invisible connection that binds us through touch. This bond is not just emotional or psychological; it's deeply rooted in our biology. Some of the key players in this story are the opioid receptors in our brains - specifically, the μ-opioid receptors (MOR). Opioid receptors are like special docking stations in our brains and nervous systems where certain substances, including natural "feel-good" chemicals produced by our body, can attach. When these substances latch on to the opioid receptors, they trigger feelings of pleasure and well-being. It's a system designed for reward and bonding.

In a fascinating study, scientists used a method called positron emission tomography (PET) to see how these receptors work during social touch. They found that when participants received non-sexual, caring touches from their partners, there was increased activity in these opioid receptors in certain areas of the brain. These areas include the thalamus, striatum, and various cortices, which are regions associated with emotion, pleasure, and social connection. This discovery isn't just about us; it's a trait we share with our primate relatives. In non-human primates, enhancing the function of these opioid receptors leads to more social grooming – an essential activity for their social bonds and well-being. This similarity hints at a deep evolutionary link, suggesting that our need for physical connection is more than just a human quirk; it's a fundamental part of our biology.

Studies have consistently shown that individuals in close relationships characterized by regular physical affection, such as cuddling and non-sexual touch, often exhibit lower blood pressure and heart rates. This correlation is attributed to the stress-reducing effects of physical contact, a phenomenon supported by Dr. James Coan's research. In his study, individuals holding hands with a loved one showed lower stress responses and a calmer demeanor during stressful situations, compared to those without physical support. This calming effect is further enhanced by releasing oxytocin, known for reducing cortisol levels – the body's primary stress hormone – and increasing serotonin production, thereby improving emotional wellbeing and relationship satisfaction.

Reflecting on our instinctual responses towards those in pain further underscores the pivotal role of physical touch. For instance, the intuitive act of a woman clutching her partner's hand during childbirth, a parent's gentle kiss on an injured child's wound, or a friend's reassuring back rub to someone feeling unwell, all serve as profound examples of touch as a natural analgesic. These gestures, deeply ingrained in human behavior, exemplify our innate tendency to provide comfort and alleviate pain through physical connection.

Additionally, the comforting aspect of physical touch plays a pivotal role in pain management. The act of touch, ranging from gentle strokes to hand-holding, can significantly diminish pain perception. This pain-relieving effect is largely mediated by the release of endorphins, the body's natural painkillers, activated by tactile stimulation. Beyond pain relief, regular physical touch in relationships contributes to overall health benefits, including reduced anxiety and improved immune function. These findings highlight the deep-seated biological need for such interactions in human relationships, emphasizing Physical Presence's integral role in promoting physical and emotional health.

In reality, touch encompasses a wide spectrum of interactions, each with distinct emotional and physiological connotations. As a sensory interface, the skin is equipped with a myriad of nerve endings that respond to different kinds of touch – sexual, cooperative, friendly, and more. This variety underscores the misconception that touch is inherently sexual, which may lead to severe psychological and physical impacts. It may lead to touch deprivation in scenarios where non-sexual physical contact would be beneficial. The release of oxytocin, a hormone that promotes feelings of bonding and reduces stress, is stimulated by physical contact. Therefore, a lack of touch can lower oxytocin levels, affecting emotional wellbeing and social bonding.

Hugging friends can greatly enhance emotional wellbeing, yet these gestures may be avoided due to the fear of misinterpretation. This misunderstanding may be particularly impactful in societies with strict gender norms, where expressions of physical affection between friends or family members of the same gender may be stigmatized. Such touch deprivation can result in heightened stress, loneliness, and reduced emotional support, particularly for individuals who do not conform to traditional gender stereotypes.

Research has indicated that the lack of non-sexual physical contact can have varying impacts on health, potentially exacerbating health disparities related to gender stereotypes. For example, men in cultures where physical affection is limited may experience higher levels of stress and less emotional support than women, as women's social interactions often include more physical touch. This disparity can contribute to differences in coping mechanisms and overall mental health between genders.

Even though there are common grounds for the importance of touch in all human relationships, the feelings and exact experiences vary individually depending on several factors. The diverse perspectives and experiences brought by individuals of varied sexual orientations and gender identities enrich how physical and emotional connections are formed and expressed. This diversity contributes to the adaptive complexity of human relationships, reflecting an evolutionary advantage in our ability to create nuanced and supportive physical connections.

The concept of Inclusive Fitness, introduced by evolutionary biologist W.D. Hamilton, provides a framework for understanding the evolutionary benefit of behaviors that seem, at first glance, not to contribute to individual reproduction directly. Inclusive Fitness theory posits that behaviors that support the group can be advantageous from an evolutionary standpoint if they contribute to the group's survival as a whole. This theory can be extended to understand the role of individuals with diverse sexual orientations and gender identities, who may contribute to a community's social and cooperative fabric in ways that support the group's overall wellbeing and survival.

Historically, many indigenous cultures recognized and often revered individuals who embodied diverse gender identities or sexual orientations. For example, the Two-Spirit people in many Native American tribes were seen as holding unique social and spiritual roles, contributing to the tribe's wellbeing through their distinct perspectives. Two-Spirit is a term used to describe certain people in Native American communities who embody both masculine and feminine spirits. This identity is deeply rooted in the spiritual and cultural life of the tribe, often associated with possessing a blend of gender traits and fulfilling specific ceremonial roles. Anthropologists, such as Dr. Sabine Lang, have documented these roles, illustrating how gender diversity was integrated and valued in these societies, contributing to their social richness and adaptability.

From an evolutionary perspective, the work of biologist Joan Roughgarden in her book 'Evolution's Rainbow' challenges the traditional Darwinian narrative of gender and sexual behavior. She argues for a broader understanding of sexuality and gender roles within the animal kingdom, including humans. Her research suggests that diversity in gender and sexual behavior is a common and natural occurrence, providing various adaptive advantages such as enhanced group cooperation and social bonding. Besides the variety in Physical Presence, the work of psychologist Simon Baron-Cohen, who understands empathy and social intelligence, highlights the benefits of diverse cognitive styles. His research suggests that various cognitive approaches, such as those found in people with different gender identities and sexual orientations, can enhance a society's overall empathy and social understanding.

BENEFITS AND CONSIDERATIONS:

The Physical Presence relationship style, characterized by the importance of physical closeness, touch, and shared physical space, offers benefits beyond mere physical comfort. It taps into the basic human need for physical contact and connection, playing a crucial role in the emotional and psychological well-being of individuals in a relationship.

Physical touch is a powerful tool for enhancing emotional intimacy. Without words, one may express care, support, and understanding via simple acts like holding hands, comforting embraces, or applying a light touch. When one partner or a friend is experiencing stress or sadness, a comforting embrace from the other can provide a sense of security and connection, conveying empathy and care more effectively than words alone. Regular physical contact, such as cuddling, hand-holding, or sitting close to each other, fosters a sense of trust and security in a relationship. These small but significant gestures of closeness can create a safe and reassuring environment, which is particularly important in times of uncertainty or distress. A couple who makes a habit of cuddling each night, and friends who make a habit of hugging each time they meet may find that this routine strengthens their bond and provides a sense of stability and comfort in their lives. Non-verbal communication plays a pivotal role in Physical Presence. Gestures, facial expressions, and physical closeness can convey complex emotions and sentiments. For a couple or friends, a knowing glance or a gentle touch can be a subtle yet powerful way of communicating affection, understanding, or reassurance, reinforcing the bond without needing words.

Sharing physical space, such as living together or engaging in activities that require physical proximity, nurtures a sense of belonging and unity. This shared space allows for shared experiences and memories, integral to the relationship's identity. For instance, a couple that cooks together in the kitchen or works on home improvement projects engages in activities that reinforce their sense of partnership and teamwork. Physical Presence also highlights the comfort that can be found in silent companionship. Sitting together in silence, whether reading, enjoying nature, watching TV, or simply being in the same room, can be deeply comforting and bonding. It allows couples or friends to enjoy each other's company without needing constant conversation, appreciating the tranquility and peace of just being together. Regular physical contact and presence serve as ongoing affirmations of commitment and care in a relationship. Each hug, kiss, or touch is a small reaffirmation of the bond and affection between partners. For example, a simple daily ritual of a goodbye kiss before leaving for work can be a small yet signifi-cant reaffirmation of love and commitment.

In times of conflict or after disagreement, Physical Presence and touch can play a crucial role in the healing process. A sincere hug or holding hands can break down walls, bridge emotional distances, and pave the way for forgiveness and reconciliation. This physical reconnection can signify the desire to move past disputes and maintain the strength of the relationship.

The Physical Presence relationship style, centered on the im-portance of touch, closeness, and shared space, can greatly en-rich relationships. However, navigating its nuances thoughtfully is crucial to ensure it aligns with the comfort levels and bound-aries of all involved. While physical closeness can strengthen a relationship, balancing this with maintaining individual inde-pendence is essential. Each person should be able to pursue their interests and spend time apart. Over-reliance on Physical Presence can lead to issues of codependency, where personal identity and independence are diminished. Couples must find a healthy balance between enjoying shared space and respecting each other's need for individual space and activities.

One of the key considerations in a relationship emphasizing Physical Presence is understanding and respecting each individ-ual's boundaries regarding physical touch and space. Comfort levels with physical closeness can vary widely based on person-al, cultural, or past experiences. For instance, one partner may enjoy constant physical affection, while the other might require more personal space. Recognizing and honoring these differ-ences is crucial to ensure both partners feel comfortable and respected. Open communication about preferences and needs regarding Physical Presence is vital. This includes discussing how much physical touch is appreciated, what types of touch are preferred, and when and where each person feels most com-fortable being physically close. For example, one partner may appreciate holding hands in public, while the other may not feel comfortable with public displays of affection. Regularly checking in and communicating about these preferences ensures that both partners' needs are met and respected. Understanding and responding to non-verbal cues is crucial. Not everyone may be comfortable verbalizing their need for space or touch, so being attentive to body language and non-verbal signals is important. For instance, if one partner seems to withdraw from a hug or hand-holding, it's essential to recognize this signal and respond sensitively.

Circumstances such as health issues, stress, or life changes can affect one's desire for physical closeness. For example, a person's need for physical space or touch might change during illness or emotional distress. Partners need to be attuned to these changes and adapt their behavior accordingly. Being flexible and understanding during these times helps maintain a healthy dynamic, ensuring the relationship remains supportive and nurturing. Circumstances may sometimes require physical separation, such as during travel or due to long-distance living situations. In such cases, finding ways to maintain the connection is important. This might involve regular communication through calls or video chats, writing letters, or finding other creative ways to express affection and maintain closeness despite the physical distance.

Finally, and most importantly, consent should be at the forefront of all physical interactions. Both partners should feel free to express when they are comfortable or uncomfortable with physical touch without fear of judgment or pressure. Ensuring that all physical interactions are consensual and mutually comfortable is fundamental to a healthy and respectful Physical Presence relationship style. The norms and customs surrounding physical touch have varied across different civilizations and time periods, shaped by numerous social, religious, and cultural influences. However, the fundamental need for physical connection in human relationships has remained a constant, underlying thread in our evolutionary story. Physical touch releases oxytocin, known as the 'love hormone,' which promotes feelings of bonding and trust and stimulates the release of endorphins, providing happiness and stress relief. Regular physical touch, like kissing and cuddling, is also associated with higher levels of relationship satisfaction and intimacy. Simple gestures like hugging when a partner comes home, or a random embrace can significantly deepen emotional connections. Sensate Focus exercises involve partners taking turns touching each other in ways that feel good, enhancing physical intimacy and communication about preferences. Non-sexual touch, such as giving backrubs, embracing each other on the couch, foot massages, or simply sitting close, can be nurturing forms of touch that promote connection and relaxation. Understanding and respecting each other's preferences for physical touch is crucial, ensuring open communication about comfort levels and boundaries regarding physical intimacy to maintain consent in all kinds of relationships. This understanding will ensure that Physical Presence remains a positive and enriching relationship aspect.

YOUR RELATIONSHIP REVIVAL:

Physical Presence is about enriching your relationship through touch and activities that foster physical closeness. Here's a list of activities to enhance this tactile aspect of your relationship:

1. **Dance Together**: Enroll in dance classes for couples. Dancing brings you physically close and builds harmony and connection through movement.

2. **DIY Home Spa Experience**: Set up a DIY spa day at home with homemade face masks, relaxing music, and a soothing bath.

3. **Vary Physical Affection Routines**: Introduce variety in your routines of physical affection, like surprise hugs, random kisses, or playful tickling, to keep the spark alive.

4. **Furniture Rearrangement**: Shift your house furniture around to create new, cozy spaces for sitting or lounging together, altering your environment to encourage closeness.

5. **Date Nights with Physical Touch**: Plan date nights that involve activities requiring physical closeness, such as couple's massages or a cooking class where you can work side by side.

6. **Daily Touch Rituals**: Incorporate different forms of touch into your daily life, like cuddling during movie nights, holding hands on walks, or giving each other a shoulder massage while watching TV.

7. **Open Discussions on Physical Affection**: Have open conversations about exploring new forms of physical affection, ensuring comfort and consent in your physical connection.

8. **Build a Fort**: Create a cozy fort in your living room with blankets and pillows, offering a playful, intimate space to relax together.

9. **Sunrise or Sunset Walks**: Go for walks together during sunrise or sunset. The beauty of nature combined with physical closeness can be incredibly romantic and grounding.

10. **Playful Physical Challenges**: Engage in light-hearted physical challenges like a three-legged race or a playful wrestling match, adding humor and playfulness to your physical interaction.

11. **Sensory Experiences**: Experiment with sensory experiences, like blindfolded taste testing or gentle feather touches, to explore and heighten your physical senses together.

Revitalizing Physical Presence in your relationship is about exploring different forms of touch and activities that bring you physically closer. These experiences enhance physical and emotional intimacy and maintain the strength of your connection. Embrace these activities to keep the physical spark alive and foster a sense of comfort and security with each other. Physicality in relationships is about connection. Integrating this with different styles, such as Playful Teasing or Inspirational Support, can deepen the physical bond in unexpected ways.

Places to Pick:

Couples' retreats, wellness and spa centers, dance studios for couples, quiet cafes, scenic parks, beachfront walks, couples' massage workshops, romantic dining spots, botanical gardens, scenic hiking trails, cozy bookstores with reading nooks, sunset viewing spots, couples' cooking classes, picnic areas, scenic boat rides, ice skating rinks, couples' fitness classes, secluded cabins, rooftop terraces.

Literary Echoes:

"You're more likely to talk about nothing than something. But I just want to say that all this nothing has meant more to me than so many somethings." — Meg Ryan, an actress and producer.

"Physical Presence provides chemical, relational, psychological, and physiological effects that virtual relationships cannot. Our brains change in the presence of another person and their behavior." — Henry Cloud, American clinical psychologist.

"The best gift you can give is your presence. When you are fully present, you are truly alive." — Thich Nhat Hanh, Vietnamese Buddhist monk and peace activist.

"The best thing to hold onto in life is each other." — Audrey Hepburn, British actress and humanitarian.

"Where I live if someone gives you a hug, it's from the heart." — Steve Irwin, Australian zookeeper and conservationist.

"Kissing her was like talking to her. There was that same sense of effortless compatibility." — Sean Norris, author.

"Wherever she is, that's where my home is." — Nicholas Sparks, American novelist, from "The Notebook."

"That's how you know you love someone, I guess, when you can't experience anything without wishing the other person were there to see it, too." — Kaui Hart Hemmings, American writer.

"We need 4 hugs a day for survival. We need 8 hugs a day for maintenance. We need 12 hugs a day for growth." — Virginia Satir, American author and therapist.

"A hug is like a boomerang - you get it back right away." — Bil Keane, American cartoonist.

"In true love, the smallest distance is too great, and the greatest distance can be bridged." — Hans Nouwens, author.

"To touch can be to give life." — Michelangelo, Italian sculptor, painter, architect, and poet.

"If you're angry at a loved one, hug that person. And mean it. You may not want to hug, which is all the more reason to do so. It's hard to stay angry when someone shows they love you, and that's precisely what happens when we hug each other." — Walter Anderson, editor and artist.

REFLECT AND DISCUSS:

The Role and Impact of Physical Presence:

1. Share an experience where physical proximity helped you and your partner or friend overcome a challenge or conflict.

   _____

   _____

   _____

2. Can you recall a time when a simple act of physical affection had a profound impact on your mood or perspective?

   _____

   _____

   _____

3. Touch releases oxytocin, sometimes called the 'cuddle hormone.' Share how physical touch plays a role in your relationship. Can you think of a moment when a simple touch communicated more than words?

   _____

   _____

   _____

Navigating Physical Presence and Space:

4. How do you maintain the balance between physical closeness and personal space in your relationship, especially in
   times of stress or busy schedules?

   _____

   _____

   _____

5. Discuss the challenges and solutions when Physical Presence is limited in your relationship, such as in long-distance
   situations.

   _____

   _____

   _____

Expressions of Care and Support Through Physical Gestures:

6. Discuss the importance of Physical Presence in moments of
   vulnerability or emotional need. How has this affected your
   relationship?

   _____

   _____

   _____

7. How do you express care and affection through physical gestures in your relationship?

   _____

   _____

   _____

Chapter Eleven

9. Inspirational Support

Moments You'll Recognize:

Meet Sophia and Jun, two best friends whose bond was forged and strengthened through a shared journey of inspiration and achievement. Their friendship, a beautiful collage of mutual encouragement and support, was a testament to the power of having someone in your corner who believes in you, pushes you, and celebrates your victories, big and small. Sophia, a budding entrepreneur, and Jun, an aspiring musician, met during university. What started as casual conversations about their dreams and aspirations soon evolved into a deep and enduring friendship rooted in a common desire to make their mark on the world. They became each other's biggest fans, advisors, and motivators.

Sophia's journey into entrepreneurship was fraught with challenges, yet Jun's unwavering faith in her vision continually bolstered her resolve. He was there for her brainstorming sessions, offering fresh perspectives and creative ideas. When Sophia hit roadblocks, Jun was the voice of reason, reminding her of her capabilities and the progress she had already made. He celebrated her milestones, whether securing her first investor or making her first sale, with genuine pride and joy.

Sophia's support equally bolstered Jun's musical journey. She was his sounding board, listening to his compositions, providing honest feedback, and encouraging him to push his creative boundaries. When self-doubt crept in, Sophia was there to remind him of his unique talent and the emotive power of his music. She organized small gigs for him, helped him network with industry professionals, and cheered the loudest at his performances.

Together, they set individual and collective goals and held each other accountable. They embarked on a 'goal buddy' system where they would set monthly check-ins to review progress, offer constructive feedback, and set new targets. This system kept them on track and deepened their understanding of each other's passions and struggles. Their encouragement extended beyond their professional lives. When Sophia decided to run a marathon, Jun was there every step of the way, from training runs to crossing the finish line. He created playlists to keep her motivated and joined her for early morning jogs. Similarly, when Jun decided to explore mindfulness and meditation to enhance his creativity, Sophia joined him in workshops and retreats, embracing the opportunity to grow alongside her friend. Their friendship was a vibrant mesh of encouragement and motivation. They celebrated each other's successes, not as mere spectators but as integral parts of each other's achievements. Their belief in each other's potential was unwavering, their support unflinching.

Sophia and Jun's story is a beautiful illustration of how the power of Inspirational Support in friendships can propel individuals toward their dreams. Their relationship style went beyond mere companionship; it was a partnership in the truest sense, marked by a shared commitment to seeing each other succeed and flourish. Their journey together showed that any goal, no matter how lofty, becomes attainable with the right support and encouragement.

Defining The Style:

Inspirational Support in relationships is centered around mutual motivation, encouragement, and uplifting each other to achieve personal growth and goals. It involves actively inspiring each other to pursue goals, dreams, and personal growth, being a positive force in each other's lives. This approach can increase self-confidence, deepen mutual respect, and create a more profound sense of connection, fostering a supportive environment where individuals feel empowered to achieve their aspirations. Examples of Inspirational Support include celebrating each other's successes and milestones, encouraging each other during challenging times or new endeavors, and sharing inspiring stories or motivational insights.

Unveiling Historical and Scientific Treasures:

Inspirational Support style plays a crucial role in achieving personal and shared goals. Whether these goals pertain to health, fitness, business, education, or other areas of life, having a partner or friend who offers support and encouragement can significantly enhance the likelihood of success.

In health and fitness, the role of a supportive partner is significant. Studies, like the one by Indiana University's Department of Kinesiology, demonstrate that couples who pursue fitness goals together have a lower dropout rate compared to those who participate individually. For instance, having a partner who shares the same goal or offers encouragement in weight loss journeys can lead to greater accountability and motivation. The famed National Weight Control Registry, which tracks over 10,000 individuals who have maintained significant weight loss, reports that many successful participants credit having support from a partner or friend as a key factor in their success.

In business and entrepreneurship, the power of a supportive relationship is equally evident. The Harvard Business Review highlights that entrepreneurs with supportive partners are more likely to take calculated risks, leading to potentially higher rewards. An inspiring example is the story of Kevin and Julia Hartz, co-founders of Eventbrite. Their mutual support and complementary skills have been instrumental in growing their business from a startup to a successful global enterprise.

Alex and Leila Hormozi's story is another inspiring example of unwavering support and mutual belief in one another's potential. When Alex expressed his fear of being a 'sinking ship' and offered Leila the option to leave, she displayed her steadfast faith in him, affirming that she would stay by his side even in the direst circumstances, even if the two would have to sleep together under the bridge. This deep level of commitment and support fortified their personal relationship and laid the foundation for their professional success. Together, they navigated the challenges of entrepreneurship, eventually leading to the creation of Acquisition.com and other ventures. Their journey, marked by resilience and mutual inspiration, culminated in them becoming successful entrepreneurs with a substantial net worth. Their story is a testament to the power of Inspirational Support.

Supportive relationships significantly bolster educational pursuits. Research from the University of Georgia shows that students with supportive partners are more likely to pursue higher education and achieve academic success. The shared encouragement and understanding between partners can create a highly conducive environment for learning and personal development.

Even in creative endeavors, the presence of an Inspirational Support system is pivotal. Renowned author Stephen King, in his memoir 'On Writing,' credits his wife's encouragement and belief in his work as a critical factor in his early career. When King was close to giving up on his now-iconic novel 'Carrie,' it was his wife who rescued the manuscript from the trash and urged him to continue. Without her determined Inspirational Support, the well-loved novel would never have reached its readers.

The human brain's evolution, particularly in abstract thought and deep emotional connections, underpins our ability to inspire and motivate each other, as illustrated by our storytelling and communication skills. This evolutionary advancement is not solely a matter of cognitive intelligence; it also encompasses our ability to inspire and motivate each other. Neuroscientists have found that some brain regions, like the prefrontal cortex, which is involved in planning and complex social interactions, also play a role in how we perceive and are influenced by others' actions and achievements. This suggests an evolutionary advantage to being able to inspire and be inspired, as it fosters cooperation, learning, and the progression of societies, which is also reflected in our storytelling and communication skills. Anthropological studies have shown that sharing stories and knowledge has been integral to human societies from early history. These narratives, passed down through generations, were both informational and inspirational, serving to unite groups, instill values, and motivate collective action.

In the primate world, although their behaviors are simpler compared to humans, we can see the beginnings of how being inspired and motivated by others in their communities plays a role. Primates, particularly great apes, engage in social learning and mimicry, which are fundamental for transferring knowledge and skills within a group. While this might not be 'inspirational' in the human sense, it highlights the evolutionary roots of learning from and being motivated by others' actions. Moreover, primates exhibit complex social structures and relationships, including cooperation and social bonding elements. These relationships can be seen as precursors to the more nuanced forms of Inspirational Support observed in humans. The social dynamics within primate groups, such as working together to solve problems or supporting each other in conflicts, lay the groundwork for understanding the evolution of cooperative and supportive behaviors.

Inspirational Support in relationships has deep historical roots, with notable examples dating back to ancient civilizations. In ancient Mesopotamia, a civilization renowned for its contributions to law, literature, and governance, the development of kingship played a pivotal role in societal structure. During this era, rulers were often perceived as divinely chosen, tasked with the responsibility of maintaining order, justice, and prosperity. The effectiveness and legitimacy of these leaders were closely tied to their ability to inspire and guide their subjects. This early form of Inspirational Support was crucial in establishing and maintaining social order and cohesion.

A quintessential example of Inspirational Support in relationships from Mesopotamian literature is found in the Epic of Gilgamesh. This epic, one of the oldest known works of literature, not only illustrates the role of kingship but also delves deeply into the themes of friendship, loyalty, and the human condition. The narrative follows Gilgamesh, the king of Uruk, on his quest for understanding and wisdom. A significant aspect of this journey is his relationship with Enkidu, who starts as a rival but becomes a close companion. Their friendship and the challenges they face together are central to Gilgamesh's development as a leader and individual. The relationship between Gilgamesh and Enkidu is emblematic of Inspirational Support in its early form. Enkidu's companionship, loyalty, and the challenges he presents to Gilgamesh are crucial in the king's journey toward self-awareness and wisdom. This bond exemplifies how relationships based on mutual support and challenge can lead to significant personal growth and understanding.

Historical friendships and mentorships have also been sources of motivation and support. For example, the bond between teachers and students in ancient philosophical schools, such as those led by Confucius, a Chinese Philosopher, often went beyond academic instruction, encompassing moral and spiritual guidance. Confucius, stemming from his ambitions and inspirations, had philosophized friendships on the concept of "do not have as a friend anyone who is not as good as you are." Confucius's emphasis on surrounding oneself with virtuous individuals reflects the essence of Inspirational Support in relationships. His advice underscores the importance of fostering connections with those who inspire personal growth and uphold moral standards. In the domain of Inspirational Support, this translates to choosing relationships that are not only supportive but also challenge and motivate one to become a better version of oneself.

Confucius believed that the quality of our relationships directly influences our personal development and moral character. By engaging with friends who embody virtues such as integrity, kindness, and diligence, individuals are more likely to emulate these traits, enhancing their own ethical and personal growth. This philosophy encourages us to seek out and nurture friendships and mentorships that inspire us to pursue our goals, adhere to our values, and strive for excellence. In an Inspirational Support dynamic, each person plays a dual role: that of a mentor and a mentee. This mutual exchange of guidance and encouragement mirrors Confucius's idea of elevating one another's moral and intellectual capacities. Relationships built on this foundation are emotionally fulfilling and instrumental in achieving personal aspirations and maintaining ethical integrity.

Expanding on the theme of Inspirational Support in relationships, it is insightful to explore how historically influential figures often had partners or close companions who played a pivotal role in their journeys, offering support, inspiration, and partnership that contributed significantly to their successes. These relationships exemplify the Inspirational Support relationship style, where the mutual exchange of support and encouragement fosters personal and collective growth.

Mahatma Gandhi, a central figure in India's struggle for independence, is a prime example. His wife, Kasturba Gandhi, was instrumental in his life, though less often in the spotlight. She was a companion who endured the hardships of his political life and supported his endeavors, offering emotional strength and personal sacrifice. Her support was as a spouse and partner in the nonviolent struggle for justice, embodying the values Gandhi championed.

Nelson Mandela, known for his fight against apartheid in South Africa, also had a strong network of supportive relationships. His wives, particularly Winnie Mandela, played significant roles in the anti-apartheid movement. These partnerships were not without their complexities, but they were crucial in providing Mandela with emotional and political support, contributing to his resilience and perseverance.

Martin Luther King Jr., a symbol of the Civil Rights Movement in the United States, similarly had a foundation of support in his wife, Coretta Scott King. Coretta was an activist in her own right and played a vital role in Dr. King's life, offering support as a wife and partner in the struggle for civil rights. Her involvement extended beyond King's lifetime, as she continued to advocate for justice and equality.

In the scientific domain, the union between Marie Curie and her husband, Pierre Curie, both trailblazers in physics and radioactivity, exemplified a powerful partnership fueled by mutual intellectual curiosity and inspiring support. Their collaborative work in radioactivity led to groundbreaking discoveries and exemplified a partnership where each individual's strengths were recognized and harnessed. Pierre's support of Marie's scientific endeavors, particularly at a time when women faced significant barriers in the field, was crucial for her remarkable achievements.

These historical examples underscore the importance of supportive partnerships in Inspirational Support. The presence of a partner or companion who shares, encourages, and challenges one's aspirations can be a powerful catalyst for achievement and impact. Whether through emotional backing, intellectual collaboration, or shared activism, these relationships demonstrate how mutual support and respect can propel individuals to remarkable heights and, in turn, inspire others.

Today, the life stories of figures like Gandhi, Mandela, and the Curies continue to inspire contemporary relationships, emphasizing mutual support and respect. The principles they embodied—such as courage, perseverance, and compassion—remain relevant in guiding how we form and nurture our relationships. Empirical research studies of helping relationships and social support have increased since the 1960s. It initially focused on understanding the dynamics of help-giving and receiving within social contexts, which laid the foundation for later studies on more specific aspects like Inspirational Support in relationships. The early work by Latané and Darley on the bystander effect was particularly influential in shaping our understanding of how individuals respond to others in need within a social context.

In more recent times, the field of social support in relationships has expanded significantly. This includes a comprehensive understanding of how emotional, informational, and appraisal support contribute to personal development and growth within relationships. Modern theories have increasingly focused on the complexity of support processes in intimate relationships, recognizing their multidimensional nature and impact on relationship dynamics. This shift reflects a broader societal focus on individualism, personal fulfillment, and the importance of emotional wellbeing. Inspirational Support in relationships is now often seen as a vital component of a healthy, fulfilling relationship, where partners or friends actively encourage and support each other's personal goals and aspirations. Unlike in the past, where traditional roles or societal expectations might have more defined relationships, modern relationships often prioritize personal development, emotional support, and mutual inspiration. The historical and contemporary context of Inspirational Support in relationships highlights a shift from a more passive understanding of support to an active, dynamic process that involves mutual growth and development.

The concept of Inspirational Support within relationships is deeply intertwined with biological and hormonal factors. Human brains are fundamentally wired for social connections, as neuroscientist Matthew Lieberman highlights in his book "Social: Why Our Brains Are Wired to Connect." This neural wiring underpins our ability to empathize, cooperate, and support each other from birth. Specific brain circuits are dedicated to empathic care and cooperative behavior. For instance, neuroscientist Tor Wager identified a brain circuit, which promotes feelings of warmth and care, encouraging selfless acts and compassion. Biobehavioral Synchrony, where behavior and biology mirror those of a social contact, prepares individuals for future relationships and enhances feelings of closeness and support of shared inspirational goals.

The concept of brain plasticity, neuroplasticity, and its role in personal development highlights our brains' dynamic and adaptable nature, suggesting that our habits, behaviors, and thought patterns can evolve over time through interactions with others. In the context of relationships, this means that partners or friends who positively influence and inspire each other contribute to the formation of new neural pathways, thereby facilitating changes in the brain. Furthermore, collaborating on shared goals can reinforce positive behaviors and habits, while fostering a sense of joint accomplishment. This process is enhanced through regular, open communication and active listening, enabling both individuals to grow, adapt, and thrive within the context of their relationship, thus exemplifying the transformative power of interpersonal connections on cognitive and emotional development.

An interesting discovery in neuroscience within the domain of neuroplasticity is the evolution of Inspirational Support in relationships. The evolutionary significance of Inspirational Support is evident in the way our brains and bodies have adapted to encourage and reward such behaviors. The anterior Mid-Cingulate Cortex (aMCC), a brain region crucial for tenacity and persistence, is integral in situations that require determination and overcoming challenges. This area is associated with cost/benefit computations necessary for enduring difficult tasks and is stimulated by activities that test our limits.

From an evolutionary perspective, the development and enhancement of the aMCC is a response to the benefits of facing and overcoming challenges, an aspect central to survival and success. Inspirational Support in relationships, where individuals motivate and push each other to take on challenges, aligns perfectly with this evolutionary adaptation. By encouraging each other to step out of their comfort zones and tackle difficulties, people in such relationships activate and nurture this part of the brain, fostering growth in areas related to willpower and resilience.

Additionally, dopamine, a neurotransmitter associated with reward and motivation, is significant in this context. The release of dopamine during challenging situations, especially when successfully navigated, suggests an evolutionary mechanism that rewards and reinforces tenacity and perseverance. This reward system can be seen as an evolutionary tool to encourage behaviors that lead to personal growth and, by extension, the success and survival of the species. Incorporating this knowledge into the context of Inspirational Support, it can be inferred that engaging in challenging activities and inspiring each other to face difficulties could stimulate the aMCC, fostering growth in areas related to willpower and resilience.

Exploring the concept of motivation and its dual nature – approach and avoidance – within the framework of Inspirational Support reveals its integral role in shaping human behavior and relationships. Approach motivation, fueled by neurochemicals signaling anticipated enjoyment, aligns with the positive reinforcement and encouragement found in supportive relationships. Conversely, avoidance motivation, driven by a 'fight or flight' response, highlights the importance of providing reassurance and understanding in challenging situations. These motivational types develop in childhood, where intrinsic drivers like natural curiosity and the pursuit of mastery play a pivotal role. Supportive partners or friends can act as external motivators, reinforcing these inherent drivers through encouragement and recognition, thereby enhancing feelings of satisfaction and achievement. Moreover, neurotransmitters such as dopamine play a significant role in motivational behavior, influencing a wide range of actions from decision-making to physical activities. Supportive relationships can positively impact the brain's motivation systems, providing the necessary responsive interactions to counter feelings of helplessness or the negative effects of addictive behaviors and substances.

According to Maslow's hierarchy of needs, the need for belonging and esteem are crucial for psychological wellbeing. Shared goals provide a sense of belonging to a group or a relationship, fulfilling this need. Additionally, achieving these goals contributes to self-esteem and self-actualization. The concept of Flow, introduced by psychologist Mihaly Csikszentmihalyi and previously discussed in the context of 'Starting from Within,' is also highly relevant in shared inspirational activities. When individuals are deeply engaged in a challenging and rewarding activity, they enter a state of flow. This state is characterized by complete immersion and enjoyment in the activity, enhancing the experience of shared goals and activities. This state not only enhances individual wellbeing but can also strengthen relationships as partners or groups experience this state of heightened engagement together. Research indicates that individuals who experience positive emotions are more creative, persistent in the face of failure, efficient in decision-making, and exhibit high intrinsic motivation. These traits benefit relationships as they contribute to a more supportive, empathetic, and understanding dynamic.

BENEFITS AND CONSIDERATIONS:

Inspirational Support in relationships acts as a catalyst for personal growth and achievement. When individuals feel supported and encouraged by their partner or friend, they are more likely to pursue their goals and aspirations. For instance, a partner encouraging their significant other to pursue further education or a new hobby instills confidence and belief in their capabilities. This support can transform dreams into tangible achievements, enhancing personal fulfillment and satisfaction. Regular encouragement and positive reinforcement in a relationship contribute significantly to building confidence and self-esteem. When individuals know that their efforts and achievements are recognized and valued by their partner, it boosts their self-worth and motivation. A simple acknowledgment of a partner's progress in a fitness journey or a new business venture can positively impact their self-esteem and drive. Beyond personal growth, Inspirational Support also inspires the growth of the relationship itself. As each individual evolves and achieves, the relationship also benefits from these positive changes.

In creativity and personal growth, there exists a common misconception known as the Creative Cliff Illusion. This illusion suggests that an individual's creative potential peaks at a certain point, after which it supposedly declines. However, research in cognitive psychology and neuroscience tells a different story. Studies indicate that creativity isn't confined to a specific age or stage of life; instead, it can flourish continuously with experience, practice, and proper stimulation. Relationships enriched with Inspirational Support can play a crucial role in dispelling this illusion, fostering personal and relational growth.

The belief in a decline in creativity stems from societal stereotypes and a limited understanding of the brain's creative processes. Research conducted by psychologists like Dr. Adam Grant has demonstrated that creativity is not a static trait but a dynamic skill that evolves. Neuroplasticity, the brain's ability to reorganize itself by forming new neural connections, is integral to this continuous development. As individuals engage in diverse experiences and challenges, the brain adapts, enhancing creative thinking and problem-solving abilities.

In the context of relationships, be they romantic or platonic, the role of Inspirational Support becomes invaluable in transcending the Creative Cliff. When individuals are encouraged by their partners or friends, they are more likely to take risks, explore new ideas, and push past their perceived limitations. For instance, consider the story of Ella and Dmitri. Ella, an aspiring writer, felt her creativity waning as she approached her forties. However, her partner, Dmitri introduced her to new genres, encouraged her to attend writing workshops, and provided constructive feedback. This support rekindled Ella's creative spark, leading her to publish her best novel.

Challenging the Creative Cliff Illusion is not just about sustaining creativity; it's about personal transformation. As individuals confront their self-imposed boundaries, they discover reservoirs of resilience, adaptability, and confidence. In relationships, when one partner supports the other in this journey, it leads to a deeper understanding and appreciation of each other's potentials and vulnerabilities. For example, when John encouraged his partner Lihua to pursue her passion for painting despite her doubts about starting late, Lihua rediscovered her artistic talent. She developed a newfound confidence that permeated other areas of her life.

In a relationship, facing the Creative Cliff together fosters a unique intimacy. Partners or friends who support each other's creative endeavors often find their bond strengthened by shared victories and challenges. Their relationship becomes a safe harbor for exploration and self-expression.

Inspirational Support style is pivotal in enhancing emotional well-being and personal growth. To understand and quantify the impact of this style in relationships, the Multidimensional Scale of Perceived Social Support (MSPSS), developed by Professor Zimet and his team, serves as an invaluable tool. The MSPSS offers a comprehensive view of how individuals perceive the support they receive and its effectiveness in their lives by assessing perceived support from three sources: family, friends, and significant others.

In the framework of Inspirational Support, this scale helps in understanding how the encouragement, motivation, and emotional backing from these sources contribute to an individual's sense of well-being and resilience. For instance, the support perceived from a significant other, a crucial component of the MSPSS, aligns directly with the principles of Inspirational Support within intimate relationships. This includes encouragement for personal goals, emotional backing during challenging times, and constructive feedback for personal development.

Through the lens of the MSPSS, the benefits of Inspirational Support become quantifiable and tangible. High scores in the significant other domain of the MSPSS often correlate with the effective implementation of Inspirational Support in a relationship. This manifests as improved mental health, increased resilience, and greater personal fulfillment. For example, individuals who report high levels of support from their partners are often more confident in facing challenges, exhibit lower stress and anxiety levels, and generally possess a more positive outlook on life.

The MSPSS's application across diverse cultural and demographic settings provides critical insights into how different groups perceive and utilize Inspirational Support. It helps identify cultural nuances in support systems and the varying effectiveness of Inspirational Support across different societies. For instance, in some cultures, family support may play a more significant role than partner support, influencing how Inspirational Support is prioritized and manifested in relationships.

The MSPSS's findings reinforce the efficacy of the Inspirational Support style in relationships. By measuring perceived support, the scale highlights the importance of emotional encouragement, information sharing, and validation in enhancing the quality of life and relationship satisfaction. It underscores the idea that supportive, motivating relationships are desirable and essential for personal and communal well-being.

Inspirational Support in a relationship leads to a deeper understanding and respect for each other's aspirations, challenges, and strengths. When partners actively engage in each other's goals, offering encouragement and constructive feedback, it shows deep care and involvement. For instance, a couple who openly discusses their career ambitions and challenges, offering each other insights and advice, builds a more comprehensive understanding of each other's professional lives and aspirations.

When partners or friends share common goals and support each other in achieving them, it strengthens their bond. Shared goals could range from fitness objectives to community service projects. Working together towards these goals creates a sense of teamwork and unity. A couple training together for a marathon experiences the ups and downs of the training process, celebrating each other's progress and supporting each other through setbacks, thereby solidifying their relationship. Inspirational

Support is especially crucial during times of adversity. When one partner faces challenges, be it professional setbacks or personal struggles, the other's support can be a source of strength and resilience. Standing by each other, offering hope and positivity, can turn challenges into opportunities for growth. If one partner is dealing with job loss, the other's encouragement and belief in their abilities can be a powerful motivator to persevere and explore new opportunities.

The presence of a supportive and encouraging partner or friend can boost an optimistic outlook on life. This attitude is contagious, creating an environment where both individuals can thrive. A friend who consistently highlights the positive aspects of challenging situations can help their friend see opportunities instead of obstacles, fostering a more optimistic approach to life's challenges.

Inspirational Support enhances communication and emotional connection, as it involves actively listening, empathizing, and responding to each other's needs and aspirations. Celebrating successes together and providing comfort during failures builds a strong foundation of trust and emotional intimacy. A partner who listens attentively to their significant other's business ideas and offers thoughtful feedback demonstrates high emotional engagement and connection.

While the Inspirational Support relationship style offers numerous benefits, it requires careful consideration to ensure that the support provided is both effective and respectful of each individual's needs. One of the primary considerations in offering Inspirational Support is understanding and respecting each other's limits and boundaries. Over-enthusiastic encouragement can sometimes lead to pressure or unintentional stress. For instance, if one partner is pursuing a weight loss journey, the other should offer support while being mindful not to push them beyond their limit or add extreme pressure. It's crucial to balance providing support with allowing autonomy. Each individual must make their own decisions and learn from their experiences. When one spouse supports the other's desire to seek a job change, for instance, they should accept the decision to go at their own speed and use their own discretion when making decisions.

When offering support and encouragement, there's a fine line between being supportive and being patronizing. It's necessary to communicate to uplift and empower rather than belittle the other person's efforts or abilities. Phrasing encouragement in a way that acknowledges their competence and capabilities is paramount. For example, saying, "I know it's challenging, but I've seen how capable you are," instead of, "Don't worry, I'll help you figure it out," can make a significant difference. Support should be genuine and relevant to the individual's needs and aspirations. Generic or unfocused encouragement may not be helpful and can sometimes be counterproductive. It is crucial to take the time to understand their specific goals, challenges, and what kind of support they truly value. If a friend is training for a marathon, understanding whether they need training advice, moral support, or help with time management can make your support more effective and appreciated. Different people are motivated by different things, and what works for one may not work for another. It's important to tailor the type and level of support to the individual's unique motivational needs. While some may respond well to enthusiastic cheerleading, others prefer quiet, steady encouragement. Understanding these differences is vital to providing effective support. A partner who is motivated by calm reassurance may feel overwhelmed by overly exuberant encouragement.

Open communication is essential in the Inspirational Support relationship style. Regularly checking in and asking for feedback on the type of support being provided ensures that it remains helpful and appreciated. It's essential for both partners to feel comfortable expressing when a particular approach is not working for them. A friend who feels overwhelmed by frequent or daily check-ins about their job search might prefer to give a weekly update.

While offering support and encouragement is positive, it's important to avoid creating a dependency where one individual relies too heavily on the other for motivation or validation. Encouraging independence and self-motivation ensures a healthier balance in the relationship. For example, if a partner is working on a personal project, instead of constantly steering their decisions, offering guidance when asked can foster a sense of independence.

Setbacks and failures are inevitable in any pursuit. How support is offered during these times is crucial. Instead of glossing over disappointments or immediately trying to fix the problem, acknowledging the setback and offering empathetic support can be more beneficial. Suppose your friend aimed to complete a marathon but fell short of their target time. Acknowledging their dedication and the frustration they might be experiencing before discussing their next race strategy shows empathy and understanding.

While offering Inspirational Support can significantly enhance a relationship, it requires thoughtful consideration of individual boundaries, motivational needs, communication styles, and the balance between support and autonomy. Mindfully navigating these considerations, the Inspirational Support relationship style can become a powerful tool for mutual growth and empowerment, fostering a relationship grounded in respect, empathy, and genuine encouragement.

YOUR RELATIONSHIP REVIVAL:

Inspirational Support is about motivating each other to pursue goals and dreams, creating a growth-oriented relationship. Here's a list of activities to foster this encouraging aspect of your relationship:

1. **Joint Goal Setting**: Set new goals together, whether it's running a marathon, learning a new language, or starting a busi-

ness venture. This shared journey towards achieving goals can significantly strengthen your bond.

2. **Celebration of Achievements**: Make it a point to celebrate each other's achievements, big or small. Acknowledging and celebrating progress is crucial for motivation and support.

3. **Encouragement Through Setbacks**: Provide unwavering support and encouragement during setbacks. Being each other's cheerleader during challenging times fosters a deeper emotional connection.

4. **Dream Board Creation**: Set up a 'dream board' in your home where you both can post your aspirations and track progress. This visual representation of your goals can be a powerful motivator.

5. **Constructive Feedback Sessions**: Regularly offer each other constructive feedback. These sessions should be aimed at helping each other grow and overcome obstacles.

6. **Learning Together**: Enroll in a class or course together to learn a new skill. This could be anything from a cooking class to an online course on a shared interest.

7. **Adventure in Entrepreneurship**: If starting a business is a mutual dream, take the first steps together. Plan, brainstorm, and navigate this entrepreneurial adventure as a team.

8. **Fitness Challenges**: Engage in fitness challenges or activities together. Train for a physical event, like a 5K run or a hiking expedition, supporting each other's fitness goals.

9. **Book Club for Two**: Start a private book club where you read and discuss books that inspire personal and professional growth.

10. **Visionary Travels**: Travel to places that inspire or hold meaning to your aspirations. These trips can offer new perspectives and deepen your understanding of each other's goals.

11. **Skill Swap**: Teach each other skills in which you individually excel. This allows for personal growth and deepens appreciation for each other's talents.

12. **Milestone Celebrations**: Create special rituals or ways to celebrate milestones in each other's journey, reinforcing the joy and importance of each achievement.

Remember, Inspirational Support is about continuously pushing and encouraging each other towards personal and shared aspirations. This mutual support enhances your bond and provides a profound sense of shared accomplishment. Embrace these activities to inspire and uplift each other in every step of your journey together. Being an Inspirational partner means motivating and uplifting each other. You create a multifaceted bond when you blend this with Caring Companionship, Adventurous Bonding, or different styles to try new things together.

Places to Pick:

Personal development workshops, motivational talks, fitness classes, hiking trails, volunteering events, community service projects, business networking events, educational seminars, goal-setting retreats, innovation conferences, language learning centers, art and creativity workshops, entrepreneurial meetups, self-improvement book clubs, skill-building courses, career development centers, leadership training sessions, health and wellness seminars, public speaking clubs.

Literary Echoes:

"Don't make friends who are comfortable to be with. Make friends who will force you to lever yourself up." — Thomas J. Watson, American businessman and CEO of IBM.

"A soulmate is someone who you carry with you forever. It's the one person who knew you and accepted you and believed in you before anyone else did or when no one else would." — "Dawson's Creek," American television series.

"Surround yourself with only people who are going to lift you higher." — Oprah Winfrey, American media proprietor and philanthropist.

"The right person will bring out the best version of yourself." — Multiple authors, commonly attributed.

"When we love, we always strive to become better than we are." — Paulo Coelho, Brazilian lyricist and novelist.

"Help others achieve their dreams and you will achieve yours." — Les Brown, American motivational speaker.

"A dream you dream alone is only a dream. A dream you dream together is reality." — John Winston Ono Lennon, English singer-songwriter.

"Love does not consist in gazing at each other, but in looking outward together in the same direction." — Antoine de Saint-Exupéry, French writer and aviator.

"Find a group of people who challenge and inspire you, spend a lot of time with them, and it will change your life." — Amy Poehler, American actress and comedian.

"Coming together is a beginning, staying together is progress, and working together is success." — Henry Ford, American industrialist.

"If you want to lift yourself up, lift up someone else." — Booker T. Washington, American educator and author.

"It is literally true that you can succeed best and quickest by helping others to succeed." — Napoleon Hill, American self-help author.

"Success is best when it's shared." — Howard Schultz, American businessman and former CEO of Starbucks.

REFLECT AND DISCUSS:

Encouragement and Overcoming Challenges:

1. Discuss the role of positive reinforcement and encouragement in your relationship. How do you practice this?

   _____

   _____

   _____

2. Share how you've helped each other overcome self-doubt or hesitation in pursuing new opportunities.

   _____

   _____

   _____

3. Reflect on a situation where your partner or friend's perspective or advice led you to a breakthrough in a personal or professional challenge.

   _____

   _____

   _____

4. Reflect on a historical figure whose supportive relationship with a partner or friend played a crucial role in their achievements. How does this inspire the way you offer support in your own relationship?

   _____

   _____

   _____

Celebrating Successes and Balancing Independence:

5. How do you celebrate each other's successes and milestones? Share an example of a meaningful celebration.

    _____

    _____

    _____

6. Discuss how you balance offering support and allowing space for independent growth in your relationship.

    _____

    _____

    _____

7. How do you deal with situations where one partner's success might create challenges for the other?

    _____

    _____

    _____

Collaboration and Shared Goals:

8. Share an experience where working together towards a common goal brought a deeper sense of connection and purpose to your relationship.

    _____

    _____

    _____

Chapter Twelve

10. CARING COMPANIONSHIP

Moments You'll Recognize:

M ei and Kai's relationship was a stunning amalgam made with alloys of deep care, shared responsibilities, and a heartwarming dedication to family. Their journey together was a testament to the strength and depth that Caring Companionship can bring to a relationship. From the outset, Mei and Kai understood that their bond was more than just romantic; it was a partnership built on mutual respect, support, and a shared commitment to nurture not only each other but also those they loved. Their days were filled with small acts of care that spoke volumes about their deep connection.

In the mornings, Kai would prepare breakfast, ensuring Mei had a healthy start to her busy day as a schoolteacher. Mei, in return, would pack Kai's favorite snacks for his long shifts as a nurse. This mutual nurturing extended beyond the kitchen. They shared household responsibilities seamlessly, each taking up tasks without needing reminders or requests. Laundry, cleaning, and grocery shopping were activities they often turned into opportunities for quality time, chatting about their day, or planning for the future.

Their approach to parenting was equally cooperative and caring. They had two children and later decided to adopt a third, a decision that came naturally to them, given their immense capacity for love and care. Mei and Kai were hands-on parents, actively involved in every aspect of their children's lives, from school activities to bedtime stories. They believed in leading by example, teaching their children the value of kindness, empathy, and responsibility.

A cherished ritual was their weekly 'family day' every Saturday. From park picnics to museum visits or cozy movie nights at home, they held these days sacred, dedicated to creating memories and fortifying their family bond.

Gift-giving in their relationship was not confined to special occasions; it was a regular expression of their thoughtfulness and deep understanding of each other's preferences. Kai had a knack for picking out books that Mei would find captivating, and Mei always remembered to get Kai his favorite artisanal coffee beans, a simple yet meaningful gesture that showed how well she knew him.

Their journey took a new turn when they decided to adopt a child. This decision was a natural extension of their nurturing nature. The process was challenging, but their untiring support for each other made it a journey of growth and love. Watching Mei and Kai with their adopted child was heartwarming; they showered the child with the same love and attention as their biological children, seamlessly integrating them into the family.

Their Caring Companionship was evident in every aspect of their life. From raising their children and managing household tasks to supporting each other's personal and professional goals, Mei and Kai showcased what it means to be true partners in life. Their relationship was a beautiful blend of love, care, and mutual respect, setting a shining example of what Caring Companionship looks like in its most genuine form.

Defining The Style:

Caring Companionship in relationships embodies a profound and supportive bond between individuals, marked by mutual respect, trust, and a commitment to each other's well-being. This relationship style goes beyond conventional companionship, incorporating commitment and interdependence. It is one of the most expansive relationship styles, centrally focused on the notion of *'care.'* This care incorporates accountability, sharing household responsibilities, and jointly raising children. We decided to include financial aspects of relationships within this style because if these weren't provided within a Caring Companionship, they could cause more harm than good. Care is vital for emotional and mental health, providing validation, mentoring, encouragement, and perspective. It can be life-changing and even lifesaving, helping individuals navigate life's challenges.

Unveiling Historical and Scientific Treasures:

From an evolutionary perspective, caring behaviors are seen as essential for survival. In early human societies, caring for one another, especially in the contexts of child-rearing and supporting fellow group members, was vital for the propagation of human beings. This nurturing behavior ensured the well-being and protection of offspring and facilitated strong group cohesion, which is crucial for facing external threats and challenges.

Unlike many other mammals, humans have evolved a complex system of shared parenting or 'alloparenting,' where individuals other than the biological parents partake in child-rearing. This unique aspect of human social structure is a response to the extensive demands of raising human offspring, who require prolonged periods of care and nurturing due to their slow maturation process. The evolutionary benefits of alloparenting are multifaceted. Anthropologist Sarah Hrdy's research into cooperative breeding highlights how shared caregiving increases the chances of a child's survival, particularly in environments where resources are scarce or threats are abundant. By distributing child-rearing responsibilities among several adults, parents can better manage the substantial investment of time and energy required to raise a child. This communal approach to parenting allows for a more efficient allocation of resources and provides a safety net of care for the child.

Biologically, caring for a child, even one that is not genetically related, can trigger hormonal changes in both males and females. Oxytocin and vasopressin play a crucial role in fostering attachment and nurturing behaviors. Studies have shown that both adoptive parents and alloparents experience changes in these hormones similar to biological parents, facilitating emotional bonding and caregiving behaviors. Furthermore, the evolution of the human brain, with its increased capacity for empathy and understanding, has been crucial in the development of Caring Companionship as a relationship style. The human brain's ability to understand and respond to the emotional needs of children, whether one's own or others', has been a critical factor in the success of alloparenting strategies.

The prolonged dependency period of human children also necessitates a more extended period of learning and development, during which they acquire complex social and survival skills. In this context, alloparenting provides a rich learning environment, as children are exposed to a broader range of adult role models and caretakers, each contributing different skills and knowledge.

In psychology, caring is understood as a manifestation of Altruism, empathy, and compassion. These qualities are fundamental for building and maintaining both intimate and communal relationships. Psychologists have identified various caring behaviors as vital for healthy relationships. These behaviors include listening attentively, showing appreciation, providing emotional support, and engaging in acts of kindness and generosity. These include simple acts like preparing a meal, giving a thoughtful gift, or offering a comforting touch. Research in relationship psychology indicates that these caring behaviors significantly contribute to relationship satisfaction and longevity. They signal to the partner that they are valued, loved, and respected, thereby enhancing the emotional bond between them. Caring creates a sense of belonging and mutual support. In families, caring actions contribute to a nurturing environment, which is essential for the healthy development of children. While the importance of caring is universally recognized, its expression can vary significantly across cultures. In some cultures, caring may be expressed more through collective activities or communal support, while in others, it may focus more on individualistic expressions of care. These cultural differences reflect the adaptability and diversity of human social behaviors.

The development of sharing resources in human societies, a practice unusual in the animal kingdom, has been pivotal in our evolution. Around 2.5 to 1.5 million years ago, the emergence of the hunter-gatherer lifestyle marked a significant evolutionary transition. This lifestyle, still observed in communities like the Hadza of Tanzania and Aché of Paraguay, relied heavily on sharing resources. The energy-intensive nature of hunting and gathering necessitated cooperation and sharing as behavioral adaptations, setting the stage for the evolution of modern humans. Such sharing behaviors fostered survival and the development of social bonds and communities.

In primitive caveman cultures, giving gifts was also a common way to show love and affection. Early humans exchanged simple items like unusually shaped rocks, animal teeth, or tree bark. These gifts, although simple, held significant emotional value and were a means of expressing care and strengthening social bonds. In ancient Egypt, gift-giving was a gesture of reverence, often involving offerings to deities, reflecting beliefs in the afterlife. Temples like the Karnak Temple in Thebes and the Temple of Luxor were adorned with valuable treasures such as golden statues of Ra, intricate jewelry dedicated to Hathor, and finely crafted figurines of Anubis, all meticulously presented as tokens of devotion to the gods and as provisions for the deceased in their journey to the next world. These offerings, known as "ka" statues, were vital to religious ceremonies and rituals, symbolizing the profound spiritual connection between the living and the divine.

In ancient Greece, it played a vital role in fostering relationships between individuals and city-states, usually consisting of food, wine, and precious artifacts. In other ancient cultures, gifting items to temples or statues in exchange for divine blessings was a common practice. For instance, Croesus, King of Lydia, sent large and expensive items as gifts to Apollo at Delphi to impress the Greeks and gain favor with the oracle. Additionally, during the Panathenaic Games held in Athens, it was customary for the city to present a specially crafted amphora filled with olive oil as a grand prize, a symbol of their devotion to the goddess Athena and a gesture of goodwill to strengthen diplomatic ties among Greek city-states.

Among the Bedouin tribes of Arabia, gift-giving has been an important part of social bonding. They shared tokens of wealth to reduce tensions and foster a broad network of relationships. For instance, the exchange of Arabian horses was a cherished tradition within the Bedouin culture. A Bedouin leader might gift a prized horse to another tribal leader as a symbol of trust and goodwill. These magnificent animals served as a practical means of transportation and survival in the harsh desert environment. Such gifts of horses were a way to solidify alliances and resolve conflicts peacefully, maintaining harmony among the tribes. Furthermore, fine jewelry, often intricately designed with precious stones and metals, was another form of gift-giving among the Bedouin tribes. These ornate pieces were valuable possessions and symbols of social status and prosperity. Sharing jewelry with fellow tribesmen or neighboring tribes created a sense of unity and comradeship, reinforcing the bonds that were essential for survival in the arid and challenging desert landscapes.

The tradition of potlatch, practiced by Native American tribes in the Northwest Pacific region, is an exemplary illustration of Caring Companionship. This complex social ceremony, involving the exchange and sometimes deliberate destruction of wealth, serves as a compelling example of how caring and giving are deeply embedded in the fabric of communal life. The potlatch ceremony transcends the simple act of giving; it is a multifaceted social event steeped in symbolism and cultural significance. During potlatch, leaders and members of the tribe would distribute their wealth and possessions among other community members. This distribution was not merely a show of personal affluence but a deliberate act of caring for the community. The givers reinforced their social status by sharing resources and demonstrating their commitment to the tribe's well-being. Giving in potlatch was a way to nurture relationships, establish social harmony, and ensure the redistribution of wealth within the community. Furthermore, the potlatch practice embodied the principles of reciprocity and balance. Those who received gifts were expected to reciprocate in the future, either through their own potlatch or other forms of support. This system of reciprocal giving fostered a network of interdependence and mutual support, crucial for the survival and prosperity of the community. The principles underlying the potlatch - generosity, reciprocity, and communal care - are universally relevant and can be seen as foundational elements in nurturing Caring Companionships in any cultural setting.

Human cooperation and resource sharing have evolved due to our reliance on social networks. These networks facilitate the exchange of resources and services, playing a critical role in the survival and prosperity of communities. This cooperative nature, while beneficial, can encounter challenges when individual self-interests conflict with the collective good. The evolution of these cooperative behaviors underlines the intricate balance between individual needs and the welfare of the group, a balance that is essential for the continued survival and evolution of our species.

In the 19th century, relationships and courtship were guided by strict societal norms. Courtship was structured and formal, prioritizing societal expectations, proper behavior, respect, and family involvement. Marriage was seen more as a social and economic institution than for romantic love, with women primarily focusing on domestic duties and obedience to their husbands. However, as the 20th century progressed, there was a shift towards companionate marriage, reflecting changes like women's independence and growing youth culture, which emphasized Caring Companionship, mutual respect, and emotional support. The principle of sharing responsibilities is integral in caring for modern relationships. It involves partners or members of a social group equally contributing to various tasks and obligations, be it in domestic, professional, or social spheres. This equitable distribution of duties is underpinned by mutual respect and consideration for each other's well-being and personal commitments.

From birth, humans are biologically prepared to form bonds. The brain's reward system is activated during cooperative interactions, suggesting that our brains are wired for Altruism and social connection. Interactions between a mother and infant, involving synchronized heart rhythms, brain activity, and hormone release, prepare the infant for future relationships. This synchronization also occurs in other relationships, such as romantic partnerships and friendships.

In the sphere of relationships, Caring Companionship is inextricably linked with emotional intelligence (EQ), reflecting Friedrich Nietzsche's observation: 'It is not a lack of love, but a lack of friendship that makes unhappy marriages.' EQ involves recognizing, understanding, and managing our own emotions and perceiving and influencing others' emotions. This skill is fundamental to Caring Companionship, facilitating deep, meaningful discussions that are anchored in personal and psychological insights, thereby enriching the connection. For example, when partners engage in a thoughtful analysis of their emotional reactions to an artwork or a political event, they are not just sharing opinions but are delving into a profound exploration of their underlying values and beliefs. Such interactions require a fusion of excellent care, keen intellect, and emotional depth, enabling partners to understand and empathize with each other's emotional experiences truly. This intricate dance of the mind and heart, where intellectual understanding meets emotional empathy, epitomizes the essence of Caring Companionship, showcasing its pivotal role in nurturing deep, fulfilling relationships.

The biological and endocrine dimensions of Caring Companionship manifest through hormonal responses when it involves gift-giving, assisting with daily tasks, or child-rearing. For instance, giving gifts triggers dopamine release, a neurotransmitter linked to pleasure and reward, thus enhancing happiness and fortifying bonds. Gift-giving and participating in household chores and other life tasks together promotes the release of oxytocin, which is released during collaborative activities, strengthening feelings of trust and togetherness. This shared responsibility can increase the sense of satisfaction and fulfillment derived from working together. When partners share financial responsibilities and engage in activities like gift-giving or managing household tasks, it's not just an economic and responsibility-based exchange, but also a hormonal interaction that enhances feelings of trust, security, and partnership, which is vital in sustaining long-term relationships.

Erik Erikson's theory of Psychosocial Development posits that human development occurs in eight stages, each marked by a specific psychosocial conflict. In a Caring Companionship, as defined in our book, several of these stages are particularly pertinent:

1. Intimacy vs. Isolation (Young Adulthood): This stage focuses on forming intimate, loving relationships with others. Caring Companionship directly addresses this need with mutual respect, trust, and commitment. The shared responsibilities and emotional support inherent in this relationship style help prevent feelings of isolation, fostering a deep sense of closeness and connectedness.

2. Generativity vs. Stagnation (Middle Adulthood): Generativity involves creating or nurturing things that will outlast oneself, often by parenting or other forms of caregiving and productivity. In Caring Companionship, activities like jointly raising children or managing household tasks are expressions of generativity. This shared contribution gives individuals a sense of purpose and belonging, aligning with Erikson's view that contributing to the next generation is a vital aspect of adult life.

3. Ego Integrity vs. Despair (Older Adulthood): In later life, individuals reflect on their lives. A successful resolution of this stage, resulting in ego integrity, comes from feeling fulfilled with one's past and a sense of wisdom. The mutual caring and shared experiences of a Caring Companionship provide a foundation for looking back on life with satisfaction, not regret.

The financial aspects of Caring Companionship, such as managing finances together, strengthen trust and mutual respect. This collaborative approach aligns with Erikson's theory by fostering interdependence and shared responsibility, key elements in nurturing emotional and psychological health throughout the various stages of development.

In essence, Erikson's theory underscores the importance of supportive relationships in each stage of life. Caring Companionship, emphasizing mutual care, responsibility, and emotional support, embodies the positive outcomes envisaged in Erikson's model for healthy psychosocial development.

BENEFITS AND CONSIDERATIONS:

Historically, the concept of care extended beyond mere survival and played a crucial role in forming and maintaining relationships. Caring and giving, whether in the form of resources or emotional support, was often seen as an expression of love and commitment. However, the intent behind these acts of care is crucial. When giving is motivated by control or received with entitlement, it can lead to imbalance and harm in relationships. Imbalances in care, often stemming from a lack of mutual agreement or understanding, can lead to resentment and conflict. Incorporating the concept of Caring Companionship in relationships involves acknowledging the profound impact of emotional support on our well-being. Emotional and mental support is a pillar of strength during such times, enabling individuals to process feelings and endure transitions more effectively. This support involves practical aspects like navigating joint child-rearing and understanding each other's financial philosophies. It's about being there for each other in times of need, offering guidance, and providing a sense of security and comfort.

In practical life, sharing household responsibilities and joint child-rearing are pivotal elements of Caring Companionship. This equitable division of labor in everyday tasks, from cooking and cleaning to managing finances, breeds a sense of fairness and teamwork. Caring Companionship emphasizes collaborative involvement in the upbringing of children, regardless of the parents' relationship status. Parents or guardians who jointly navigate the challenges and joys of raising children provide a stable and loving environment, essential for the children's healthy development. Parents sharing responsibilities such as attending school events, discussing discipline strategies, or supporting children's hobbies, ease individual burdens and model teamwork and mutual support to their children.

Jointly raising children requires a harmonious blending of different parenting styles. This blending is not always straightforward, as each parent may have their own set of beliefs and methods based on their upbringing or personal values. Continuous dialogue is key in navigating these differences. Parents might find that while they have distinct approaches to discipline, education, or recreational activities, they can reach a consensus that respects both perspectives and works in the child's best interest. For instance, one parent may emphasize academic achievement while the other focuses on creative expression. Finding a balance that nurtures all aspects of the child's development can be fulfilling for both parents and children.

Financial support and security are forms of care that can prevent stress and conflict. It strengthens the relationship when partners work together to manage finances, make budgeting decisions, and support each other through financial highs and lows. This could be as simple as jointly saving for a family vacation or as significant as supporting a partner through job loss or career transition. Financial aspects must be navigated with care and transparency. Money matters, often a source of contention in relationships, require a collaborative approach to ensure both partners feel involved and respected. This might involve setting joint financial goals, openly discussing expenditures, or establishing a budget that aligns with both partners' values and priorities. When one partner earns significantly more than the other, it's essential to approach financial decisions sensitively, ensuring that both voices are equally heard and valued. Creating a financial plan that accommodates both partners' comfort levels and aspirations can prevent potential conflicts and foster a sense of teamwork and mutual support. Including financial aspects in a Caring Companionship style introduces the need for fairness and clarity. Disagreements over financial management can strain a relationship. A joint approach to budgeting, expenses, and investments, where both partners clearly understand and agree on financial goals and responsibilities, helps prevent conflicts.

Within a Caring Companionship, giving gifts must be driven by a motivation of care, love, and affection. Gifts in this context are not mere material offerings but are imbued with thoughtfulness and consideration of the other person's needs and preferences. Gift-giving in Caring Companionship is more than a transactional exchange. Thoughtful gifts that resonate with the partner's needs, interests, or aspirations can have a profound emotional impact. These gifts, whether material or in the form of experiences, serve as tangible expressions of love and appreciation. For instance, gifting a weekend retreat to a partner who has been stressed can show understanding and empathy, reinforcing the supportive nature of the relationship. A thoughtful gift that shows appreciation for the partner's efforts or acknowledges their challenges can significantly enhance the feeling of being cared for and valued.

Understanding and utilizing the concept of "Bids for Connection" can be instrumental in nurturing Caring Companionship. Developed by relationship experts Drs. John and Julie Gottman, bids for connection represent the various ways, both significant and subtle, through which we reach out to our partners seeking emotional closeness, support, and validation. These bids may manifest as a subtle look for reassurance across a crowded room, a gentle squeeze of the hand seeking comfort, or an explicit request for a conversation after a long day. Even something as simple as pointing out a bird outside the window or asking which mug you would prefer for tea can represent a small bid for connection. Ignoring these moments or responding dismissively—by saying something like "So?" or "I don't care about the mug"—can subtly harm the relationship. Conversely, responses like "Aw, I think that's a goldfinch!" or "I'd love the mug with the cats on it, thanks!" accept these bids, taking every small opportunity to connect and affirm the care you have for one another.

Each time we recognize and respond affirmatively to our partner's bids, we affirm their needs and feelings and fortify the foundations of trust, understanding, and mutual respect that underpin our relationship. This dynamic process is pivotal in signaling to our partners that they are seen, valued, and supported.

However, engaging effectively with bids for connection can sometimes pose challenges. Distractions, misinterpretations, or simply the ebb and flow of daily life can lead to overlooked bids, leaving our partners feeling neglected or unseen. Navigating these challenges requires cultivating mindfulness and attentiveness within our interactions. By consciously tuning into our partner's verbal and nonverbal cues, we can become more adept at recognizing the subtle and overt ways they reach out for connection. Furthermore, the willingness to engage openly and vulnerably in responding to bids fosters a climate of empathy and understanding. It encourages a reciprocal exchange of care and affection, where both partners feel empowered to express their needs and desires. This cycle of positive reinforcement strengthens the relationship, building a reservoir of goodwill and affection that can buffer against the inevitable challenges and conflicts that arise.

In Caring Companionship, sharing household responsibilities goes beyond merely ticking off tasks on a list. It's about understanding and appreciating the effort that goes into managing a home and family life. When one partner takes on more than their fair share of household duties, it can lead to resentment or being undervalued. Open discussions about the division of labor, recognizing each other's contributions, and showing appreciation for each partner's mundane yet essential tasks can strengthen the bond and sense of partnership in the relationship. This mutual recognition and appreciation transform everyday chores into acts of love and care, enriching the relationship.

Life is replete with changes and transitions, and a Caring Companionship must be flexible enough to adapt. Whether it's the arrival of a new child, a move to a new city, or dealing with aging parents, these transitions can strain a relationship. Being open to adjusting how care and responsibilities are shared during these times is crucial. This flexibility ensures that the relationship survives and thrives through these changes. In a relationship that heavily involves caregiving, particularly during illness or emotional distress, recognizing caregiving's emotional and physical burden is crucial. Providing care can also be taxing. Providing support to a partner dealing with health issues is commendable, but it's also necessary to be mindful of one's well-being and to seek external support when needed. The caregiving partner needs to acknowledge their limits and seek support when needed. This might involve asking other family members to step in, hiring professional help, or simply ensuring they take breaks and practice self-care to prevent burnout. The health and well-being of the caregiver are as important as that of the person receiving care.

The importance of reciprocity cannot be overstated in Caring Companionship. This doesn't necessarily mean an exact 50/50 split in every aspect but rather an overall sense of give and take. There might be times when one partner needs more support, and at other times, the roles may reverse. While one partner may be the primary caregiver or supporter at one point, there should be a balance over time, where both partners have the opportunity to give and receive care. What's important is that both partners feel that their giving and receiving are balanced over the long term. This sense of reciprocity fosters a deep-seated feeling of fairness and mutual respect, which is essential for the longevity and health of the relationship.

While the concept of Caring Companionship has been largely explored in families and romantic partnerships, its principles are equally applicable and vital in friendships. Friendships, often undervalued in their depth and commitment, can embody the same level of care, support, and mutual respect as seen in romantic or parental relationships. Living together, for instance, is a scenario where friends, as roommates, engage in a shared life experience that extends beyond the casual interactions of typical friendships. In such arrangements, the division of household responsibilities becomes essential to their relationship. Friends who live together navigate the nuances of shared spaces, from deciding on décor to managing chores and bills. This shared living experience can strengthen the bond as friends learn to accommodate each other's habits and preferences, fostering a deeper understanding and respect.

Financial support is another dimension where the principles of Caring Companionship manifest in friendships. There are instances where friends may lend or borrow money, support each other through job losses, or even invest in joint ventures. This financial interdependence requires high trust and transparency, mirroring the dynamics often seen in familial or romantic financial arrangements.

In many cultures, the role of friends extends to familial responsibilities. Friends might step in to babysit each other's children, offering much-needed respite to parent friends. In some cases, friends become integral to family functions, helping with organizing events or providing support during family crises. This involvement in each other's family lives is a testament to the depth and significance of their friendship, often blurring the lines between friendship and family.

The exchange of gifts and celebrating significant milestones, such as birthdays or professional achievements, is another aspect where Caring Companionship in friendships shines. These celebrations are more than mere social obligations; they are heartfelt expressions of care and appreciation. A friend might spend considerable time choosing a gift that resonates with the other's interests or needs, reflecting a deep understanding and connection. Moreover, the emotional support aspect of Caring Companionship is particularly prominent in friendships. Friends often become confidantes, offering a safe space to share thoughts, fears, and dreams. This emotional scaffolding is a crucial component of the support system that friends build with each other.

However, as with any relationship, maintaining a healthy balance is crucial. The dynamics of living together, financial interdependence, involvement in family matters, and emotional support require a careful understanding of boundaries, mutual respect, and continuous communication. Friends must navigate these waters sensitively, ensuring that their actions and involvement align with each other's comfort levels and expectations.

Caring Companionship represents a holistic approach to relationships, where care is the driving force in all aspects, from emotional support to practical life management. Caring Companionship has been linked to better physical health, reduced stress and anxiety, and increased happiness and well-being. It allows sharing of experiences, thoughts, ideas, and values, enriching one's life through shared journeys. It also involves maintaining honesty, trust, and understanding between partners. It respects individual space and personal interests, balancing togetherness and individuality for a healthy relationship. Moreover, sharing responsibilities demands essential communication, problem-solving, and empathy skills. It requires individuals to understand and accommodate each other's strengths and weaknesses, leading to a deeper understanding and appreciation of one another. This shared approach can enhance intimacy and partnership in romantic relationships, as it involves navigating challenges together and supporting each other's goals.

YOUR RELATIONSHIP REVIVAL:

Caring Companionship is about continuously finding new ways to express care and support for each other, keeping the relationship nurturing and fresh. Here's a list of activities to enhance this compassionate aspect of your relationship:

1. **Surprise Acts of Service**: Regularly plan surprise acts of service to show your care and appreciation. This could be anything from preparing a favorite meal to taking over a chore your partner usually does.

2. **Memory Book Creation**: Collaborate on creating a memory book or scrapbook that captures special moments in your relationship. Include photos, mementos, and notes that reflect your journey together.

3. **Heartfelt Letter Writing**: Write and exchange heartfelt letters, expressing your feelings, gratitude, and appreciation for each other.

4. **Shared Activity Routine Changes**: Introduce new shared activities into your daily routines, like morning walks, joint cooking sessions, or evening reading time.

5. **Care Days**: Dedicate days focused on doing small, meaningful acts for each other. This could include organizing a relaxing spa day at home or creating a special movie night experience.

6. **Explorative Shopping Trips**: Go shopping together in a new mall or area, making the experience fun and explorative. Look for innovative gift ideas or items that add a unique element to your home.

7. **Surprise Day for Children**: If you have children, plan a surprise day filled with activities they love. This shared act of caring strengthens the family bond.

8. **Joint Projects**: Share responsibilities in new projects like gardening or home decorating. Working together on these projects can strengthen your teamwork and shared sense of accomplishment.

9. **Meaningful Gift Practice**: Make it a habit to give each other meaningful gifts, not just on special occasions but as spontaneous gestures of affection.

10. **Plant a Garden Together**: Start a garden together, whether it's a few pots on a balcony or a plot in the backyard. Caring for plants can parallel nurturing your relationship.

11. **Health and Wellness Focus**: Take an interest in each other's health and wellness. This could include planning healthy meals, exercising together, or supporting each other in mental health practices.

12. **Personalized Playlist Exchange**: Create and exchange playlists of songs that remind you of each other or your significant moments.

13. **Memory Lane Adventures**: Revisit places that hold special memories for you both, or recreate past dates or experiences that were meaningful in your relationship.

Remember, Caring Companionship nurtures relationships through thoughtful actions, continuously discovering and addressing evolving needs to keep the bond strong and supportive. Caring is at the heart of deep connections. Adding elements from other styles, like the Intellectual stimulation of deep conversations or the Playfulness of light-hearted activities, enhances the care you share.

Places to Pick:

Workshops on various hobbies, family-friendly parks and museums, personal time retreats, couple spa days, home improvement classes, cooking courses, community cultural events, local theater performances, gardening clubs, arts and crafts fairs, outdoor adventure groups, pet adoption events, weekend road trips, family game nights, couple's therapy workshops, relationship coaching sessions, DIY home decor studios, couples' photography sessions.

Literary Echoes:

"There's nothing like a really loyal, dependable, good friend. Nothing." — Jennifer Aniston, American actress.

"Love is that condition in which the happiness of another person is essential to your own." — Robert A. Heinlein, American science-fiction author.

"Love is worthless unless it acts out, unless it's expressed in deed and behavior." — David Jeremiah, American author and televangelist.

"One person caring about another represents life's greatest value." — Jim Rohn, American entrepreneur and motivational speaker.

"We have to recognize that there cannot be relationships unless there is commitment, loyalty, love, patience, persistence." — Cornel West, American philosopher and political activist.

"The best way to raise positive children in a negative world is to have parents who love them unconditionally and model the behavior they wish to see." — Zig Ziglar, American author and motivational speaker.

"I grew up babysitting and always enjoyed it. I love family. A couple of my closest friends have kids, and I'm their godfather, and that's one of my greatest pleasures in life, just picking them up from school and hanging out with them." — Matthew Perry, American and Canadian actor.

"Acts of service, like doing the dishes or vacuuming, can be powerful expressions of love and care in a relationship." — Gary Chapman, American author.

"Love is a condition in which the happiness of another person is essential to your own." — Robert A. Heinlein, American science fiction author, aeronautical engineer, and naval officer.

"Money is an opportunity to reach unity in marriage. When couples work together, they can do anything." —Dave Ramsey, bestselling author, radio host, and founder of Ramsey Solutions.

"Money is either the best or the worst area of communication in our marriages." —Larry Burkett, American radio personality.

"Friendship is always a sweet responsibility, never an opportunity." — Khalil Gibran, Lebanese-American writer, poet, and visual artist.

Reflect and Discuss:

Parenting and Family Care:

1. Share an experience where you and your partner worked together to overcome a parenting challenge. How did providing care to your children affect your care for each other?

    _____

    _____

    _____

2. Share an instance where you both had to care for a family member or friend together. How did this shared responsibility affect your relationship?

    _____

    _____

    _____

Household Management and Everyday Acts of Care:

3. Discuss how you divide household responsibilities. How has this duties-sharing strengthened your companionship and view of what constructs care?

    _____

    _____

    _____

4. Can you recall an instance where a small act of everyday care (like making a meal or doing a chore) was significant? How do you celebrate such moments?

    _____

    _____

    _____

Support During Emotional Challenges:

5. Discuss how you support each other as friends or partners during emotionally challenging times, such as grief or stress.

_____

_____

_____

6. Discuss the importance of nurturing each other's mental health. Can you share a time when this was particularly crucial?

_____

_____

_____

Special Needs and Individual Care:

7. Reflect on a time when caring for a partner or friend with special needs brought new insights or depth to your relationship.

_____

_____

_____

8. How do you approach caregiving responsibilities if one partner becomes the primary caregiver for the other?

_____

_____

_____

Significant Decisions and Life Transitions:

9. Share how you approach decision-making on significant matters, such as financial planning, children's education, or health issues.

_____

_____

_____

10. How have you and your partner adapted your caring roles during major life transitions, such as moving, career changes, or retirement?

_____

_____

_____

Maintaining Equality and Nurturing the Relationship:

11. How do you ensure that both partners feel equally valued and cared for in the relationship?

_____

_____

_____

12. Discuss ways you've managed to keep the spark alive in your relationship while juggling caregiving responsibilities, whether for children, aging parents, or each other.

_____

_____

_____

Expressing Affection and Appreciation:

13. Share a memorable instance where a thoughtful gift or gesture deeply touched your partner or friend.

_____

_____

_____

Chapter Thirteen

11. EMPATHETIC CONVERSATION

Moments You'll Recognize:

Ishana and Jay's relationship was a compilation of gentle words mixed with languages of deep understanding, affirmations, and a unique ability to listen to one another honestly. Their connection was a beautiful example of how Empathetic Conversation can create an unbreakable bond between two people.

One crisp autumn evening, they sat together on their pleasant porch, wrapped in blankets, watching the sunset. It was their cherished time for heartfelt conversations, a moment where they could share their thoughts, feelings, and experiences openly and without judgment. Jay started by sharing his concerns about a challenging project at work. As he spoke, Ishana listened intently, her eyes reflecting genuine interest and concern. "I can see how much this means to you, Jay, and I understand why it's weighing on you," she said softly after he finished. Her words were an affirmation of his feelings, making him feel seen and heard.

Ishana then shared her excitement about a volunteer program she recently joined. "It's wonderful to see you so passionate about helping others," Jay responded, his voice warm with admiration. "Your kindness and dedication are truly inspiring." His words were compliments and a testament to his deep appreciation for who she was.

As they continued to talk, the conversation shifted to their plans for the future. Jay expressed his gratitude for Ishana's unwavering support in his career. "Thank you for always believing in me, even when I doubt myself," he said, reaching out to hold her hand. Ishana smiled, squeezing his hand gently in return. "I am always here for you, just like you've been for me. We're a team, remember?"

The conversation flowed seamlessly from serious topics to lighter ones, each listening attentively and responding thoughtfully. When Ishana mentioned her recent anxiety about an upcoming family gathering, Jay quickly offered reassurance. "I know these gatherings can be overwhelming for you, but I'll be right there by your side. We can navigate it together."

As the sky darkened and the stars began to twinkle, they ended their conversation with expressions of love and gratitude for each other. "I am so grateful for these moments with you," Jay said, his voice filled with emotion. "They remind me of how lucky I am to have you in my life." Ishana leaned in, resting her head on his shoulder. "And I am thankful for your presence in my life, for your listening ear, and for your kind heart." Their Empathetic Conversation was a series of elegant exchanges of words and emotions, where each phrase, each nod, and each smile was a step in a beautiful rhythm. It was a conversation that strengthened their bond, nourished their love, and deepened their understanding of each other.

DEFINING THE STYLE:

Empathetic Conversation relationship style represents a holistic approach to communication within relationships. It is an approach where active listening, affirmative speaking, and a profound understanding of emotional undercurrents blend, creating an environment where everyone feels deeply seen, heard, and valued. Empathetic Conversation goes beyond the basic need to feel loved or validated. It recognizes that healthy communication is a two-way street, where the desire to hear words of love and affirmation stems not from a personal, sometimes selfish need for validation, but from a mutual, empathetic understanding. In this relationship style, both parties are actively involved in giving and receiving emotional support, ensuring that love, gratitude, and understanding are shared in a balanced and reciprocal manner.

Active listening is paramount in Empathetic Conversation. It involves a combination of attentiveness and empathy that enables individuals to fully absorb and resonate with the speaker's message. Techniques like paraphrasing for clarity, validating emotions, and responding thoughtfully without immediate judgment are crucial. These practices elevate conversations beyond one-sided exchanges, fostering mutual involvement and respect.

Moreover, affirmative speaking is a critical component of Empathetic Conversation. It involves choosing words that build up rather than tear down and expressing solidarity and understanding rather than indifference or opposition. By choosing the name Empathetic Conversation for this relationship style, we highlight the importance of empathy as the foundational element of communication in relationships. It underscores the significance of mutual understanding and a shared desire to foster a loving, supportive environment, ensuring that every interaction is not only about being understood but also about understanding the other person in a deeper, more empathetic manner.

Unveiling Historical and Scientific Treasures:

Before the advent of complex language, our ancestors relied on a more primitive form of communication, likely consisting of gestures, facial expressions, and rudimentary sounds, which was crucial for survival in a world where cooperation meant the difference between life and death. Empathy, in these contexts, was expressed through actions and non-verbal cues. Researchers like Michael Tomasello have studied the evolutionary aspects of human communication, suggesting that cooperative communication – the ability to share intentions and attention – is a fundamental aspect that differentiates humans from other primates.

With the evolution of Homo sapiens, our capacity for intricate language flourished, opening new horizons for empathy and connection. This linguistic evolution provided a significant advantage: the ability to share detailed information, express emotions more intricately, and form deeper social bonds. The development of language allowed for a more nuanced expression of empathy. Words became tools not just for conveying information, but for understanding and expressing feelings and intentions.

The human brain's evolution, with the development of specialized speech, listening, and communication areas, provides compelling evidence of our inherent disposition towards Empathetic Conversation as a relationship style. This neurological evolution underscores our species' adaptive preference for social interaction and emotional connection, which are integral to our survival and well-being. Brain regions like Broca's area and Wernicke's area specialize in speech production and comprehension, illustrating the intricate design of our brain for sophisticated communication. The development of these regions facilitates complex verbal communication, allowing for the expression and interpretation of a wide range of emotions and thoughts. This capability is a functional tool for conveying information and forming empathetic connections with others.

Moreover, the linkage of these linguistic areas with parts of the brain involved in emotional processing, such as the limbic system, further highlights the integral role of Empathetic Conversation in human relationships. When we engage in meaningful dialogue, not only are the language centers activated, but so are the emotional processing areas. This activation lets us empathize with the speaker's emotions, understand their perspective, and respond appropriately. It is a neurobiological dance where language and emotion intertwine, allowing for a depth of understanding and connection that is uniquely human.

Additionally, neuroimaging studies have shown that listening to someone speak activates similar brain areas to those used when speaking. This mirroring effect suggests that our brains are wired to facilitate empathetic engagement during conversations, enabling us to 'tune in' to others' emotional states and intentions.

Evolutionarily, the development of these brain regions and their interconnections likely offered significant advantages. Early humans who were better at communicating and forming emotional bonds would have been more successful in cooperative endeavors, from hunting and gathering to raising children and building communities. The ability to empathize and communicate effectively would have been crucial for maintaining social cohesion and resolving conflicts, essential factors for the survival of social groups.

The influence of language on both the physiological and psychological development of children is a testament to the profound power of words in shaping human growth. The foundation of this concept lies in the understanding that children, even in the womb, can hear and respond to external sounds, including the human voice. Research by Dr. Eino Partanen and his team at the University of Helsinki has demonstrated that fetuses can recognize and react to sounds by the third trimester. Their study found that newborns could recognize and show a preference for melodies to which they were exposed while in the womb. This early exposure to sound and speech plays a crucial role in auditory and cognitive development.

The influence of words continues to be significant after birth. Renowned pediatrician Dr. T. Berry Brazelton has highlighted the importance of verbal communication with infants in fostering language development, emotional bonding, and social interaction. Engaging in 'baby talk' or 'parentese,' characterized by high-pitched, melodious tones, captures infants' attention and enhances their ability to learn language nuances.

The words children hear in their early years can shape their psychological development profoundly. Psychologist Dr. Albert Bandura's Social Learning Theory posits that children learn behaviors, norms, and values through observation and imitation. The child will likely internalize and mirror the language and communication styles modeled by parents and caregivers. Positive, affirming words encourage a sense of security and self-worth, while negative or harsh language can have the opposite effect, potentially leading to issues with self-esteem and emotional well-being.

From a neurological perspective, the language children are exposed to significantly influences their brain development. Neuroimaging studies have shown that positive verbal interactions are associated with more significant brain growth and connectivity, especially in language and emotional regulation regions. Conversely, a lack of exposure to enriching verbal communication, often termed 'language poverty,' can delay language development and cognitive processing. Furthermore, the emotional content of words and the tone in which they are spoken can influence a child's emotional development. Warm, supportive language fosters a sense of belonging and emotional security, while critical or emotionally charged language can contribute to anxiety and emotional distress.

The role of empathy in education and therapeutic contexts highlights its significance in facilitating understanding and growth. The language used by teachers and the verbal environment in classrooms can impact children's learning attitudes and academic performance. Positive reinforcement and constructive feedback help build confidence and resilience, which are essential for academic and personal success. Teachers who employ empathetic communication foster a more inclusive and supportive learning environment. Similarly, in therapy, the therapist-client relationship heavily relies on empathetic communication to build trust and facilitate healing.

Empathetic Conversations may transform our somatic states more profoundly than we might realize. Studies have found that our physiological responses can become remarkably synchronized during deep, empathetic engagements. For instance, research has shown that individuals' breathing patterns tend to align when they engage in meaningful conversations, highlighting the unconscious mirroring that facilitates a sense of connection. Similarly, pupil dilation, a marker of attention and arousal, has been observed to synchronize among individuals in high mutual understanding, suggesting an unconscious, shared emotional state. Furthermore, scientists have explored the phenomenon of brainwave synchronization, revealing that during successful communication, the brainwaves of speakers and listeners can exhibit strikingly similar patterns, an effect termed 'neural coupling.' This synchronization of neural activity suggests a fundamental biological basis for our capacity to connect and empathize with others.

Historically, cultures across the globe have recognized and emphasized the significance of empathetic communication. For instance, in ancient philosophical texts, the significance of understanding and responding to others' emotions is a recurring theme. Philosophers like Aristotle and Confucius spoke of the importance of understanding others to cultivate ethical and harmonious relationships. In his work 'Nicomachean Ethics,' Aristotle emphasized the importance of empathy in friendship and ethical living. He believed that true friends hold a mirror to each other, allowing for deep understanding and mutual growth. For Aristotle, empathy in conversation was not just about listening but about understanding the other's perspective, sharing joys and sorrows, and fostering moral development. Confucius, on the other hand, in his teachings compiled in the 'Analects,' emphasized the concept of ren or benevolence, which includes the ability to empathize and understand others. He advocated for the 'Golden Rule' – "Do not do to others what you do not want done to yourself" – highlighting the significance of considering others' feelings and perspectives in communication.

Empathetic communication has also been a crucial element in storytelling and narrative construction. From the ancient epics like Homer's "Iliad" and "Odyssey," which echo themes of human emotions and relationships, to the poignant plays of Shakespeare that delve into the complexities of the human psyche, empathy in language has been pivotal.

In Homer's "Iliad" and "Odyssey," we find early and profound examples of empathetic communication. These epics are tales of heroism and adventure and elaborate narratives of human emotion and relationships. In "The Iliad," characters like Achilles and Priam demonstrate a deep understanding of each other's grief and pain. When Priam, the king of Troy, begs Achilles for the body of his slain son Hector, Achilles is moved by the older man's words. They share a moment of mutual sorrow, transcending the enmity and violence of war. This scene exemplifies the power of Empathetic Conversation to bridge divides and foster understanding. Similarly, "The Odyssey" explores the emotional odyssey of its characters, notably in Odysseus' interactions with his crew and the various beings he encounters on his journey home. His ability to listen, understand, and respond to others' emotions aids in his survival and eventual return to Ithaca. The epic underscores the importance of empathy and understanding in navigating the complex web of human relationships.

Shakespeare's plays are a treasure trove of Empathetic Conversation. His characters often engage in profound dialogues that reveal their innermost thoughts and feelings. In "Hamlet," for instance, the titular character's soliloquies are not mere reflections but invitations to the audience to empathize with his existential dilemmas. His conversations with other characters, like Ophelia and Horatio, demonstrate his ability to articulate deep emotional states, inviting empathetic responses from them and the audience. In "Romeo and Juliet," the balcony scene is a stellar example of Empathetic Conversation. Romeo and Juliet share their feelings openly, listening to each other intently and responding with deep understanding. Their dialogue is an affirmation of love and a testament to the power of empathetic communication in forging strong emotional bonds.

Poetry has long been a medium for expressing and evoking empathy. Rumi, a 13th-century Persian poet, is renowned for his mystical poetry that transcends the boundaries of time and culture. His work is imbued with themes of love, both earthly and divine, and the profound understanding of the human soul.

In his poem "The Guest House," Rumi portrays emotions as transient visitors, each serving a purpose and bringing a lesson. This perspective invites readers to engage in Empathetic Conversation with themselves, acknowledging and embracing their feelings with compassion and wisdom. Another of Rumi's famous poems, "The Lovers," beautifully captures the essence of love and connection. He writes of lovers as being mirrors to each other, reflecting their inner worlds. This reflection is not just about seeing oneself in another but understanding and empathizing with the other's emotions and experiences. Rumi's poetry often explores this interconnectedness, highlighting how empathy and love intertwine to deepen our connections.

Emily Dickinson's poetry, characterized by depth and introspection, often explores the themes of love, loss, and human connection. Her ability to capture profound emotional experiences in just a few lines makes her work a rich source of Empathetic Conversation. For example, in her poem "If I can stop one heart from breaking," Dickinson expresses a profound sense of altruism and empathy. She speaks of the importance of easing another's pain, a sentiment at the heart of Empathetic Conversation and connection. In "Hope is the thing with feathers," Dickinson personifies hope as a bird singing within the soul. This metaphor resonates with the comforting aspect of Empathetic Conversation – the ability to offer solace and encouragement in times of despair, much like a quiet, enduring song of hope.

In modern literature, the theme of Empathetic Conversation continues to be a pivotal element. In novels like "To Kill a Mockingbird" by Harper Lee, the character of Atticus Finch embodies the principles of Empathetic Conversation. His guidance to his children, especially in understanding and empathizing with others, is a cornerstone of the novel's moral framework.

The Kite Runner" by Khaled Hosseini is a compelling narrative that revolves around themes of friendship, betrayal, redemption, and empathy. The protagonist, Amir, embarks on a journey of self-discovery and atonement, where empathy plays a crucial role. His relationship with Hassan, marked by complexity and deep emotional undercurrents, is a testament to the power and necessity of understanding and compassion in human relationships. Amir's journey to redeem himself and his efforts to understand Hassan's unyielding loyalty and love are touching examples of how Empathetic Conversation, both internal and with others, can lead to profound personal growth and healing. The narrative demonstrates how empathy can bridge gaps created by guilt and regret, leading to reconciliation and deeper understanding.

These examples from literature and poetry beautifully illustrate the principles of Empathetic Conversation. They show how understanding, listening, and responding with empathy are tools for effective communication and integral to the human experience, shaping our relationships and understanding of the world. These literary works serve as timeless reminders of the power of Empathetic Conversation in understanding and connecting with one another.

Cultural norms surrounding communication have evolved alongside societies. In many ancient societies, oral traditions were not just storytelling methods but also means of preserving and transmitting cultural values and empathetic understanding. Take, for instance, the Griots of West Africa - they were multi-talented figures embodying the roles of historians, storytellers, musicians, and diplomats. Their mastery of language was pivotal in forging social cohesion and resolving conflicts. Empathetic communication styles vary across cultures. For example, Asian cultures often emphasize non-verbal cues and the importance of understanding implicit messages, whereas Western cultures might focus more on explicit verbal expression and active problem-solving in empathetic exchanges.

The term "empathy" itself has experienced a remarkable evolution over time. Originating from the German word *Einfühlung*, meaning "in-feeling," in 1908, empathy initially referred to projecting one's feelings onto objects, particularly in the context of art. This early notion of empathy was more about emotional engagement with art, like sensing movement in paintings or being uplifted by certain lines and shapes. By the early 20th century, psychologists broadened the scope of empathy to include understanding other people's emotions and perspectives. This marked a critical transition from an aesthetic to a psychological and social understanding of empathy. By the 1930s, empathy began to be seen as crucial for clinicians to accurately comprehend their clients' thoughts and feelings.

Today, Empathetic Conversations are recognized as multifaceted interactions that involve the emotional understanding of others' feelings, cognitively grasping another's thoughts, and sometimes acting caring towards others. It is essential for building and maintaining interpersonal relationships and is a core element of effective communication. Empathy now includes actively listening, engaging with others, and understanding their perspectives and emotions. This involves interpreting nonverbal cues, paraphrasing, responding attentively and understandingly, validating others' feelings, and creating a supportive, non-judgmental environment for open communication.

The rise of digital communication has introduced new complexities and opportunities for Empathetic Conversations. While technology has enabled us to connect across vast distances, it has also raised concerns about losing empathy in digital interactions. As we look to the future, the evolution of Empathetic Conversations will likely intertwine with technological advancements. The development of AI and machine learning presents possibilities for enhancing empathetic communication, but also poses ethical questions about the nature of empathy and human interaction.

In the Empathetic Conversation relationship style, the power of expressing gratitude and appreciation through simple yet profound phrases such as 'thank you,' 'I love you', 'I like your music list,' or other affirming comments holds significant physiological, psychological, and biological benefits. This style of interaction, grounded in empathy and understanding, contributes positively to the well-being of both the giver and receiver of such expressions.

From a physiological perspective, expressions of gratitude and positive affirmation trigger the release of neurotransmitters such as serotonin and dopamine, which are key neurotransmitters that play a vital role in regulating mood and facilitating emotional connections during Empathetic Conversations. These 'feel-good hormones' are exceptionally responsive during interactions characterized by expressions of love, gratitude, and deep understanding.

During Empathetic Conversations that convey love and appreciation, the raphe nuclei in the brainstem become activated and initiate the secretion of serotonin. This neurotransmitter is closely linked with feelings of happiness and well-being, playing a crucial role in mood regulation and fostering a sense of satisfaction and emotional balance. For example, a heartfelt expression of gratitude towards a partner's actions or recognizing their positive attributes can boost serotonin levels, thereby elevating the mood of both parties. The importance of serotonin in stabilizing mood underscores the transformative power of positive language in enhancing emotional well-being and mitigating symptoms of depression and anxiety.

Furthermore, expressions of affection and thoughtful gestures activate the brain's reward pathways, such as the ventral striatum and the orbitofrontal cortex. The brain perceives these expressions as rewarding, prompting the ventral tegmental area to produce dopamine. This neurotransmitter, linked to feelings of pleasure and fulfillment, rewards and reinforces positive verbal exchanges in a manner akin to the brain's reaction to tangible rewards like food or companionship. Dr. Christian Ruff and his team's research emphasizes that the brain's reward system responds similarly to both material and social rewards, utilizing the same neural circuits.

Moreover, these empathetic exchanges can create a feedback loop of positive emotions. As one partner expresses love and gratitude, and the other receives and reciprocates these feelings, there is a continual release of serotonin and dopamine. This biochemical exchange deepens the emotional intimacy of the relationship, making each interaction more meaningful and rewarding. The impact of these neurotransmitters extends beyond the immediate conversation. Over time, regular empathetic interactions that stimulate serotonin and dopamine can lead to lasting improvements in mood, emotional resilience, and relationship satisfaction. They contribute to a foundation of emotional support and mutual understanding, essential elements for a fulfilling and enduring partnership.

In integrating the research findings of Dr. Martin Seligman and Dr. John Gottman, we can observe the profound impact of positive communication and expressions of gratitude on relationship dynamics and individual well-being. Dr. Seligman, a leading figure in positive psychology, has emphasized the role of gratitude in enhancing life satisfaction and reducing depression symptoms. His research suggests that recognizing and appreciating the positive aspects of life and relationships shifts the focus from negative to positive, fostering a more optimistic and resilient mindset. Similarly, Dr. John Gottman's work in relationship dynamics underlines the importance of positive communication for the longevity and health of relationships. Gottman's research indicates that regular expressions of gratitude and positive affirmations contribute significantly to building and maintaining solid emotional bonds, trust, and mutual respect between partners. These practices are essential for relationship satisfaction and the emotional well-being of the individuals involved. The combined insights from Seligman and Gottman highlight the integral role of empathetic communication in fostering healthy relationships.

Furthermore, the benefits of such empathetic interactions extend to physical health, particularly in stress management and immune function. Regular expressions of gratitude and positive social interactions have been shown to lower cortisol levels, the body's primary stress hormone. This stress reduction can lead to improved immune response and a lower risk of chronic diseases. Empathetic Conversation in relationships can significantly influence both mental and physical health, primarily through its effects on inflammation, a critical factor in many physical pathologies and psychiatric conditions. Research has demonstrated that strong emotion regulation skills, which include empathetic communication, are associated with lower inflammation, while poor emotion regulation can lead to higher inflammation. This connection is particularly evident in chronic diseases such as rheumatoid arthritis, where emotional stress and poor coping strategies can exacerbate inflammation.

When it comes to mental health, the suppression of emotions has been linked to heightened inflammatory responses. Conditions like depression, characterized by emotional dysregulation, often co-occur with increased inflammatory markers. Furthermore, chronic emotional suppression can have physical manifestations, such as eczema or other autoimmune disorders, where the body's immune response becomes dysregulated. Conversely, positive coping strategies, expression of emotions and validation, and seeking social support, which are integral to Empathetic Conversation, can help regulate health-harming inflammatory activity. The biological mechanisms underlying these effects include changes in immune function and stress response systems, thereby reducing the risk of such conditions.

Empathetic Conversations in relationships can positively impact our biological health by influencing inflammatory markers and hormones. For example, effective emotional expression and conversation validation can lower levels of pro-inflammatory cytokines like tumor necrosis factor-alpha (TNF-α) and interleukins (IL-6, IL-1β). These cytokines are typically elevated in states of chronic stress or emotional suppression, contributing to various health issues. Empathetic interactions also stimulate the release of oxytocin, known for its anti-inflammatory properties and ability to enhance social bonding and trust. Some studies have shown that Empathetic Conversations have proven effects on preventing cancer and strengthening our immune system. This hormonal and biochemical modulation underscores the healing potential of empathetic communication in relationships, both psychologically and physically. The bi-directional relationship between emotion regulation and inflammation highlights the potential of psychosocial interventions in managing both psychiatric and somatic illnesses.

The physiological impact of positive verbal communication goes beyond immediate emotional responses. Prolonged exposure to a positive linguistic environment can yield lasting changes in brain structure, especially in regions linked to emotional regulation and positive thinking. This phenomenon, known as neuroplasticity, indicates that our brain's structure can be modified over time based on our experiences, including the language we use and are exposed to.

The amygdala, an almond-shaped cluster of neurons nestled in the brain's medial temporal lobe, is instrumental in emotion processing, particularly those related to fear and pleasure. Research has shown that positive words and compassionate speech can directly impact the amygdala's activity. In studies using functional magnetic resonance imaging (fMRI), researchers have observed that positive words can help reduce the stress response typically associated with amygdala activation. For instance, a study by Dr. Richard Davidson, a renowned neuroscientist, demonstrated that engaging in positive verbal communication or even exposure to positive words can lessen the reactive response of the amygdala, leading to lower stress and anxiety levels.

The history and evolution of Empathetic Conversations reveal much about our species – our social structures, psychological complexities, and cultural diversities. From prehistoric times to the digital age, the way we use empathy in communication has continually adapted, reflecting the changing landscapes of our societies. It underscores the inherent human need to connect, understand, and be understood. As we continue to evolve, so will our ways of empathetic communication, shaping the future of human relationships in profound ways. Empathetic Conversation, including active listening and affirmative language, is vital for building and maintaining strong, healthy relationships. It's about understanding and responding to the emotional content of the conversation, not just the factual content.

Benefits and Considerations:

Empathy is integral to the health and depth of friendships and romantic relationships. Empathy turns simple word exchanges into meaningful communication and disagreements into growth opportunities, deepening emotional intimacy and creating a mutually respectful relationship. Empathetic Conversation allows for intuitive feeling and shared alignment, essential for deep connections and making partners and friends feel heard and understood. Suspending oneself to understand another's perspective can greatly enhance connectedness and understanding.

Active listening is an essential component of Empathetic Conversation. This requires paying close attention to the speaker and going beyond mere hearing to fully understand what's being conveyed. It demands total concentration, responding to and remembering the details of the conversation, and letting go of preconceptions and judgments to focus on the other person's emotions and needs. Techniques, such as paraphrasing, characterize this form of listening to ensure clarity and understanding. It involves acknowledging and validating the speaker's feelings, showing empathy, and a genuine interest in their perspective. When one listens actively, the conversation transforms into a collaborative exchange, where both parties feel equally involved and respected. Imagine a scenario where a person shares their anxieties about their job; an empathetic listener hears the concerns and reflects back an understanding of the emotions involved, such as stress or uncertainty, thereby deepening the connection.

Incorporating affirmative talking is another cornerstone of this communication style. It's about consciously choosing uplifting and supportive language, creating a positive and nurturing environment for the conversation. This practice expresses solidarity and understanding, using words that encourage and fortify rather than cause harm or create conflict. In situations where one might disagree or offer a different perspective, the approach is to do so respectfully and constructively, maintaining a positive tone that fosters mutual respect and understanding.

Empathetic Conversation also significantly involves interpreting and responding to non-verbal cues like body language, facial expressions, gestures, and tone. Much of what is communicated in a conversation is done so without words. Understanding a sigh, a pause, or a change in tone can provide insights into the speaker's true feelings or thoughts. Responding to these non-verbal cues empathetically can significantly enhance the depth and quality of the interaction. Picture a conversation where one person's body language – perhaps crossed arms or averted gaze – indicates discomfort or hesitation. An Empathetic Conversationalist would recognize these cues and perhaps respond by creating a more comfortable environment or gently encouraging the person to express their unspoken concerns.

Another critical aspect of Empathetic Conversation is its impact on conflict resolution. Conflicts are inevitable in any relationship, but how they are handled makes all the difference. Empathetic Conversation facilitates a more productive and less confrontational approach to finding solutions when disagreements arise. Approaching conflicts with empathy, keeping an open mind, valuing the other side, striving to understand the partner's perspective, and working collaboratively towards resolution can lead to more effective problem-solving and strengthen the relationship. It's also important to recognize when to take a break during a heated discussion to prevent escalation and to approach the situation with a calm and clear mind later.

Empathetic Conversation involves adjusting to each individual's varied communication needs and styles. Not everyone expresses or processes their thoughts and emotions in the same way. Some might need more time to articulate their feelings, while others might communicate more spontaneously. Acknowledging and respecting these differences is crucial. In the case of Attention Deficit Hyperactivity Disorder (ADHD), for instance, individuals might experience challenges with attention or may tend to interrupt during conversations. Understanding and accommodating these tendencies – perhaps by creating structured conversation spaces or gently steering the discussion back on track – can make communication more effective and respectful.

A key consideration in practicing Empathetic Conversation is avoiding misinterpretations and assumptions. It's easy to misconstrue what someone says, especially when discussing complex or emotionally charged topics. This can be particularly challenging when interacting with individuals who have mental health conditions that affect communication.

Imagine a friend who has an anxiety disorder. They might appear hesitant or overly worried during conversations about future plans or decision-making. In this case, it's essential to provide reassurance without dismissing their concerns. Active listening is critical, but so is offering support in a way that doesn't exacerbate their anxiety. For example, instead of saying, "Don't worry about it," a more empathetic response might be, "I understand why this feels worrying to you. How can I help ease your concerns?"

A partner with depression might have difficulty expressing themselves, seem disinterested, or withdraw from conversations. It's crucial to recognize that these behaviors are symptoms of their condition, not a reflection of their feelings toward the relationship. It is vital to offer patience and a non-judgmental space for them to share at their own pace. Avoid trying to 'fix' their issues with overly optimistic advice, and instead validate their feelings and offer consistent support. It is influential to show understanding and empathy, even if their experiences or reactions differ from one's own.

A person with Autism Spectrum Disorder (ASD) might have unique communication patterns. They might take things literally or struggle to understand sarcasm or idiomatic expressions. It may be essential to communicate clearly and directly, avoiding metaphors or ambiguous language. Being mindful of their comfort with eye contact and physical proximity during conversations is also important. Recognizing and respecting their communication style helps create an understanding and comfortable conversational environment.

An individual with PTSD may be triggered by certain subjects, or react unexpectedly during conversations. Being aware of topics that might be triggering and avoiding them unless they choose to bring them up is crucial. If they become distressed, focusing on grounding techniques or simply offering a calm, supportive presence can be helpful. It's also essential to ensure they feel in control of the conversation's direction.

Someone with Borderline Personality Disorder (BPD) might exhibit intense emotional shifts or have a fear of abandonment, which can manifest in conversations. Maintaining a consistent and reassuring communication style is key. It's important to acknowledge and validate their feelings, even if they seem to change rapidly. Establishing clear and consistent boundaries in communication while offering reassurance can help foster a stable and trusting conversational environment. For instance, affirming your commitment to the relationship or friendship during conversations can help alleviate fears of abandonment or rejection.

A person with bipolar disorder may have periods of elevated mood or depression, which can significantly affect how they engage in conversation. During their manic phases, they might be more talkative, with rapidly shifting topics, while during depressive phases, they might be withdrawn or uncommunicative. It's essential to stay patient and adaptable to these changes, offering support without trying to 'correct' their mood. During manic phases, listening attentively and gently guiding the conversation if it becomes too scattered is helpful. In depressive phases, offering a non-demanding presence and letting them know you're there when they're ready to talk can be comforting.

During Empathetic Conversation with individuals who have mental health conditions, it's crucial to adjust the approach to fit their specific needs. For example, individuals with ADHD may benefit from shorter, more focused conversations or may require gentle reminders to stay on topic. It's crucial to be patient and flexible, understanding that their way of processing and responding might be different. For someone with ADHD, their rapid speech or changing topics might be misinterpreted as disinterest or avoidance. It's important to ask clarifying questions and provide them with the space to express themselves entirely without jumping to conclusions.

In all these scenarios, the key lies in understanding that each mental health condition uniquely affects communication. Miscommunications may occur, and conversations might not always lead to immediate understanding or resolution. It's important to approach these interactions with a mindset of learning and growth rather than frustration. Being informed about these conditions and how they manifest and then adjusting one's approach to communication is crucial in practicing Empathetic Conversation effectively. This involves adapting to different communication styles and being sensitive to the emotional and psychological needs that underlie these styles. While Empathetic Conversation involves deep emotional support, it's essential to recognize the boundary between being a supportive friend or partner and taking on the role of a therapist. Professional help should be encouraged when necessary, and one should avoid trying to diagnose or treat mental health issues through conversation alone.

While being empathetic is central to Empathetic Conversation, it's also important to balance empathy with self-care. Engaging deeply with someone's emotions can be taxing, particularly if the conversations are intense or frequent. Practicing self-care ensures one doesn't become emotionally overwhelmed or drained, which is paramount for maintaining the capacity to provide empathetic support to others. Respecting privacy and personal boundaries is another key consideration. Not everyone may be comfortable sharing personal or sensitive information. It's crucial to respect their limits and not push for disclosure. Consent and comfort should guide the depth and direction of conversations.

Moreover, Empathetic Conversation is about creating a safe space for vulnerability and emotional sharing, where individuals can communicate their thoughts and feelings without fear of judgment or dismissal. This is crucial in building respect, trust, and mutual understanding. When both partners can freely express their thoughts and feelings without fear of judgment or retaliation, it creates a safe and supportive environment where emotional intimacy can flourish. Relationships are a two-way street, and ensuring that emotional expression is balanced and reciprocal is paramount. This means being as open to hearing and understanding the other's emotions as expressing one's own. In instances where a person shares a personal struggle or a profound experience, the ability to respond with empathy and understanding – without rushing to give advice or minimize the experience – can make all the difference. It's about being present and supportive, allowing the other person to explore and express their emotions fully.

Expressing emotions, gratitude, love, and feelings in relationships, be they romantic or platonic, is a cornerstone of deep, meaningful connections. This open expression is about sharing positive feelings and being honest with more challenging emotions, leading to a richer, more authentic relationship experience. Open communication of emotions and sentiments promotes understanding in relationships. A simple phrase like "I really appreciated your help today," can reinforce positive actions and strengthen bonds.

Expressing love and affection through words like "I love you" or "You mean a lot to me" doesn't just convey feelings; it actively nurtures the emotional connection between individuals. In friendships, expressing gratitude and appreciation can significantly enhance the bond. Acknowledging a friend's support with a heartfelt "Thank you for always being there for me" makes them feel valued and reinforces the mutual care and respect that forms the foundation of the friendship. The honest expression of emotions is equally important during challenging times. Expressing feelings of sadness or frustration, like saying, "I'm really struggling with this situation, and I feel overwhelmed," invites support and understanding. It opens the door to supporting each other emotionally and providing comfort and advice.

While expressing emotions and feelings is beneficial, it requires certain considerations to ensure it's done effectively and empathetically. Timing and approach are crucial when expressing emotions. Blurted out in the heat of the moment, even well-intentioned expressions can be misunderstood. Choosing a suitable time and approach is essential, especially for sensitive topics. Replacing something like, "You are deliberately ignoring my calls," with, "I feel hurt when you don't answer my calls," calmly and non-accusatorily can lead to a constructive conversation rather than an argument. Understanding the other person's current emotional state and receptivity is key. If a friend is going through a tough time, expressing one's minor frustrations might not be appropriate. Sensitivity to their needs and choosing a more suitable time to share are crucial for mutual respect and understanding.

While honesty is important, it should be balanced with tact. Expressing emotions should not be an excuse to be hurtful or insensitive. Phrases like, "I'm feeling a bit upset about what happened, can we talk about it?" demonstrate a willingness to address issues without placing blame compared to destructive phrases like "It's all your fault". Encouraging open dialogue and expressing a willingness to listen are as important as expressing one's emotions. Saying "I'm here if you want to talk about anything" can make the other person feel safe and supported in sharing their feelings.

Expressing gratitude, in particular, has profound benefits. It's a simple yet powerful way to acknowledge the value of the relationship and the other person's actions. Statements like "Your support means so much to me" or "I'm grateful for your friendship" can significantly boost the emotional well-being of both parties.

It's paramount to understand that Empathetic Conversation is an art that requires patience, understanding, and the ability to connect with another person's emotional state genuinely. Effective communication in a relationship goes beyond just exchanging information; it involves understanding the emotions and intentions behind the information. This can be achieved through active listening, showing unpretentious interest in the partner's feelings, and responding appropriately. In addition, effective communication includes expressing one's needs and feelings openly and honestly while respecting the feelings and needs of the partner.

YOUR RELATIONSHIP REVIVAL:

Empathetic Conversation is about connecting on a deeper emotional level, ensuring both partners feel heard, understood, and valued. Here's a list of activities to foster this profound aspect of your relationship:

1. **Video Messages of Love**: Record and send each other video messages expressing love and gratitude, especially when one of you is away or having a challenging day.

2. **Compliment Day**: Dedicate a day to give each other sincere compliments on various aspects, from personal qualities to the way each of you contributes to the relationship.

3. **Love and Gratitude Box**: Create a box where you both can drop notes of love and gratitude. Open it together once a month and read the notes aloud.

4. **Changing Conversation Settings**: Have deep conversations in different environments. Changing your surroundings can bring new insights, whether it's a park, a cozy café, or during a walk.

5. **Feelings Validation Practice**: Make it a point to validate each other's feelings during conversations. This practice strengthens emotional understanding and support.

6. **Scheduled Discussion Times**: Set aside regular times to discuss daily events, feelings, dreams, and aspirations. Consistent communication deepens your connection.

7. **Conversation Jar**: Create a 'conversation jar' filled with thought-provoking questions. Pick questions at random to spark deep and meaningful discussions.

8. **Gratitude Journaling Together**: Keep a joint gratitude journal. Regularly write down things you are grateful for about each other and your relationship, and share these entries with one another.

9. **Active Listening Practice**: Engage in active listening, where you give each other undivided attention and reflect back on what's been said to demonstrate understanding and empathy.

10. **Conversation-Stimulating Activities**: Participate in activities like visiting art exhibitions or watching plays. Discuss your thoughts and feelings about these experiences afterward.

11. **Memory Sharing Nights**: Dedicate evenings to sharing personal stories and memories, deepening your understanding of each other's past experiences.

12. **Affirmation Mirrors**: Leave loving and encouraging notes for each other on the bathroom mirror, starting their day with a warm moment of self-reflection.

13. **Dream Sharing Mornings**: Share your dreams over breakfast, discussing what you dreamt about and what you think it might mean.

14. **Cultural Exchange Evenings**: Spend an evening exploring a different culture through its storytelling traditions and discuss the themes and lessons from those stories.

Empathetic Conversation is more than just talking; it involves deep emotional engagement, active listening, and mutual respect. By embracing these activities, you ensure that your empathetic connection continues to grow, evolve, and strengthen the foundation of your relationship. Empathy allows you to deeply understand each other. Incorporating aspects from other relationship styles, like Creative Expression or Inspirational Support, can offer new ways to empathize and connect.

PLACES TO PICK:

Quiet parks, art galleries, cozy cafes, book clubs focusing on emotional intelligence, group counseling sessions, mindfulness retreats, spiritual discussion groups, poetry readings, intimate live music venues, beachside walks, scenic viewpoints, public gardens, historical site tours, cultural exchange events, storytelling nights, community discussion forums, couples' communication workshops.

LITERARY ECHOES:

"Ultimately the bond of all companionship, whether in marriage or in friendship, is conversation." — Oscar Wilde, Irish poet and playwright.

"Friendship is born at that moment when one person says to another, 'What! You too? I thought I was the only one.'" — C.S. Lewis, British writer and theologian.

"The first duty of love is to listen." — Paul Tillich, German-American philosopher and theologian.

"People think that intimacy is about sex. But intimacy is about truth. When you realize you can tell someone your truth, when you can show yourself to them, when you stand in front of them bare and their response is 'You're safe with me,' that's intimacy." — Taylor Jenkins Reid, American author.

"Trust is the glue of life. It's the most essential ingredient in effective communication. It's the foundational principle that holds all relationships." — Stephen R. Covey, American educator and author.

"One of the greatest gifts you can give to anyone is the gift of attention." — Jim Rohn, American entrepreneur and motivational speaker.

"I have been in love, and it was a great feeling. But love isn't enough in a relationship—understanding and communication are very important aspects." — Yuvraj Singh, Indian cricketer.

"Communication to a relationship is like oxygen to life. Without it, it dies." — Tony A. Gaskins Jr., American motivational speaker and author.

"Empathy has no script. There is no right way or wrong way to do it. It's simply listening, holding space, withholding judgment, emotionally connecting, and communicating that incredibly healing message of 'You're not alone.'" — Brené Brown, American professor and lecturer.

"Being heard is so close to being loved that for the average person they are almost indistinguishable." — David W. Augsburger, American Anabaptist author.

"Gratitude can transform common days into thanksgivings, turn routine jobs into joy, and change ordinary opportunities into blessings." — William Arthur Ward, American author and motivational speaker.

"Kind words can be short and easy to speak, but their echoes are truly endless." — Mother Teresa, Albanian-Indian Roman Catholic nun and missionary.

"The language of kindness is the lodestone of hearts and the food of the soul." — Abdu'l-Baha, eldest son of Bahai's faith prophet.

REFLECT AND DISCUSS:

Effective Communication and Conflict Resolution:

1. Reflect on a time when active listening was crucial in resolving a conflict in your relationship. How did it change the outcome?

   _____

   _____

   _____

2. Share an instance where acknowledging and validating each other's feelings prevented a misunderstanding or conflict. How do you maintain Empathetic Conversation during sensitive topics?

   _____

   _____

   _____

3. How do you navigate conversations where you have to deliver difficult or uncomfortable news to your partner or friend?

   _____

   _____

   _____

Expressing and Receiving Emotional Support:

4. Discuss how you and your partner practice giving and receiving affirmations. What impact does this have on your communication?

   _____

   _____

   _____

5. How do you balance expressing your emotions with being receptive to your partner's feelings during a conversation?

_____

_____

_____

Building Connection Through Gratitude and Empathy:

6. Share an experience where expressing gratitude to each other deepened your connection. How do you make gratitude a regular part of your relationship?

_____

_____

_____

7. Historical figures often wrote letters to express deep emotions. Imagine writing a letter to each other expressing your feelings. What would you say, and how might this exercise enhance your empathetic communication?

_____

_____

_____

Maintaining Open and Non-Judgmental Dialogue:

8. Share techniques you use to maintain open and non-judgmental communication in your relationship.

_____

_____

_____

Chapter Fourteen

More Practicalities: The Philosophy of "Pick a Place, then a Face!" Plus, a Surprise!

Congratulations on exploring the depths of maintaining your relationships and friendships through the insights shared in this book. But why stop there? Whether you're blissfully married or single, enriching your life with new connections is always a refreshing adventure. While it might be challenging for adults to form new connections due to their great commitment and shortage of time, we promise you that you will be delighted if you stick with us to the end of this chapter about the unique solutions we will provide. It's time to expand your social horizons and discover new connections with people who share your interests and passions. Our philosophy of "Pick a Place, then a Face!" intertwines seamlessly with the science and insights explored earlier in this book.

Current dating apps, while widely used, often present challenges that hinder the formation of meaningful connections. Statistically speaking, around half of the users find these platforms inadequate for their relationship needs. In the ever-evolving landscape of technology and human interaction, there arises a need for an innovative approach to forming relationships, both platonic and romantic. This is where the last third of this book becomes pivotal, as it examines the psychology behind the shortcomings of these apps and reinventing novel solutions.

The common pitfall lies in an external approach to connection, where the focus is more on superficial attributes rather than deeper, intrinsic compatibilities. As we have proposed, the first step to solve this is to start from within – to understand and embrace our relationship style. This self-awareness takes us to the next foundation of our approach, encapsulated in the philosophy of 'Pick a Place, then a Face.' Imagine an app that transcends the conventional approach of other platforms. Rather than the traditional method of selecting potential matches based on their profiles or images, this new app encourages users to first choose a location or activity on the map that resonates with their relationship style. In support of this philosophy, that's TerriTie for you! Our app's foundation is based on a map interface. Here's how it works: you select a destination you'd love to visit - let's say, a local tennis court, a local restaurant you've always wanted to try, or your favorite cafe. Once you register your interest in this location, you can see who else is interested in the same spot and go through a matching process with them- as simple as that! This innovative approach lets you connect with others who genuinely share your interests.

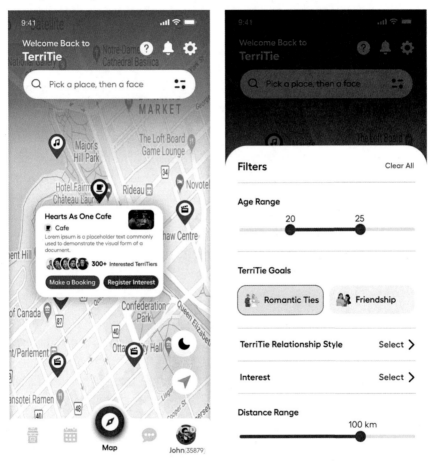

For example, a user inclined towards the Playful Teasing style might select a comedy show, while someone who identifies with Adventurous Bonding might opt for a rock-climbing gym. By prioritizing shared activities and locations, TerriTie shifts the focus from superficial criteria to shared experiences and interests, which are more likely to lead to lasting and fulfilling relationships. This method aligns users with compatible companions and offers a more enjoyable and authentic way to explore potential connections. It allows individuals to engage in activities they love, in settings where they feel most comfortable, thus providing a natural and relaxed environment for relationships to blossom.

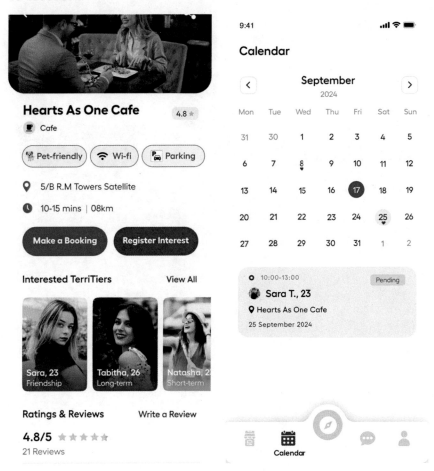

MORE PRACTICALITIES: THE PHILOSOPHY OF "PICK A PLACE, THEN A FACE!" PLUS, A SURPRISE!

261

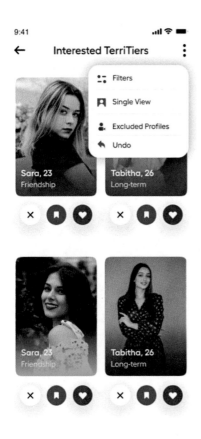
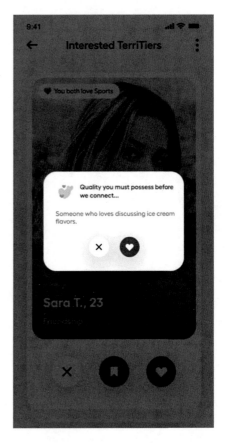

To ensure everyone's time is valued, and to encourage face-to-face, meaningful interactions, TerriTie requires you to confirm your plans – like booking your cinema tickets – and agree on a date through our pre-designed message templates that will mark the date into the built-in calendar. Texting and calling features unlock approximately 48 hours before your confirmed date, and only if you've confirmed your booking. We're all in support of face-to-face interactions as this is how you can truly know the other side. Safety is paramount to us, which is why we encourage all users on TerriTie to complete profile verification. While profile verification is not mandatory, it is strongly recommended to enhance the safety and trust within our community. Additionally, we listen to user feedback and may adjust the 48-hour window to better suit user preferences in the future.

9:41

← Tabitha P.

Why It's Great

1. **Encourages Real Interaction:** It promotes face-to-face interactions during the actual date instead of prolonged virtual communication.
2. **Reduces Miscommunication:** With limited texting time, users are encouraged to communicate more effectively and avoid potential misunderstandings.
3. **Builds Anticipation:** By restricting communication, it builds excitement and anticipation for the actual date."

9:41

← Tabitha P.

Set chat theme

Unmatch

Block and Report

Congratulations on your match! Arrange your date using our easy, pre-designed messages. Unlimited messaging and video calls will become available once both of you have agreed on the date details and confirmed. This feature activates 24 hours prior to your scheduled date, giving you the perfect window to connect and chat more freely.

Initial Interaction

Conditions

Date Planning

Special offer: Now, let's talk about something exciting! We have a special offer for those of you who purchased this book. As a token of appreciation, when you buy $10 worth of TieCoins from our app or website, we will give you the book's value ($3) PLUS $1.5 MORE in the form of TieCoins - our in-app currency used to secure dates and confirm bookings. Remember, TieCoins are not a cryptocurrency; they're a simple, stable way for users to engage with and enjoy the unique offerings of the TerriTie, much like PokéCoins from Pokémon or MineCoins from Minecraft games. We'll give you $4.5 worth of TieCoins, which is 450 TieCoins.

To give users a practical perspective on the value of TieCoins, consider the cost of securing a date through the app. The cost range for arranging a date on TerriTie is set between 4 to 8 USD. This pricing structure translates into 400 to 800 TieCoins, respectively. By establishing this straightforward conversion rate, users can easily comprehend and utilize their TieCoins for various activities and features within the app, such as securing dates or buying items from the TerriTie store.

Join & Earn:

Be one of the pioneers in the TerriTie community! As a special incentive, we're offering 500 TieCoins, equivalent to $5, towards your first date for the first 10,000 users who create an account on our website. This is a limited-time offer, so don't miss your chance to get a head start in enjoying our app with this exclusive bonus.

Refer & Earn Program:

We're excited to introduce our 'Refer & Earn' program, designed to enrich your experience with TerriTie. Our program offers a unique and engaging approach to referrals, rewarding you with 50 bonus TieCoins for EVERY member who joins through your post or link.

Here's how you can earn TieCoins:

❖ **Share your relationship style test results or test prompts**: Depending on what you choose to share, you can engage your friends and family with your personal insights or challenge them to discover their own styles.

❖ **Recommend locations from the TerriTie map**: Help others find great spots for their dates and earn rewards.

❖ **Suggest potential matches**: Connect your friends and family with compatible matches and get rewarded.

❖ **Share your unique referral link**: Simply share your personal referral link, and earn TieCoins for every new member who joins through it.

This tailored approach allows you and your friends to explore your relationship styles together, enriching your TerriTie experience. Discover, connect, and earn easily.

Visit our website for immediate access and start earning Tie-Coins now! www.territie.com

See the screenshot below for an example of what shared online test results would look like!

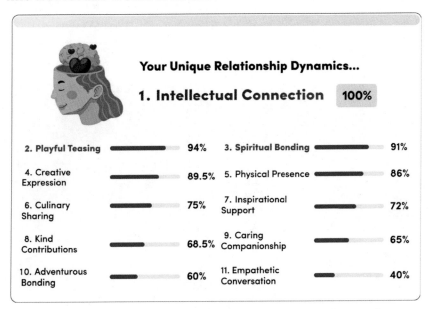

Your Unique Relationship Dynamics...

1. Intellectual Connection `100%`

2. Playful Teasing — 94%	3. Spiritual Bonding — 91%
4. Creative Expression — 89.5%	5. Physical Presence — 86%
6. Culinary Sharing — 75%	7. Inspirational Support — 72%
8. Kind Contributions — 68.5%	9. Caring Companionship — 65%
10. Adventurous Bonding — 60%	11. Empathetic Conversation — 40%

Strengthening Local Communities

In addition to our passion for creating a flourishing web of social connections through TerriTie, we are happy to have the opportunity to support local communities and businesses. At TerriTie, we wish to build community and extend allyship to other causes, using innovative and fun advertising that benefits both our users and local and up-and-coming businesses. We've developed an engaging way for businesses to connect with potential customers in their immediate area via our app's unique feature: an interactive balloon gift on the TerriTie map. Clicking on this balloon rewards users with free TieCoins and displays an ad from local businesses matching their interests. This benefits users in a dual fashion - not only are the free TieCoins usable anywhere in the app, not just with the business that issued them, but this is also an easy way for people to find out about new spots in their area, like a cozy new coffee shop or a tucked-away cinema. Additionally, a unique feature of our app allows upcoming events and discounts to be found when venues are selected or preferred spots are searched for, enabling users' immediate access to local offers and happenings. This transparent approach is a win-win situation, smoothly connecting businesses and their potential clients, spreading information, and bolstering the community.

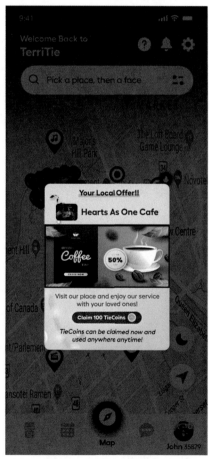

Incorporating the 'Picck A Spice' Framework

The app also includes a sophisticated system that aligns with the 'PICCK A SPICE' framework, allowing you to connect with others based on the 11 relationship styles discussed in this book. Whether you're looking for a partner to explore culinary delights, someone who shares your passion for creative arts, or a companion for intellectual discussions, TerriTie makes these connections possible. TerriTie is not just another dating or social app; it's a platform that embodies the principles of Starting from Within and connects people through shared interests and preferred environments. So, as we prepare to unveil how you can be part of this opportunity through our app or website, we invite you to first immerse yourself in the rest of the book about the current dating and friendship apps.

Exciting news for our early adopters: TieCoins are now on pre-sale at a special discounted rate on our website—a limited-time offer exclusively for you, our early adopters. By purchasing TieCoins directly, you'll enjoy a significantly lower price than what will be set in the app upon its release. Importantly, we're committed to maintaining a lower price for TieCoins on our website even after the app launches. This means that whether you're buying TieCoins during our pre-sale or after the app is live, you'll always find a more favorable rate on our website compared to in-app purchases. This pricing advantage is made possible as our website transactions bypass the additional fees imposed by the Appstore and Google Play Store. Furthermore, for a frictionless experience, any TieCoins purchased and accounts registered on our website will be fully integrated with your app account, ensuring you can effortlessly use your TieCoins across both platforms. Take advantage of this exclusive offer to maximize your investment with TieCoins at the best possible rate now and in the future.

TerriTie, named to signify our connection to the Earth ('Terri' from Terrestrial) and the ties that bind us in relationships ('Tie'). We chose this name to focus on the emphasis of earthly connections, face-to-face connection, as opposed to digital connections. It's a community, a new way to engage, and a safe platform to form meaningful connections, both platonic and romantic. So, are you ready to embark on this new journey with us? Stay tuned for more details on how to join TerriTie and claim your TieCoins - the first step towards new, authentic, and rewarding connections.

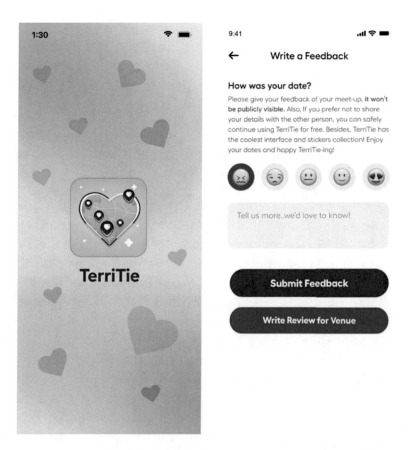

The 'Pick a Place, then a Face' philosophy is grounded in the idea that the best relationships often stem from shared interests and authentic experiences with people that resonate with your relationship style. Reflecting on the 'Places to Pick' sections highlighted in each relationship style chapter is essential. Whether you're seeking a romantic partner or a new friend, this section serves as a practical guide, helping you navigate the map of the TerriTie app to meet individuals who resonate with your preferred style. They are your starting points for finding compatible, fulfilling connections. This approach encourages you to engage in environments and activities you are passionate about, thereby attracting individuals with similar values. Within the TerriTie app, you'll find features that allow you to select venues or activities that interest you – from coffee shops and bookstores to hiking trails and art galleries. This selection process is guided by an understanding of your dominant relationship styles, ensuring that your choices reflect your true self. By focusing on the place first, TerriTie encourages you to engage in experiences you enjoy, creating a natural and relaxed environment for meeting new people.

We're thrilled to announce that TerriTie is set to launch at the end of August 2024. Join our website or follow us on social media to receive an announcement when our app comes to life. Links are at the end of the book.

As we conclude our exploration of the 'PICCK A SPICE' framework, it's crucial to understand that these relationship styles are not mutually exclusive but rather comprehensive of the diverse spectrum of human connections. Unlike some frameworks that categorize connections into rigid types, often labeling some as healthy and others as unhealthy, the 'PICCK A SPICE' styles are instinctive and healthy and may overlap with each other. The eleven relationship styles we unveiled are deeply rooted in our evolutionary history, with each style being backed by scientific research. It's entirely natural and healthy to be drawn to individuals with different or similar relationship styles. Our framework celebrates this diversity, acknowledging that human connections are dynamic and constantly evolving. Applying these styles thoughtfully and understanding their interplay can lead to transformative experiences in both romantic and platonic relationships. Furthermore, the existence of other theories focusing on personality types, attachment styles, or brain types does not contradict our framework. Each theory has its place and relevance in specific contexts. The 'PICCK A SPICE' framework is designed to be inclusive and adaptable, providing a broad and holistic understanding of the myriad ways individuals connect and interact. It's a testament to human relationships' rich complexity and adaptability, offering insights that complement rather than compete with other theoretical models.

Before diving into the exciting opportunity to be part of TerriTie's journey, we believe it's essential for you to make an informed decision. With this in mind, the rest of this book is dedicated to providing you with comprehensive insights into what sets TerriTie apart from other apps in the market. In the following pages, we'll investigate the psychology behind dating apps and present how TerriTie leverages the latest technology and psychological insights to offer a unique and effective way to form new relationships. From its consumer-focused philosophy and user-friendly interface to its commitment to safety and authenticity, TerriTie stands as a testament to the potential of technology in enhancing human connections.

TerriTie, a visionary user-centric application, stands at the forefront of this revolution, embodying a unique blend of psychology, human nature, science, and technology. TerriTie's core philosophy, 'Pick a Place, then a Face,' is a groundbreaking approach in the world of dating and social apps. This philosophy shifts the focus from profile browsing to fostering genuine connections based on shared interests and activities. The genesis of TerriTie is rooted in a profound understanding of relationship styles, the limitations of existing dating apps, and comprehensive market research. It represents a harmonious fusion of these diverse domains, aimed at transforming how technology facilitates the formation of earthly, meaningful connections. Join us in this transformative experience.

Although TerriTie is at the forefront of modern dating and social connectivity, our insights have far-reaching applications beyond the digital sphere. As we resume the following chapters, we invite all readers, regardless of their interest in the app, to join us on this journey and explore fascinating psychological theories and scientific research that offer practical wisdom and enlightening perspectives. These insights are not just for the digitally connected or those navigating the dating world; they are universal tools that can enrich every aspect of your daily interactions and relationships, whether it's understanding the subtleties of communication, the complexities of emotional connection, or the art of maintaining lasting bonds.

Chapter Fifteen

Reinventing Dating and Friendship Apps

INTRODUCTION

V isualize a festival of light where each lantern floats in its own bubble, unable to merge with others. Every lantern glows beautifully, but in solitary spheres, they hover – close yet distant. This sea of individually encapsulated lights mirrors the isolated connections of our digital world. Technology, with its dazzling brilliance, often confines us within our own digital spheres, dimming the potential for deeper, collective human experiences.

Now, imagine the transformation as these bubbles dissolve. The lanterns, no longer confined, begin to drift and mingle. Some join in vibrant clusters, forming colorful constellations of friendship, their lights dancing together in joyful harmony. Others gravitate towards a single lantern, their colors blending into a new hue, a testament to the deep, intimate glow of romantic connection. As they come together, the night sky blossoms into a mosaic of lights, each grouping unique in its pattern and beauty. This magnificent vista represents the potential richness of our relationships when we step beyond the digital veil – a spectrum of human emotions and connections, from the platonic warmth of companionship to the passionate fire of love.

While technology has introduced unprecedented convenience, it has also built invisible walls, confining us to a digital sphere and transforming the essence of our relationships and interactions. This section explores breaking free from this digital confinement and rediscovering the authenticity and joy of real-world connections. The knowledge displayed offers a journey towards more fulfilling, genuine interactions, guiding us from our encapsulated digital bubbles into a world rich with human connection and warmth. It's about moving beyond the isolated glow of screens to a brighter, more connected human experience.

Growing up as a millennial in a small, close-knit community where everyone knew each other was a fortunate experience for me. Embracing the digital changes early, I quickly adopted online platforms. I observed firsthand the unimaginable ways in which they began reshaping our social connection. Dating and friendship have undergone a substantial transformation in this landscape. From the days of traditional unions and romantic matchmaking to the era of digital networking, how we form and nurture relationships has changed.

During my teenage years in the early 2000s, online dating websites such as Match.com and eHarmony laid the groundwork, moving away from personal ads, dating agencies, and matchmaking services to algorithm-based partner suggestions. Social media platforms such as Facebook, Instagram, and X (Twitter) brought a new dimension to digital relationships. Fast forward a few years, and many of us now spend more time online than engaging in real-life socialization. Although not explicitly designed for dating or making friends, these platforms have significantly influenced how we connect, share experiences, and maintain relationships.

With technological advancements, the platforms evolved as well. The advent of apps such as Tinder, Bumble, and OkCupid revolutionized online dating, shifting it from a meticulous process to a swift, swipe-based system. This shift catered to a growing desire for immediate interactions, aligning with the fast-paced lifestyle of contemporary years. Alongside dating apps, platforms dedicated to forming friendships and professional connections emerged. Apps such as Meetup and Bumble BFF broadened online connectivity, accommodating various relationship types.

While popular and widely adopted, these platforms have not been immune to criticism. Privacy issues, superficial connections, and the paradox of choice have dominated discussions regarding online dating and friendship platforms. Whether these platforms enhance or hinder genuine human relationships remains a topic of debate.

Digital platforms have broken down geographical barriers, expanded our networks, and facilitated reconnections with old friends and family. Social apps have solved and simplified many issues in our societies. Nonetheless, they have introduced complexities in how we perceive and manage relationships. They have disrupted how we view the world and caused a lot of confusion for our evolutionary instincts. This is the first time in human history that we've faced such an extensive array of changes to our way of life.

Problems like ghosting, catfishing, and transactional relationships have become more prevalent. Impersonal interactions and detachment from accountability are on the rise. It has become alarmingly easy to harm others, treating them as mere images rather than actual human beings. These platforms have shifted public focus towards valuing quantity over quality, diminishing the enjoyment of present moments. Reducing love and friendship to mere algorithms and swipes raises significant concerns. Genuine human interactions diminish as people favor algorithmic matches and social media feeds over organic chemistry.

A survey reveals that 47% of singles find dating more challenging now than a decade ago. Approximately 45% of online dating users report dissatisfaction with the process, citing various reasons. Given that many industries strive for a dissatisfaction rate of 5% or less, with some even aiming for 1%, a 45% rate of customer frustration is considered exceptionally high. This indicates a significant need for improvements in dating apps.

My personal experiences with the challenges posed by social and dating apps have led me to conclude that a significant element is missing in the app market (more on my personal experience in Digital Deceptions and the Perils of Online Scams). I couldn't find what I was looking for. The concept of building a new app that would solve the problem lingered in my mind for many years. Driven by a determination to address these issues, I initiated extensive market research, laying the foundation for launching a new app.

Fully aware of the human tendency for confirmation bias, I deliberately sought diverse perspectives to validate my views. This journey started with conversations with friends and family, but I quickly expanded my research to include a broader demographic, engaging with people from various backgrounds on the streets of Auckland City. This multicultural city, bustling with tourists year-round, provided a rich collection of opinions and insights. This comprehensive approach helped me balance my innate biases with real-world data, strengthening my conviction in my cause. The potential to create a transformative digital solution far outweighed the risks of investing my time, savings, and efforts. Committing to the development of this app was a decision fueled by my belief in its potential, a belief shaped by listening to diverse perspectives on dating and friendship apps. My strong faith in my vision and ambition to offer something unique to society mirrors the conviction that I encourage you, dear reader, to have in your own visions.

The evolution of digital dating and friendship platforms is still ongoing. We are at the threshold of a new interval set to reshape the social and dating landscape once more. Built on the advancements of its predecessors, TerriTie aims to address the critical issues that users face. It is designed to enhance how we form relationships, fostering deeper connections and prioritizing user safety and authenticity. I welcome your feedback and suggestions via our website and social channels. I am building this app for society. Everyone's voice matters. I believe in inclusivity and equality and will try to cater to all your needs and suggestions when launching the app or in future updates. Stay tuned and be part of this exciting development journey and the eventual launch of TerriTie. In the next chapters, I'll examine the current challenges of relationship platforms, informed by thorough market research.

CHOICE OVERLOAD AND PERCEPTUAL COMPLETION IN DATING APPS

Imagine yourself in front of a grand carousel, where each horse is a seat taken by a potential date. As the carousel spins, you have but a moment to decide whether to reach out and sit next to someone. Each rotation brings new faces into view, and with them, your indecision grows. You hesitate, pondering whether the next turn might reveal someone more compatible or captivating. This carousel serves as a metaphor for the ceaseless cycle of choices in dating apps, where an overload of options fosters hesitation and a fear of making the wrong choice, often resulting in missed opportunities.

Relationship apps come with various psychological and social implications. In digital dating, users are often confronted with an overwhelming array of choices. Though connecting with numerous potential partners is easily accessible, it can also be overwhelming. While seemingly advantageous, giving the illusion of increased chances of finding a match, it leads to the paradox of choice, where too many options can lead to decision paralysis and decreased satisfaction. Digital connections, while fast-paced, often lack depth. Relationships that might have developed gradually and organically in the past now tend to start (and sometimes end) with a rapidity that can leave both parties feeling unfulfilled.

Barry Schwartz, a professor of social theory, in his seminal work 'The Paradox of Choice,' articulates how having too many options can lead to worse decision-making outcomes. Our brains are wired to seek pleasure (potential matches) and avoid pain (rejection). In the context of dating apps, this theory manifests in users feeling overwhelmed by the high number of possible partners. Most people perceive rejection in the real world as more painful and humiliating than in the digital world. If you get rejected behind the screen, no one will know, and it won't affect your daily relationships. The risk is shallow, and the entry is effortless.

As users swipe through endless profiles, the initial thrill of repetitive swiping exhausts their decision-making capacity. Such fatigue may lead to either hasty, unconsidered decisions or a complete reluctance to make any choice. For the average user, this gets worse every day they use the app. Refer to the accompanying diagram for a clearer visualization of this problem.

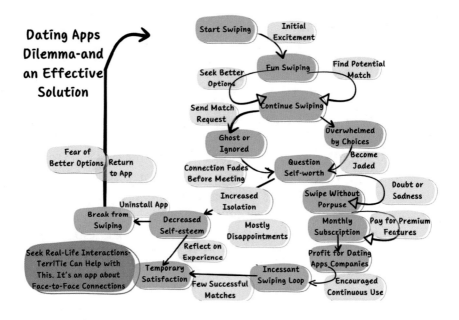

Swiping on dating apps can create a loop of decision paralysis. The euphoria turns into a relentless pursuit of something better, leading to a cycle of fleeting connections and self-doubt. Users might swipe past potential good matches in hopes of finding the 'perfect' option, often influenced by the illusion of unlimited possibilities. This mindset can diminish the satisfaction with current matches and escalate a sense of regret, even when good connections are made.

Gender disparities are also evident. Studies released by different organizations reveal that while women on online dating sites are more likely to feel overwhelmed by the volume of messages they get, males are more likely to feel insecure about the lack of responses.

Upon making a match, instead of engaging deeply, users might persist in swiping, enticed by the app's design, to see more prospects, which can lead to superficial interactions and ghosting behaviors. The more users swipe, the more they pay, regardless if they made a real connection or not, feeding into the app's profitability rather than fostering genuine relationships. This investment becomes more about playing the game than finding companionship.

The few successful matches are overshadowed by the constant barrage of choices that breed confusion and self-doubt. Users may internalize this as a personal failure, questioning their worth and desirability. This negative loop is exacerbated by the app's monetization model, which thrives on users' indecision and prolonged app usage. Most dating apps prioritize a monetization strategy that emphasizes user engagement with superficial features like browsing profiles, swiping, and sending likes. This approach contrasts starkly with what might be a more meaningful revenue model: charging users only upon achieving the app's primary goal of forming successful matches, real dates, and meaningful connections.

"I found myself swiping for hours, but instead of feeling hopeful, I felt more indecisive and skeptical," shared Sam with me, a user of a popular dating app. Their experience resonates with many users, who similarly find themselves adrift in a sea of options.

Research indicates that individuals may exhibit lower satisfaction levels with their current relationships due to constant comparison and the 'what-if' scenarios that abundant choices bring. The overflow of choices has impacted relationship dynamics and how we perceive and value relationships. Thinking that a better person is only a swipe away can undermine the investment in existing connections. Rejection rises by around 30% among individuals who review more than 50 possible online matches' profiles. While the grass is sometimes greener on the other side, it is more often that the grass is as green as we nourish it. Relationships flourish with effort.

"Even when I met someone great, I couldn't help but think there might be someone better out there," confessed Alex after using a popular dating site. This sentiment is increasingly common among digital daters, reflecting the impact of the illusion of infinite options.

The trend towards maximization is encouraged through social media posts presenting the perfect side of our lives. Our brains like to fill in the gap. When we see only part of a picture, our brains instinctively fill in the rest. A phenomenon rooted in a concept known as *perceptual completion*. Perceptual completion is a cognitive process where the brain constructs a complete, coherent picture from partial visual information. This phenomenon is deeply rooted in the Gestalt Principles of Perception, a theory first introduced by German psychologists in the early 20th century, including Max Wertheimer, Wolfgang Khler, and Kurt Koffka.

During the COVID-19 pandemic, the widespread use of medical masks has provided a unique illustration of how our brains strive to interpret and complete partial visual information. This phenomenon aligns with the Gestalt Principles of perceptual organization, particularly the law of closure. According to this principle, our minds are inclined to perceive incomplete shapes as whole by filling in the missing contours or gaps. Thus, when we encounter individuals wearing medical masks, our brains instinctively reconstruct the obscured parts of their faces, often relying on our pre-existing perceptions or biases to do so. The removal of the mask can challenge our brain's filled-in image, confronting us with the reality that our presumptions may not accurately represent the individual's actual appearance. The Gestalt psychologists posited that the human brain prefers to perceive complete, organized patterns rather than disparate elements. The same thing can be said regarding images of friends and couples on social media. Our brain fills in the gap in other people's lives based on what we see in their profiles and selected feeds.

Neuroscientific research supports the idea of perceptual completion. Studies involving neuroimaging techniques like fMRI (Functional Magnetic Resonance Imaging) have shown that certain areas of the brain, especially the visual cortex, are active when individuals perceive incomplete stimuli. Pioneering neuroscientists like V.S. Ramachandran and Richard Gregory have explored how the brain processes visual information, suggesting that the brain uses perceptual 'shortcuts' or assumptions based on past experiences to fill in gaps. Perceptual completion is also a result of *top-down processing*, a concept where our perceptions are shaped by our expectations, knowledge, and experiences. This cognitive approach implies that what we perceive is not merely a product of the sensory data presented to us but is also heavily influenced by our mental framework and understanding of the world. Another relevant theory is Predictive Coding, proposed by scientists like Karl Friston. This theory suggests that the brain constantly generates and updates a mental model of the environment. When sensory input does not provide complete information, the brain relies on these models to predict and fill in the missing pieces.

Understanding perceptual completion has practical implications when navigating relationships in the digital world. The more time we spend online talking to people, the more our brains leverage this principle unconsciously to create perceptions about others that don't reflect their realities. The clear solution to this problem is reducing our time on online platforms while increasing the time we seek real-world experiences, both of which are actively encouraged by TerriTie's unique features.

Territie intends to address many of the new complications of our digital age by introducing features that promote thoughtful decision-making and foster deeper, more meaningful connections. Some bustling urban environments, like New York City, London, Delhi, and Tokyo, have over 10 million active users in their traditional dating apps. In these situations, finding a good match might seem like finding a needle in a haystack. In tackling the challenge of choice overload, particularly in highly populated cities, TerriTie introduces an innovative approach. Our philosophy of 'Pick a Place, then a Face' adds a layer of precision and personalization that narrows down the overwhelming array of choices. This also ensures that the connections you make are more aligned with your interests and lifestyle. By integrating our unique 11 Relationship Styles compatibility framework, TerriTie enhances the likelihood of connecting with someone who shares your passions and preferences.

Moreover, TerriTie addresses the issue of perceptual completion, where digital interactions often lead to misconceptions and unrealistic expectations. We believe in the power of face-to-face interactions. Sharing real-life experiences allows for a more authentic understanding of a person, beyond the digital facade. This hands-on approach enables you to see potential matches for who they truly are, aiding in making more informed decisions about compatibility and connection.

We encourage our users to choose public places for initial meetups, aligning with our commitment to safety. However, we offer flexibility ensuring that you can select a venue that matches your comfort level while still enjoying the adventure of meeting someone new.

Our requirement for booking confirmations from both parties before a date adds an additional layer of commitment and sincerity. For those concerned about safety during meet-ups, TerriTie offers the option to share GPS locations with a family member, a friend, or with your partner if you are already engaged and looking to meet a new friend. This feature is designed for your peace of mind, allowing for a secure and comfortable meeting experience.

Besides, we have committed that if users are going to pay, they will only pay for confirmed dates with potential partners or friends. People won't be paying to use the basic functions of the app like browsing and matching. We will accomplish this through an innovative booking system that allows users to choose the time and place of their first meeting. TerriTie, designed for ease of use, aims to significantly reduce factors contributing to decision paralysis. It's designed to help you know the other individual by meeting them in person. TerriTie intends to shift the focus from quantity to quality, helping users make more deliberate and meaningful choices.

Challenges in Adult Friend-Making

Imagine a vast library where each book symbolizes a potential friendship or connection. As an adult, you wander the aisles, sometimes finding a book that seems interesting, but often they're placed just out of reach, , nestled on towering shelves that stretch into uncertainty. This library is the adult world of making connections, where forming new bonds can be challenging and daunting, filled with missed opportunities and uncertainty on how to initiate.

Most current adult apps focus on dating, leaving a gap in facilitating platonic relationships. Research indicates that while the swiping style may hold some effectiveness in dating, it performs significantly worse in fostering friendships. This shortfall is largely due to mismatched intentions and the style's inherent lack of encouragement for real-life meetings, which is crucial in building platonic relationships. Recent studies reveal that adults typically find it more challenging to forge new friendships due to various factors. Unlike in childhood or adolescence, adults face constraints like limited time, frequent relocations, and evolving life stages, which can hinder the development of new social connections.

Personal anecdotes further illustrate these challenges. For instance, a 31-year-old accountant, Robbie, shares, "Since moving to a new city for work, I've found it incredibly hard to meet new people. Everyone seems busy with their own lives." Such stories are not uncommon and highlight the struggle many adults face in expanding their social circles.

Psychological barriers, including social anxiety and introversion, also play a significant role in adult friend-making. The fear of rejection or feeling out of place in new social settings can deter many from attempting to make new friends.

Experts in psychology and social sciences emphasize the importance of maintaining a healthy social life at all stages of adulthood. Adult friendships are crucial for mental well-being but require effort and stepping out of one's comfort zone. TerriTie incorporates features that balance the social needs of adults for both friendship-making and dating by creating time-efficient ways to connect, facilitate real-life meetings, and build suitable personalized settings, all while ensuring safety and privacy and catering to diverse life stages. Let us say that you like playing badminton, going to one of the French cafés nearby, or going to a dancing session, and none of your friends is interested in joining you. TerriTie will help you find people who have registered their interests in the same places you want to visit. TerriTie's approach helps you build confidence, knowing the other person is also looking for someone to share an experience with.

THE SWIPE EFFECT - SUPERFICIALITY VS INTUITION IN MODERN DATING

Imagine a conveyor belt in constant motion, carrying items representing potential partners. As you stand before it, you quickly swipe items off — some to the left, others to the right, based on a fleeting glance. This conveyor belt symbolizes the swipe culture of online dating, characterized by rapid judgments and a ceaseless stream of options, fostering a superficial approach to matchmaking, focusing on swiping and, often, bypassing deeper considerations.

Envision a gallery lined with portraits, each portraying only the most flattering images of individuals. Visitors stroll through, making snap judgments based on these images, often missing the stories behind them. This gallery mirrors online dating scenarios, where profiles display idealized personas, prompting superficial evaluations, often overlooking the deeper, more meaningful aspects of a person's character.

Another issue with swipe-based apps is promoting a culture based on external superficial factors related to other people. Relationships, in general, and dating specifically, should Start from Within. Physical appearance has become the primary criterion in these split-second decisions. We are not against being attracted to others based on their appearances. It is entirely natural and healthy to a high degree. However, due to how technology exploits it, we tend to start relationships based on exterior influences. Shouldn't we start relationships from within ourselves? Imagine that you are choosing the driving force for your life. Do you wish this influential force, guiding how you spend your time, to originate from within yourself or from external sources? This choice directly impacts who controls your life and how you spend your time. Additionally, through qualitative and quantitative research data, numerous studies have shown that users of swipe-based dating apps report lower satisfaction with their faces and bodies than non-users, indicating an appearance-focused culture's impact. Research also demonstrates elevated levels of anxiety and depression among swipe-based dating app users.

We will allow you to choose based on appearances in TerriTie. However, the most significant change we are making is that you will have to Start from Within yourself and move forward. While this might sound complex, rest assured, we have designed our app to be user-friendly and efficient, thanks to our intuitive features. First, you will be able to select your primary relationship styles and interests that determine how you want to spend your time. Then, our strategy is to Pick a Place, then a Face! Our app is map-based. You can register your interest in visiting a particular show or the nearby museum and view other people who also put their names there so you can match each other on common grounds, platonic or romantic. This approach will also eliminate awkwardness and misunderstanding, as both of you will have the same expectations after going through the matching process in our app and viewing each other's profiles. Our app will help you book and schedule the perfect date and time for both parties with our calendar and booking system.

Some people argue that quick decisions in dating can be intuitive and accurate as humans can make fast, instinctive, often correct judgments. To address this argument, while intuition plays a role in human decision-making, relying solely on split-second judgments can be limiting in the context of complex and nuanced areas like forming friendships or dating. Would it be fair if employers selected new staff based on their profile pictures rather than checking their resumes and interviewing them? Balancing instinct with deeper reflection is essential to create more well-rounded and meaningful connections. Alexander Todorov, a psychology professor who has spent over a decade studying facial psychology, emphasizes that while first impressions can be powerful, they are not infallible. In fact, they can be downright wrong. Todorov's research at Princeton University's Social Perception Lab suggests that faces with softer features are generally perceived as more trustworthy. In contrast, those with harsher features are often seen as less trustworthy. Additionally, faces with mature characteristics tend to be viewed as more dominant, whereas those with youthful or child-like features are perceived as more submissive. "It can be dangerous to rely too much on the face because these judgments are not based on rational thought," Todorov says. "It happens in job interviews, it happens with police, it happens with your online dating profile — we look at faces, and immediately we assume that we have a window to people's personalities, even without talking to them or interacting with them at all."

A balance of intuition and thoughtful consideration is key to making sound decisions when forming new connections. Intuition is stronger when paired with intellect and reflection. You can understand people on a deeper level when you meet them face-to-face, without filters or Photoshop, and share an experience with them. Facilitating these interactions is the strategy we provide in TerriTie. Meeting someone is the best way to get to know them. This preference for personal interaction is why more than 70% of companies still favor in-person interviews despite other options being more cost and time-efficient.

There's a growing need for platforms that encourage users to look beyond the surface. While traditional dating agencies continue to serve some clients, their services often come at a substantial cost, typically ranging between $250 to $500. TerriTie steps in with a more thoughtful, cost-effective approach, aiming to reduce these costs significantly – to about 1% to 4% of traditional agency fees. This positions TerriTie as the most viable option for a wider audience seeking genuine connections without the hefty price tag.

It is well-documented that everyone holds unconscious beliefs about various social and identity groups. It is another way our minds try to fill the gap and figure out environmental patterns. We evolved those tendencies to categorize social worlds to survive. Unconscious biases are often incompatible with our conscious values and are far more prevalent than conscious prejudice. That is why it is essential to pair intuition with reflection. Unconscious biases frequently sway quick decisions on social apps. These biases can be based on physical appearance, leading to stereotyping or discrimination, and often go unrecognized by the individual. Moreover, the act of swiping through profiles can inadvertently lead to the dehumanization of potential matches, reducing people to images. Users may begin to view profiles not as people with their own stories and personalities but as mere images to be accepted or rejected. This reductionist view can diminish the sense of empathy and connection towards others. The impersonal nature of swiping on a picture minimizes the realization that there is a real person behind each profile.

In addressing the challenges posed by swipe culture, TerriTie advocates for a transformative approach to forming connections, beginning from a foundation of personal reflection, growth, and preference. You will choose your main relationship styles and the activities you most align with before selecting the person. This inward focus ensures that the journey towards finding meaningful relationships starts with self-awareness and authenticity. By helping users be more genuine within themselves, TerriTie creates a foundation for expanding outward to others who are similar or complementary. Sharing experiences sets the stage for connections that are more likely to resonate on a deeper level. This approach nurtures relationships based not just on initial attraction but on mutual development and understanding. It fosters a more thoughtful and intentional method of connecting with others, where shared interests and values take precedence, and TerriTie's innovative features will make this process smooth and enjoyable. By starting the journey from within, TerriTie is not just offering an alternative to existing dating apps but redefining how we connect in the digital age.

Algorithms and Human Intuition in Digital Dating

Picture a futuristic city where everyone wears virtual reality (VR) devices that echo their thoughts and mirror their preferences. Over time, people only hear reverberations akin to their own and see news feeds that imitate their viewpoints, leading to an echo-chambered dystopia. Intrigued by the diverse world, a young inhabitant switches off the device and begins to explore the city, uncovering a rich panorama of thoughts and ideas previously unheard. This journey illustrates the importance of stepping out of algorithmically curated zones to experience the richness of diverse human connections.

Unconscious biases can significantly affect AI matching algorithms, leading to a snowballing effect. AI relies on training models that continually learn from loops of data feeds. AI's vulnerability to making mistakes may shape user decisions in ways that do not align with their natural inclinations or desires.

Users frequently view algorithmic selections as the most accurate or appropriate choices. While algorithms are powerful, they are not infallible. They may not capture the complexity and unpredictability of human relationships since they are designed on specific parameters and data points. It is an illusion of algorithmic perfection. Algorithms can become biased in a number of ways. Even after removing sensitive factors such as gender, color, or sexual orientation, AI systems draw conclusions based on their training data, which may contain biased human decisions or represent historical or societal inequities. A few years ago, Amazon abandoned one of its recruiting algorithms when it was shown to prefer candidates with resumes that included terms like "executed" or "captured," which were more frequently seen on applications from men. Inaccurate data sampling, wherein some groups are over or underrepresented in the training set, is another cause of bias. For instance, Joy Buolamwini of MIT and Timnit Gebru found that possibly due to unrepresentative training data, face analysis systems had higher error rates for minorities, particularly minority women.

The mere reliance on algorithms can lead to a homogenization of choices, where users are repeatedly presented with similar profiles. This can inadvertently narrow the range of experiences and connections, limiting exposure to potentially fulfilling matches outside these algorithmic parameters. Exploration is one of the most wonderful things we can do in our lifetime, so this would be a shame.

Algorithms provide a data-driven approach to matchmaking, missing the nuanced understanding and emotional intelligence inherent in human interactions. This gap often leads to a disconnect between algorithmic suggestions and the organic chemistry that can develop in person. Studies in behavioral psychology suggest that while technology can aid in the initial stages of matchmaking, a relationship's ultimate success depends on human factors — communication, emotional compatibility, and shared experiences.

Another issue with data-driven algorithms is their primary reliance on user input. People can tailor their profiles to reflect different personalities than in real life, intentionally or unintentionally. This might keep potential matches away from your radar.

Acknowledging AI's limitations, TerriTie aims to find an ideal balance between algorithmic precision and the depth of human intuition, blending these with in-person experiences and exploration. Meeting in person and sharing experiences is the best way to capture the nuances of complex human attraction and emotional dynamics, which are unquantifiable, at least at this stage.

Loneliness and the Human Need for Connection

In an era where digital tools are designed to enhance connectivity, a paradoxical trend emerges: heightened feelings of loneliness and social isolation. This paradox is particularly evident in online dating and social networking. Humans are social creatures. It is in the genetic disposition of most people to seek physical and emotional connection.

Social media creates an illusion of connectivity. Psychologist Dr. Sherry Turkle's research into online communication and social media has shown that while these platforms offer the illusion of constant connectivity, they frequently lead to a superficial engagement that lacks the nuances and emotional richness of in-person interactions. Social media platforms, by design, encourage users to present curated versions of their lives, leading to comparisons, unrealistic expectations and a distorted sense of reality. This phenomenon has been linked to feelings of inadequacy and isolation, as found in other studies by researchers like Jean Twenge and Keith Campbell, who explore the impact of social media on psychological well-being. To serve their true purpose of helping people socialize, social apps need to foster confidence, inspire exploration, and motivate users to venture beyond their screens into the real world. This is TerriTie's vision.

Studies have shown a concerning trend in the rise of loneliness across various demographics. The Cigna 2023 US Loneliness Index found that about 60% of the 330 million Americans reported feelings of loneliness, up from 54% in 2018, highlighting a growing societal issue. Young adults are twice as likely to be lonely than seniors, with around 80% of adults between the ages of 18 and 24 reporting feeling lonely. The staggering statistics show that we are lonely and getting lonelier. Termed the 'loneliness epidemic' by many, this trend has adversely impacted various aspects of life, from our mental health to productivity and happiness.

Research findings in multiple studies show that people who use social media to keep up with their friends and seek relationships feel lonelier than others who use it for different reasons, even if they spend the same amount of time online. While social media can help people connect, it might not offer the kind of interaction that people looking to form or maintain relationships really want.

Humans have a fundamental need for connection. We are inherently social beings, and our need for connection is directly related to our emotional fulfilment and is critical to our survival and well-being. These connections are genetically driven, as they provide reproductive opportunities and cooperative advantages regarding resource sharing and protection. Alarmingly, studies have shown declining trends in physical relationships and sexual activity, particularly among younger generations. Scientists express concern that our increasingly disconnected society could threaten our species' survival due to its impact on reproduction rates and societal vitality. The decline in forming relationships and engaging in sexual activity poses potential long-term consequences for demographic trends.

In many developed nations, there's a noticeable trend towards later-life marriages and declining birth rates. For instance, the United States has seen its lowest birth rates in three decades, according to a report from the National Center for Health Statistics. In 2023, the U.S. birth rate hit a historic low, with only 11.99 births per 1000 people, a decline from the previous year. Similarly, countries like Spain and South Korea are experiencing significant declines in their population growth, attributed partly to the younger generation's changing attitudes towards relationships and family formation. Japan, known for its aging population and low birth rates, continues to see a decline. In 2023, the birth rate was 6.825 births per 1000 people, reflecting a 1.68% decrease from 2022. Italy's birth rate in 2023 is 7.036 births per 1000 people, marking a 1.65% decrease from the previous year. Italy has the worst fertility rate in Europe and the sixth worst globally, with only 1.24 births per woman. The replacement level fertility rate is typically around 2.1 births per woman. This rate is necessary to maintain a population's size, assuming no immigration or emigration influences the population numbers. Many developed countries are well below this threshold. Such low fertility rates can lead to aging populations and potential challenges in maintaining economic and social stability.

Beyond romantic relationships, friendships are crucial to mental and physical health. The decline in forming deep and lasting friendships contributes to the 'loneliness epidemic', affecting overall societal well-being. The American National Social Network Survey reports a decline in the average size of Americans' social networks in recent years. Approximately one in five Americans reports having no close confidantes in their primary social network.

With the convenience of digital communication, there's a tendency to substitute deep, in-person interactions with more superficial online exchanges, which are less effective in fulfilling emotional and psychological needs.

Research in social psychology indicates that the quality, not the quantity, of social interactions determines feelings of social fulfillment and well-being. The format of most online dating platforms, focusing on quick judgments and transient interactions, contributes to a lack of genuine connection, leaving individuals feeling more isolated despite being digitally 'connected.' This paradox is at the heart of modern social dynamics. Dr. Julianne Holt-Lunstad's studies on loneliness and social relationships suggest that lacking meaningful connections can have negative consequences on both mental and physical health, comparable to well-established risk factors like smoking and obesity.

Recognizing the significant impact of this 'loneliness epidemic', TerriTie is dedicated to devising accessible methods for connecting people beyond their digital screens by emphasizing real-life meetings to build fulfilling social and romantic relationships, contributing to healthier, happier individuals and societies.TerriTie's approach is built on rigorous market research and psychological principles that emphasize the importance of self-love and self-care, using these principles as a vehicle for building social relationships and personal well-being.

The Impact of Ghosting and Rejection in Digital Dating

Imagine a masquerade ball where everyone weaves through a gigantic ballroom, wearing elaborate masks as they intermingle. You strike up a connection with someone, but suddenly, in the middle of a conversation, they vanish into the crowd like smoke, leaving you alone and bewildered. Imagine this happening again and again for no apparent reason. This ballroom, filled with masked faces appearing and disappearing, mirrors the world of online dating, where ghosting leaves individuals confused and hurt, wondering what went wrong.

In the digital dating world, ghosting (the act of suddenly cutting off communication without explanation) and rejection have become widespread experiences, often leaving deep emotional scars. One reason ghosting is prevalent is the difficulty of forming deep connections through text messages. Digital communication serves as the primary mode of interaction in relationship apps. While it offers convenience and accessibility, it also introduces complexities that can lead to misunderstandings. Another significant factor contributing to the prevalence of ghosting is the digital environment's ability to insulate individuals from the "real world" repercussions of their actions. This virtual buffer diminishes the ghoster's sense of accountability and mitigates the guilt they might otherwise feel, as they are spared from witnessing the direct emotional fallout of their actions on the ghostee. In effect, the ghoster can disengage entirely, retreating into the digital ether and leaving unresolved emotional threads to fray in silence. This phenomenon underscores a stark contrast between digital and face-to-face interactions, where the immediate presence of the other person might otherwise deter such abrupt terminations of contact, highlighting the complex interplay between technology, human behavior, and emotional health in the context of modern relationships.

Initially, the typical inbox of dating app conversations is filled with messages like "Hey," "How are you?" and "How was your day?". Conversations that start and go nowhere. These conversations don't necessarily mean that the other person as boring. If we interpret it this way, we will probably end up labeling most people boring. The issue here is the need for more context and a fitting environment. Suppose you meet these people who wrote those messages in real-life experiences. You will be surprised at how much they can make you laugh, share interesting conversations, and bring happiness to your life. These brief messages often reflect a broader phenomenon: exhaustion with current platforms and the busyness of our lives. They don't reflect personalities.

Additionally, if conversations continue beyond that, misunderstandings are more common in texting than in person. Unlike face-to-face conversations, digital communication lacks non-verbal cues such as tone and facial expressions. Body language is non-existent, which plays a crucial role in conveying meaning and intent.

Consider two villages separated by a deep canyon, connected only by a narrow bridge. While the villagers can shout across the canyon, proper understanding and connection happen only when they dare to cross the bridge. Those who cross the chasm find deeper relationships and greater awareness on the other side. The idea of this metaphorical canyon represents the need to take brave steps out into the open air in our own lives; moving beyond superficial levels of digital communication and towards more profound, meaningful connections.

From a sociolinguistic standpoint, context is crucial in understanding communication. Digital platforms often strip away the contextual cues that help interpret messages, making it challenging to fully understand a person's intentions. Where is the other person texting from? Are they at work? Are they with their family? How did their day affect their texting style? The absence of these cues in text-based communication can lead to misinterpretations. A message meant to be humorous can be perceived as offensive. Genuine expressions may be seen as insincere.

How language is used online can differ significantly from face-to-face communication. Emojis, abbreviations, and online jargon can have different interpretations, adding layers of complexity to digital interactions. A study conducted by the Proceedings of the International AAAI Conference on Web and Social Media found that even when emojis are interpreted in textual contexts, the potential for miscommunication appears to be roughly the same as when they are interpreted in isolation. Studies also found that there's a significant chance of misinterpretation of emojis, even among users on the same platform. About 40% of the emojis tested had a sentiment misconstrual score of 2 or more, meaning that people often disagreed about whether an emoji conveyed a positive or negative sentiment. This challenges the hypothesis that textual context would significantly reduce emoji misinterpretation.

Texting can also lead to greater conflict because of anonymity. Facing an invisible person is less intimidating. When we cannot see someone's eyes, allowing our emotions to influence how we respond to them is simpler. Misinterpretation and communication hurdles might also arise when no emotional cues or indications are present. Face-to-face conversation provides insights into how the other person interprets your words. These misunderstandings can hinder the formation of connections, leading to conflicts or even the premature ending of potential relationships. All of these factors may lead to ghosting behavior. This issue isn't the fault of individuals but rather an inherent weakness in digital communication.

Ghosting and rejection can profoundly affect an individual's self-worth and esteem. When communication ends abruptly without explanation, individuals often question their value. As ghosting becomes increasingly normalized, its psychological toll, unfortunately, grows more acceptable in our culture.

Research reveals that repeated ghosting on digital platforms can lead to lower self-esteem, altered self-perception, and the development of a trait called 'rejection sensitivity'. The ambiguous nature of ghosting and the lack of closure contribute significantly to self-doubt, compounding its emotional impact. Other root causes for ghosting include fear of confrontation and lack of communication skills.

TerriTie is dedicated to nurturing the mental and emotional well-being of its users. This commitment is reflected in the app's design, which encourages healthy interaction patterns. Recognizing the damaging impact of ghosting and rejection, TerriTie aspires to offer two solutions for the problem. Firstly, TerriTie aims to create a more accountable and empathetic dating environment by encouraging face-to-face interaction. Secondly, TerriTie also significantly focuses on building resilience and confidence, as we believe relationships should Start from Within. By picking a place first, you begin to fulfill your bucket list and continue to build yourself. This approach allows for more magic to happen and helps maintain self-image regardless of external validation.

Beyond the Screen - Embracing Real Connections and Reclaiming Time

Data indicates that a substantial part of daily life is spent on digital platforms, particularly among the younger demographics. The typical working-age internet user spends around 3 hours daily on social media. For users of dating apps like Tinder, the investment of time may be measured in swipes rather than minutes. Generational differences are evident, with Gen Z users typically finding a partner after 3,525 swipes, while Baby Boomers may require as many as 6,200 swipes. On average, it takes about 60 matches for users to arrange one real-life meetup. While these platforms offer ways to connect and interact, the time spent on them raises questions about the balance between digital and real-life interactions and the potential for time mismanagement.

Prolonged reliance on digital communication can impact social skills. Face-to-face interactions have intrinsic value, involving a complex set of emotional and social cues essential for personal development and relationship building. In-person interactions offer profound emotional and psychological benefits, including developing empathy, trust, and deeper emotional bonds. Research has demonstrated that physical interactions, such as eye contact and touch, are vital for emotional well-being, reducing stress, and altering pain perception. On the other hand, excessive screen time increases the risks of depression and anxiety, while engaging in face-to-face activities enhances social skills and helps build stronger, more resilient relationships. Moreover, even negative in-person interactions have an intrinsic value, as they help impart lessons that can be valuable in forming future connections and give us confidence in how to deal with awkwardness, rejection, or rude behavior in real life. While negative digital interactions may be difficult to interpret properly, leaving us painfully mulling over or quickly forgetting them, in-person negative interactions can be more genuinely character-building. They can be worthwhile teaching moments about ourselves and/or the world.

In an age where screen time dominates, there is a growing need to reclaim our time, consciously prioritizing real-world experiences and interactions. TerriTie envisions the future of digital dating as a harmonious fusion of technology and real-world interaction, where the digital experience is a gateway to real-life connections, not a replacement for them. Therefore, in designing TerriTie, a key consideration has been the efficient and meaningful use of users' time for a more balanced lifestyle. TerriTie has built an intelligent user interface design that streamlines the interaction process, ensuring that time spent on the app is productive and fulfilling, shifting the focus towards meaningful, face-to-face interactions. TerriTie utilizes technology to ensure that users spend less time browsing and more time engaging in memorable experiences where genuine relationships can flourish.

SOLUTIONS FOR SOCIAL ANXIETY

There once was a large garden filled with numerous glittering mirrors sewn amongst the flowers. In this garden, people could see little else other than reflections of themselves. Many felt safe yet isolated and cold. One day, a gardener replaced some mirrors with windows. People started seeing others through these windows, realizing they were not alone in their fears and desires. This small change transformed the garden into a place of connection and understanding.

Online dating platforms have become a significant part of social life for many, especially for individuals with social anxiety. While these platforms can offer safe spaces for connection, they also present challenges that can exacerbate anxiety.

For many with social anxiety, online dating can act as a safe haven. It is a less intimidating way to initiate contact and form relationships. According to a study in Cyberpsychology, Behavior, and Social Networking, individuals with social anxiety and depression are more inclined to use dating apps due to the ease of communication they provide. However, the same features that make online dating appealing can also create anxiety in specific contexts. The pressure to maintain engaging conversations, the uncertainty of online interactions, and the fear of eventual face-to-face meetings can heighten tension. For some, the transient nature of online interactions and the prevalence of ghosting and rejection can exacerbate social fears and insecurities.

What's the solution? In relation to the paradox of online dating and social anxiety, a renowned clinical psychologist Goodman, in his book 'Your Anxiety Beast and You', articulates the dilemma: "People want to wait until they feel more comfortable with physically meeting up in person. But the clock keeps ticking and they never get comfortable enough because you don't get more comfortable until you start doing it. Yet their anxiety fools them into believing that if they just wait a little longer, someday they'll feel up to it. But that day will never come."

TerriTie takes the same approach supported by clinical psychology: the best way to overcome your social anxiety is to meet people more often under controlled circumstances and agreed conditions. As a result, we have taken the decision that none of the current dating apps have taken. After the matching process, users can utilize pre-designed messages to set up the first date. They can negotiate details such as offering or accepting a treat or splitting the bill. Optional texting and calling features will be unlocked 48 hours before the first date to facilitate communication en route to the location and for discussions post-date. Additionally, these messages allow users to set specific conditions for the date, such as the inclusion of a pet or a family member. The journey of meeting someone new as a friend or as a partner varies in difficulty between people. Understanding the complex relationship between online dating and social anxiety, TerriTie aims to support the development of social skills. Improved interpersonal skills can positively affect various aspects of life, including work, family, and friendships. In addition, TerriTie offers robust security features that help people feel safer and less anxious during their first interaction.

The Role of Authenticity in Digital Profiles

In a sea of digital interactions, imagine an island with a lighthouse that emits a unique light pattern for each ship, reflecting its true nature. Unaware of the lighthouse's guiding principles, the sailors masked their true selves, conforming to the sea's norms and expectations, which led to aimless wandering. However, those courageous enough to showcase their authentic light patterns were led by the lighthouse to their matching harbor, where meaningful connections awaited. This tale illustrates how authenticity in the digital world, like unique light patterns, leads to genuine and fulfilling relationships.

In the world of online dating and friendship-making, creating a digital profile is the first step in presenting oneself to potential matches. This process, however, often becomes a balancing act between portraying an idealized image and remaining true to one's authentic self. Constructing an online identity is a blend of personal reflection and adherence to social norms and expectations. This construction can impact the quality of connections formed. Users often feel pressure to curate their profiles in a way that they believe will be most appealing, which can lead to a discrepancy between their online persona and their real identity. When profiles are heavily curated or inauthentic, the resulting relationships may be based on a false premise, leading to potential mismatches and dissatisfaction.

Authentic self-representation is crucial in building trust and ensuring compatibility. Relationships founded on genuine understanding and acceptance are more likely to be fulfilling and enduring. Statistics from various sources reveal that approximately 53% of all dating profiles contain some form of false information, with about 10% to 15% being entirely fake.

In a digital dating landscape often marked by superficiality and pretense, TerriTie aims to redefine online dating as a space for sincere connections by encouraging genuine self-representation. Acknowledging the significance of integrity, TerriTie encourages face-to-face verification as a key feature to ensure authenticity. To further enhance safety, we recommend users meet in public locations. While we strive to protect minors on our platform, we encourage users to report any suspicious activity and employ advanced algorithms to detect and prevent underage usage. By fostering a culture where honesty and authenticity are valued and rewarded, we aim to create a more trustworthy and genuine dating environment.

ꝹIGITAL ꝹECEPTIONS AND THE PERILS OF ONLINE ꙖCAMS.

Though digital dating presents new opportunities for connection, it also brings significant risks, notably online scams. The FBI reported a 25% increase in online scams since 2019, with victims losing over $547 million in 2021 alone to cyber fraudsters posing as romantic interests. The reported financial losses due to romance scams increased by nearly 80% from 2020 to 2021, with the median individual loss to a romance scam being around $2,400 in 2022, indicating the profound impact these scams have on individuals. This alarming trend showcases the growing sophistication and prevalence of online dating scams.

The emotional toll is equally severe. Victims frequently experience heartbreak, depression, and embarrassment, leading to long-lasting psychological impacts. The darkest side is when these victims attempt suicide resulting in tragic loss of lives. These scams target individuals of all ages, genders, and sexual orientations, making no one immune to their reach.

I personally was in a five-year online relationship without meeting the other person, which carried significant challenges. After my arduous experience, I learned that people have it worse looking at the findings of various studies and reports. This ordeal hit me hard and revealed the stark dangers lurking behind digital profiles, highlighting not only the financial implications but also the deep betrayal of trust and the severe impact on mental well-being for many people.

Motivated by this experience, I embarked on a journey of extensive research and analysis, diving deep into the resources of evolution, science, and psychology. The insights gained from this exploration, supported by approximately 650 references, have been distilled into the book you're holding now: "Unveiling 11 Relationship Styles: Secrets Nobody Told You." This incident was a catalyst for me. It also propelled my determination to create a platform where safety, authenticity, and genuine connections are foundational pillars.

People often say, 'It's a crazy idea!'... Until it works. People tend to support those who don't need it because they don't want to be associated with failure, let alone experience failure themselves. However, successful individuals embrace failure time and again. I stand before you today as a nobody. How can I inspire you when I haven't achieved success yet? I may be a nobody, but I believe in myself, and you should too. That's how it always starts! We can all start from zero, from the Big Bang, or from God, or whatever you believe marks the beginning of the universe. It's not uncommon for the initial idea of the business or mission you want to undergo some twists and turns and require some exploring and changes in direction until the right path is found. As you progress on your journey, so will your ideas. They may evolve into something different from what you initially imagined. But the most important thing is not to stop working. I have put in a lot of effort without seeing results yet, but I believe I will start to see the fruits of my labor sometime soon. Faced with a critical decision between buying a house, tied down by a mortgage, or investing in my dream, I chose the latter. It was a hard choice with a significant risk, but one that I was willing to take. Starting something big might mean walking alone for an extended period of time. Taking a rest might be okay, but if you stop, your mission will be over. It's hard, but if you believe in it, it is worth it, and it will be satisfying one day. It's definitely easier if you go on this journey with a co-founder, but for me, this choice wasn't available.

Catfishing, creating fake identities to deceive unsuspecting victims, lies at the heart of most online romance scams. Scamalytics reports that of 3.5 million dating profiles scanned monthly, approximately 500,000 are fake. This form of deceit leads to financial loss and severe emotional distress for the victims, who often believe they have found true love. FBI data revealed over

24,000 catfishing cases in 2021, marking a 30% increase in four years. The Federal Trade Commission reported a whopping $1.3 billion in damages by over 70,000 victims of romance scams in 2022. $4,400 was the median loss recorded, which is around a 200% increase from 2021 in terms of cases and financial loss. Catfishing can manifest in various forms – from financial scams to a means of trolling, blackmail, or a result of personal insecurities. Some catfishers seek romantic attention due to self-esteem issues, while others aim to exploit their victims financially.

Other motives for catfishing include harassment or cyberbullying, with perpetrators creating fake profiles to target individuals for their political or religious views, or sometimes, simply for entertainment. Some catfishers engage in this behavior due to underlying mental health issues like antisocial, narcissistic, or psychopathic personality disorders. Furthermore, catfishers sometimes use their fake identities to coerce victims into sending compromising photos or videos, later using these for blackmail. This tactic underscores the importance of caution in digital interactions, particularly in sensitive or vulnerable situations. Victims are often targeted due to their vulnerability, with widows, widowers, and lonely singles being common targets. Catfishers fabricate scenarios, such as medical emergencies or travel expenses, to financially exploit their victims.

Minors and teenagers, a demographic especially susceptible to online exploitation, face unique risks on online relationship platforms. These risks include exposure to inappropriate content, susceptibility to grooming by predators, cyberbullying, and emotional manipulation. A 2022 study by the Australian Institute of Criminology found that 12.4% of adult dating app users had received a request to facilitate the sexual exploitation of a child. Teenagers, still developing critical thinking and emotional intelligence, might not always discern the intentions of those they interact with online. This vulnerability makes them prime targets for individuals with harmful intentions.

To counter these alarming trends, TerriTie has been meticulously designed with comprehensive features aimed at combating online threats, including protecting minors and the broader community from exploitation, fraud, and catfishing. Our platform's proactive commitment to zero fake profiles is not just a promise but a cornerstone of our user safety strategy. This commitment is supported by our unique technology, which is designed to significantly reduce fraud and ensure that all interactions on the platform are genuine and transparent. Our platform prioritizes user safety in technologies that exceed standard measures, ensuring that the individuals our users interact with are who they claim to be. We are committed to continuously advancing our technology and protocols to stay ahead of potential threats, reaffirming our dedication to creating a trustworthy and secure platform. Our commitment extends to every aspect of user interaction, affirming our dedication not just to building a community, but to protecting it as well.

Diversity and Inclusivity in Online Dating

In a vibrant village, there was a legendary weaver whose tapestries were admired for their beauty and intricacy. However, they were all woven in monochrome. One day, a traveler brought threads of various colors and textures to the village, sharing these with the skilled weaver. Initially hesitant, the weaver started incorporating these new threads. The fabric transformed into a mesmerizing piece, rich in color and depth, celebrated by all. This story mirrors the importance of embracing diversity in our communities, including online platforms, and the enriching effect this has within our social cloth, just as varied and vibrant new threads enhance a fabric.

Online dating platforms possess the potential to become inclusive spaces, accommodating a diverse array of users. Online dating has also contributed to the acceptance and visibility of different forms of relationships. Although many online platforms have made commendable strides towards inclusivity, significant scope remains for essential improvements. Numerous studies have pointed out the shortcomings of dating apps in embodying diversity, especially concerning race, ethnicity, sexual orientation, and gender identity. This lack of diversity can lead to a homogenized user experience and marginalize certain groups. Research has shown that individuals from minority groups often face unique challenges on dating platforms. Unfortunately, hate speech against minorities can manifest blatantly, as seen in profiles stating, "No Asian and No Black." In addition, users who identify as LGBTQ are more likely to encounter hate speech, including threatening, misogynistic, and transphobic remarks.

Algorithms may unintentionally uphold biases, typically rooted in the data they are trained on. This can reinforce stereotypes and exclude certain groups from the matchmaking process. Dating platforms bear the responsibility of mirroring the diversity present in society. This involves creating a space where individuals of all backgrounds feel welcomed and represented. Inclusive platforms provide a fairer experience for all users and enrich the dating pool, offering a wider range of perspectives and experiences. Diverse social interactions enrich individual perspectives, promote empathy, and lead to a more inclusive, vibrant, and understanding society. While diversity and inclusivity are often discussed in the context of romantic relationships, their importance extends to platonic friendships and broader social interactions facilitated by online platforms.

A genuinely inclusive social platform caters to diverse relationship preferences that reflect cultural, racial, and lifestyle diversity. TerriTie acknowledges diversity and inclusivity as fundamental principles in online dating and is dedicated to developing a platform embodying these values. We designed TerriTie to be a welcoming space for users of all backgrounds. TerriTie aims to actively challenge biases and stereotypes in its algorithms and community guidelines to ensure a fair and respectful dating environment for all. TerriTie maintains that continuous attention to users' feedback and suggestions is crucial for fostering inclusivity. TerriTie advocates for healthy, respectful, and honest relationship dynamics, irrespective of the form those relationships take.

ᴛHE ᴄHALLENGING ꜰUTURE OF ᴅIGITAL INTERACTIONS

Picture a garden where flowers represent relationships and friendships. Some flowers are vibrant, real, and deeply rooted, symbolizing genuine connections. Contrastingly, some are mere holographic projections: aesthetically pleasing but transient, lacking scent of life, symbolic of the ephemeral nature of AI-powered bots and fake profiles. The gardener realizes that although the artificial flowers are easier to care for, they miss the true essence and beauty of their real counterparts. The story centers on a gardener who learns to distinguish between the real and the virtual, nurturing the flowers that bring true value to their life.

The future of dating and friendships is increasingly veering towards virtual spaces, marked by technological advances that are both intriguing and concerning. Advancements in technologies such as sexbots, chatbots, and virtual avatars are offering increasingly sophisticated simulations of companionship and interaction. While these innovations provide certain conveniences, they also raise questions about the nature of human relationships. Michelle Obama, in her YouTube interview with Jay Shetty, said that one of the things that keep her up at night is that people aren't prepared for the dangers of AI. As interactions become more virtual, there's a risk of losing the essence of human connection — the emotional depth, physical presence, and complex dynamics of human relationships. Heavy reliance on virtual interactions may deteriorate crucial social skills and empathy, as virtual avatars and bots cannot replicate the nuances of human feelings and behaviors.

It is the new low-risk, low-reward paradigm. Engaging with virtual entities presents a low-risk alternative to fundamental human needs. Users can experience companionship without the vulnerabilities and complexities of actual relationships. However, this low-risk approach comes with low rewards. Virtual interactions lack the depth, growth, and fulfilment of natural human connections, eventually leading to a less satisfying and meaningful life experience.

Amidst these technological developments, TerriTie remains dedicated to restoring the human element in dating and friendships. TerriTie promotes real-life connections and experiences, encouraging users to engage in activities, meet in person, and form authentic relationships based on shared interests. By doing so, TerriTie helps users develop and enhance their social skills, empathy, and emotional intelligence.

Join the Revolution:

TerriTie transcends being merely an app; it embodies a movement geared towards reigniting the essence of human connection in our digital era. As we conclude this exploration into the current landscape of dating and friendship apps, it's clear that our goal is for TerriTie to stand at the forefront of a significant shift. Let's pave the way for a future where technology enhances, not replaces, the depth and authenticity of our relationships.

We Trust You: We've opened our vault to demonstrate our commitment to transparency and to earn your trust. Relationships, after all, are built on this very foundation—extending from personal bonds with loved ones to professional ties with suppliers and even your connections with the apps you use. Unlike our competitors, we chose to share our journey with you from the very beginning. Our app wasn't developed in secrecy, or its underlying psychology obscured. Instead, we've opted to build it alongside you, openly sharing our process and inviting your input every step of the way. We shared our science with you and we hope you share it with others.

Your Voice Matters. Your thoughts and experiences are vital in shaping TerriTie into a platform that truly reflects its users' needs. We encourage you to share your feedback and reviews, as your participation is crucial in this collaborative journey.

How to Redeem Your Code: As we promised, you will be able to claim the value of this book by TieCoins. When you purchase $10 worth of TieCoins, simply use the code attached to receive $4.5 worth of TieCoins.

Your Unique Code: kujsZhpNeWfPQR

How to Sign Up: Visit https://www.territie.com/ to join our mailing list and **receive 500 FREE TieCoins** when you create an account. Receive exclusive insights, updates, and early access information as we gear up for the launch.

- ❖ **Website**: www.territie.com
- ❖ **Social Media Links**:
- ❖ **Facebook Group**: https://www.facebook.com/groups/TerriTie/
- ❖ **Facebook Page**: https://www.facebook.com/TerriTie/
- ❖ **YouTube**: https://www.youtube.com/@TerriTie
- ❖ **TikTok**: https://www.tiktok.com/@territie.tt
- ❖ **Instagram**: https://www.instagram.com/territie.tt
- ❖ **LinkedIn**: https://www.linkedin.com/company/territie
- ❖ **Twitter/X**: https://twitter.com/TieTerri
- ❖ **Reddit**: https://www.reddit.com/r/TerriTie/
- ❖ **Threads**: https://www.threads.net/@territie.tt
- ❖ **Mastodon**: https://mastodon.social/@TerriTie
- ❖ **Quora**: https://www.quora.com/TerriTie
- ❖ **Pinterest**: www.pinterest.com/territie
- ❖ **Discord**: https://discord.gg/h5XQzpKCUk
- ❖ **Twitch**: https://www.twitch.tv/territie

PLEASE LEAVE A REVIEW

Thank you for joining me on this journey through 'Unveiling 11 Relationship Styles.' If you found the insights shared within these pages valuable, I would be deeply grateful if you could take a few moments to leave a review. Your feedback supports my work and helps others discover and benefit from these relationship styles. Use the links below to leave a review. For readers who purchased from a non-US Amazon site or another retailer not listed above, please consider leaving your review on the specific site of your purchase.

Goodreads:
https://www.goodreads.com/book/show/209438315-unveiling-11-relationship-styles

Amazon US:
https://www.amazon.com/review/create-review/?ie=UTF8&channel=reviews-product&asin=B0CW1GKQ8S

Other Retailers:
https://books2read.com/11RelationshipStyles

Chapter Sixteen

11 Relationship Styles Test

Now, with all you have learned, you are invited to embark on an exciting threshold of self-discovery with a personal test designed to illuminate the patterns of your heart. After delving into the evolution of the 11 relationship styles and gaining the knowledge of how to nourish them practically, it's time to discover their order of importance at this stage of your life. Each style resonates uniquely across the spectrum of human connection. Understanding these styles offers profound insights into our own behavior and preferences. This easy and quick quiz will take only about 5 minutes to complete. If you prefer to use the website, please visit this link so you can save the results in your account and share them on social media. www.territie.com

It's recommended to repeat this test half-yearly or annually because it is natural that life stages may change your priorities. Embrace this test with an open heart, and you may just find the keys to unlock the deeper layers of your relationship styles.

TEST: DISCOVER YOUR DOMINANT RELATIONSHIP STYLES

Instructions: For each statement, rate how much you agree on a scale from 1 (Strongly Disagree) to 5 (Strongly Agree). Tally your scores for each category to see which relationship styles are most dominant for you. This test is for both romantic and platonic relationships. Remember, by sharing your results to social media using our website, you will earn FREE TieCoins for every curious friend who joins using your post! www.territie.com.

1. Playful Teasing

❖ I feel most connected to someone when we can laugh and joke together.

<table>
<tr><td>☐</td><td>☐</td><td>☐</td><td>☐</td><td>☐</td></tr>
<tr><td>1</td><td>2</td><td>3</td><td>4</td><td>5</td></tr>
</table>

❖ I love it when my partner joins the humor in our social circles.

<table>
<tr><td>☐</td><td>☐</td><td>☐</td><td>☐</td><td>☐</td></tr>
<tr><td>1</td><td>2</td><td>3</td><td>4</td><td>5</td></tr>
</table>

❖ I don't mind when my partner jokes about serious matters.

<table>
<tr><td>☐</td><td>☐</td><td>☐</td><td>☐</td><td>☐</td></tr>
<tr><td>1</td><td>2</td><td>3</td><td>4</td><td>5</td></tr>
</table>

❖ I enjoy relationships where we can playfully challenge each other.

<table>
<tr><td>☐</td><td>☐</td><td>☐</td><td>☐</td><td>☐</td></tr>
<tr><td>1</td><td>2</td><td>3</td><td>4</td><td>5</td></tr>
</table>

❖ I enjoy visiting amusement parks, board games or comedy clubs where humor is a key part of the experience.

<table>
<tr><td>☐</td><td>☐</td><td>☐</td><td>☐</td><td>☐</td></tr>
<tr><td>1</td><td>2</td><td>3</td><td>4</td><td>5</td></tr>
</table>

❖ A witty exchange can quickly turn my day around.

<table>
<tr><td>☐</td><td>☐</td><td>☐</td><td>☐</td><td>☐</td></tr>
<tr><td>1</td><td>2</td><td>3</td><td>4</td><td>5</td></tr>
</table>

Playful Teasing Total Score: /30

2. Intellectual Connection

❖ I value deep, thought-provoking conversations in my relationships.

☐   ☐   ☐   ☐   ☐
1   2   3   4   5

❖ Intellectual compatibility is essential for me.

☐   ☐   ☐   ☐   ☐
1   2   3   4   5

❖ I am drawn to people who challenge my thinking and share knowledge.

☐   ☐   ☐   ☐   ☐
1   2   3   4   5

❖ I don't get frustrated when my partner is not interested in intellectual discussions.

☐   ☐   ☐   ☐   ☐
1   2   3   4   5

❖ Attending a lecture, a book club, or a discussion group is an ideal way to connect.

☐   ☐   ☐   ☐   ☐
1   2   3   4   5

❖ Engaging in debates about current events or philosophical topics over dinner is appealing to me.

☐   ☐   ☐   ☐   ☐
1   2   3   4   5

Intellectual Connection Total Score: **/30**

3. Creative Expression

❖ I am drawn to people who express themselves through art, music, or writing.

□	□	□	□	□
1	2	3	4	5

❖ Collaborating on creative projects is a meaningful way for me to connect with others.

□	□	□	□	□
1	2	3	4	5

❖ I feel a deep connection when sharing and interpreting art or creative work like paintings, novels, movies, or videogames.

□	□	□	□	□
1	2	3	4	5

❖ I feel disconnected if my partner isn't involved in creative activities.

□	□	□	□	□
1	2	3	4	5

❖ I enjoy visiting art galleries, concerts, or theater performances with a partner.

□	□	□	□	□
1	2	3	4	5

❖ Sharing our favorite music, writings, poetry, or creative ideas is a significant way to bond.

□	□	□	□	□
1	2	3	4	5

Creative Expression Total Score: /30

4. Culinary Sharing

❖ I feel left out if my partner isn't interested in cooking or food-related activities.

☐ 1 ☐ 2 ☐ 3 ☐ 4 ☐ 5

❖ The kitchen is a place of connection and creativity in my relationships.

☐ 1 ☐ 2 ☐ 3 ☐ 4 ☐ 5

❖ Exploring new restaurants, cuisines or cooking styles with someone is an ideal date for me.

☐ 1 ☐ 2 ☐ 3 ☐ 4 ☐ 5

❖ I feel closer to someone when we share our favorite foods and recipes.

☐ 1 ☐ 2 ☐ 3 ☐ 4 ☐ 5

❖ Culinary traditions and stories are an important part of my relationships.

☐ 1 ☐ 2 ☐ 3 ☐ 4 ☐ 5

❖ I appreciate when someone shares their family recipes or culinary traditions with me.

☐ 1 ☐ 2 ☐ 3 ☐ 4 ☐ 5

Culinary Sharing Total Score: /30

5. Kind Contributions

❖ Kindness and generosity are traits I actively look for in relationships.

☐ 1 ☐ 2 ☐ 3 ☐ 4 ☐ 5

❖ Volunteering or engaging in charitable work with someone strengthens our bond.

☐ 1 ☐ 2 ☐ 3 ☐ 4 ☐ 5

❖ I feel a strong connection with people who are empathetic and considerate.

☐ 1 ☐ 2 ☐ 3 ☐ 4 ☐ 5

❖ I feel disconnected if my partner isn't involved in charitable activities.

☐ 1 ☐ 2 ☐ 3 ☐ 4 ☐ 5

❖ I find it meaningful when we support each other's philanthropic causes or altruistic endeavors.

☐ 1 ☐ 2 ☐ 3 ☐ 4 ☐ 5

❖ Altruistic spirits naturally align with mine.

☐ 1 ☐ 2 ☐ 3 ☐ 4 ☐ 5

Kind Contributions Total Score: /30

6. Adventurous Bonding

❖ Adventure and exploration are key elements I look for in relationships.

☐   ☐   ☐   ☐   ☐
1   2   3   4   5

❖ Exploring new places and activities is my idea of quality time with someone.

☐   ☐   ☐   ☐   ☐
1   2   3   4   5

❖ Hiking, rock climbing, or participating in outdoor adventures together is exhilarating.

☐   ☐   ☐   ☐   ☐
1   2   3   4   5

❖ I enjoy planning spontaneous road trips or travel adventures with a significant other.

☐   ☐   ☐   ☐   ☐
1   2   3   4   5

❖ Exploring new cities, cultures, or off-the-beaten-path destinations with a partner is ideal.

☐   ☐   ☐   ☐   ☐
1   2   3   4   5

❖ I feel disappointed if my partner prefers routine over spontaneous adventures.

☐   ☐   ☐   ☐   ☐
1   2   3   4   5

Adventurous Bonding Total Score: **/30**

7. Spiritual Bonding

❖ Spiritual or philosophical harmony is important in my relationships.

☐   ☐   ☐   ☐   ☐
1   2   3   4   5

❖ Discussing and exploring spiritual or existential topics is a key aspect of my connections.

☐   ☐   ☐   ☐   ☐
1   2   3   4   5

❖ I find a deep connection with those who share my spiritual curiosity or path.

☐   ☐   ☐   ☐   ☐
1   2   3   4   5

❖ I feel disconnected if my partner doesn't share my spiritual interests.

☐   ☐   ☐   ☐   ☐
1   2   3   4   5

❖ I seek relationships where spiritual growth and exploration are encouraged.

☐   ☐   ☐   ☐   ☐
1   2   3   4   5

❖ I feel a deep connection when participating in religious services, spiritual ceremonies, or yoga and meditation classes together.

☐   ☐   ☐   ☐   ☐
1   2   3   4   5

Spiritual Bonding Total Score: **/30**

8. Physical Presence

❖ Physical closeness and touch are crucial components of my relationships.

☐   ☐   ☐   ☐   ☐
1   2   3   4   5

❖ I feel disconnected if my partner isn't physically affectionate.

☐   ☐   ☐   ☐   ☐
1   2   3   4   5

❖ Physical affection is a primary way I express and receive love.

☐   ☐   ☐   ☐   ☐
1   2   3   4   5

❖ A hug, a touch, or just being close physically can be deeply comforting to me.

☐   ☐   ☐   ☐   ☐
1   2   3   4   5

❖ I believe holding hands during our walks or cuddling while watching a movie is a significant part of a relationship.

☐   ☐   ☐   ☐   ☐
1   2   3   4   5

❖ Engaging in dance classes or physical hobbies together helps strengthen our bond.

☐   ☐   ☐   ☐   ☐
1   2   3   4   5

Physical Presence Total Score: **/30**

9. Inspirational Support

❖ Motivating and supporting each other's goals is a critical aspect of my relationships.

☐	☐	☐	☐	☐
1	2	3	4	5

❖ I feel sad if my partner doesn't support my goals.

☐	☐	☐	☐	☐
1	2	3	4	5

❖ I thrive in an environment where encouragement and positivity are abundant.

☐	☐	☐	☐	☐
1	2	3	4	5

❖ Supporting each other's aspirations, like starting a business or pursuing a degree, is key in my relationships.

☐	☐	☐	☐	☐
1	2	3	4	5

❖ Celebrating each other's successes, big or small, is a regular part of our relationship.

☐	☐	☐	☐	☐
1	2	3	4	5

❖ Being each other's accountability partner in personal development goals is fulfilling for me.

☐	☐	☐	☐	☐
1	2	3	4	5

Inspirational Support Total Score: **/30**

10. Caring Companionship

❖ I prioritize emotional availability, care and understanding in my relationships.

☐   ☐   ☐   ☐   ☐
1   2   3   4   5

❖ Being there for each other through ups and downs is fundamental for me.

☐   ☐   ☐   ☐   ☐
1   2   3   4   5

❖ Sharing responsibilities, caring for family members, or co-parenting effectively are crucial aspects of a caring relationship for me.

☐   ☐   ☐   ☐   ☐
1   2   3   4   5

❖ I feel cared for when my partner or friend helps me with daily tasks during tough times.

☐   ☐   ☐   ☐   ☐
1   2   3   4   5

❖ Exchanging gifts that show understanding and thoughtfulness is important to me.

☐   ☐   ☐   ☐   ☐
1   2   3   4   5

❖ I feel less cared for if my partner doesn't help with daily tasks.

☐   ☐   ☐   ☐   ☐
1   2   3   4   5

Caring Companionship Total Score: /30

11. Empathetic Conversation

❖ Active listening and affirming others' feelings are practices I prioritize in relationships.

□	□	□	□	□
1	2	3	4	5

❖ An understanding heart is what I offer and seek.

□	□	□	□	□
1	2	3	4	5

❖ Being heard and understood on an emotional level is very important to me.

□	□	□	□	□
1	2	3	4	5

❖ I don't believe in relationships where empathetic and open communication isn't the norm.

□	□	□	□	□
1	2	3	4	5

❖ Having deep conversations where we understand and empathize with each other's life experiences is vital.

□	□	□	□	□
1	2	3	4	5

❖ Being able to discuss our feelings openly and without judgment is key in my relationships.

□	□	□	□	□
1	2	3	4	5

Empathetic Conversation Total Score: **/30**

Scoring Interpretation:

Once you've tallied your scores across all categories, your total will range between 6 and 30. This score reveals the prominence of each relationship style in your life, with the highest-scoring categories highlighting your dominant relationship styles.

Reflection and Sharing:

Below, you'll find space to list your relationship styles in order of their strength based on your results. Take a moment to reflect on these styles. Think about how they shape your interactions and influence your preferences in connecting with others.

Your Unique Relationship Dynamics:

1. _____

2. _____

3. _____

4. _____

5. _____

6. _____

7. _____

8. _____

9. _____

10. _____

11. _____

We're excited to see what you discover about yourself! Share your top relationship styles with us on social media and tag us in your post. Seeing your insights truly makes our day brighter!

This test can serve as a starting point for readers to reflect on their relationship preferences and styles, fostering greater self-awareness and understanding of their interpersonal dynamics.

As you know from reading this book, we have done elaborate market research in Auckland streets. At this stage, we're so eager to expand our horizons and embrace the global pulse of dating app experiences. Your voices and stories are invaluable to us, and we invite you to share your insights on our website or social channels, or reach out directly through our contact form www.territie.com. Your feedback is the cornerstone upon which we will build a better TerriTie – an app that not only listens but responds to your desires. You are the people. You have the right to shape the social apps to serve you best! This is your stage.

Help us refine the world of digital dating by contributing your perspectives through the following questions. Together, we can craft an app that truly resonates with the needs of its users worldwide. The following questions are designed to help you reflect on your experience and help us get to know your opinion on social connectivity overall.

Chapter Seventeen

Dating and Friendship Apps Experience Test

nstructions: Reflect on your experiences with dating apps and answer the following questions. This test will help you understand your relationship with dating apps and what you might be looking for in future digital dating experiences.

User Experience & Feelings

❖ Have you ever felt overwhelmed by the number of choices on dating apps?

_____

_____

❖ Have you found it difficult to form genuine friendships through dating apps?

_____

_____

❖ Do you feel that dating apps are more geared towards romantic connections than platonic ones?

_____

_____

❖ Have you ever felt disconnected or desensitized because of the swiping format?

_____

_____

❖ Do you feel more anxious or self-conscious when using dating apps?

_____

_____

❖ Have you struggled with being your authentic self on these platforms?

_____

_____

❖ Have you encountered deceptive or misleading profiles on dating apps?

_____

_____

Interactions & Connections

❖ What do you think about prioritizing face-to-face interactions over texting and calling?

_____

_____

❖ Do you believe that the algorithms in dating apps truly understand your preferences?

_____

_____

❖ When you meet someone, do you believe more in the power of shared experience, intuition, and intellect to understand them or in AI algorithms?

_____

_____

❖ Do you feel that dating apps adequately address your need for genuine connection and companionship?

_____

_____

❖ Have you experienced challenges in transitioning from app-based chats to real-life interactions?

_____

_____

❖ How much value do you place on a genuine, real-life date compared to endless online interactions?

_____

_____

Improvements & Preferences

❖ What improvements do you like to see in dating and friendship apps to solve the loneliness pandemic?

_____

_____

❖ Why do you think ghosting and rejection happens in traditional dating apps?

_____

_____

❖ What are the top three things you dislike or find frustrating about dating apps?

_____

_____

❖ If you could change or add three things to make dating apps better, what would they be?

_____

_____

- ❖ What changes or improvements do you hope to see in these platforms?

_____

_____

Inclusivity & Authenticity

- ❖ Do you feel that dating apps cater to a diverse range of people and preferences?

_____

_____

- ❖ Have you found these platforms inclusive of different genders, sexualities, and backgrounds?

_____

_____

- ❖ How do you feel about the authenticity of the information presented on these platforms?

_____

_____

TerriTie's Approach

- ❖ What do you think about TerriTie's approach to solving choice overload?

_____

_____

- ❖ How do you feel about TerriTie's approach in bringing friends together based on mutual interests and the 11 relationship styles?

_____

_____

❖ How do you feel about features that promote face-to-face interactions over online chats?

_____

_____

Comparisons to Traditional Methods

❖ How do you think dating apps compare to traditional dating methods, such as dating agencies or setups by friends and family?

_____

_____

❖ Do you believe there's something lost in the transition from traditional dating to app-based dating?

_____

_____

Value & Pricing

❖ If there was a platform that guaranteed genuine real-life dates, what would you consider a reasonable price for such a service?

_____

_____

Scoring: Reflect on your responses and consider what they reveal about your experiences and expectations from dating apps. This test isn't about right or wrong answers but understanding your personal journey and preferences in digital dating. We will be grateful if you answer these questions on our website or if you share your answers and tag us in social media.

Acknowledgments

The support and encouragement of many individuals have immensely enriched the journey to bring TerriTie to life. I extend my heartfelt gratitude to friends, family, early adopters, and everyone who has contributed their time, insights, and feedback.

Your belief in TerriTie's vision has been instrumental in shaping this platform. Thank you for being a part of this revolutionary journey.

About the Author

Ahmad Aljazeeri, the author of this book and the innovative mind behind TerriTie, is a medical imaging technologist deeply fascinated by psychology and relationships. His unique combination of healthcare expertise, passion for human communication, and technology is the foundation of his approach to creating impactful social changes.

With his multicultural experience from various countries, Ahmad has broadened his perspective on the nuances of human connections. His active participation in community service across diverse landscapes underscores his dedication to fostering positive societal transformations.

Beyond his professional endeavors, Ahmad founded the PICCK A SPICE: 11 Relationship Styles Framework,' a groundbreaking approach to understanding and navigating the complexities of interpersonal relationships. This framework reflects his insights into the dynamics of human interaction and is central to his mission with TerriTie – to transcend traditional digital boundaries and cultivate authentic, fulfilling human connections.

Driven by firsthand observations of digital dating and social media limitations, Ahmad is committed to building TerriTie. A platform enhances the depth and authenticity of human relationships, guided continuously by community feedback and his belief in the transformative power of technology.

Unmasking the Layers of Relationships:

1. Liesen, L. (2007). Women, behavior, and evolution: Understanding the debate between feminist evolutionists and evolutionary psychologists. *Politics and the Life Sciences, 26*(1), 51-70.

2. Vandermassen, G. (2008). Can Darwinian Feminism Save Female Autonomy and Leadership in Egalitarian Society? *Sex Roles, 59*, 482–491.

3. Goleman, D. (1995). *Emotional Intelligence.* New York, NY: Bantam Books.

Starting and Maintaining Relationships: From Within and Habituation:

4. Rogers, C. R. (1951). *Client-centered therapy: Its current practice, implications, and theory.* Boston: Houghton Mifflin.

4. Cohen, I. S. (2020, October 8). Defining a Self While in a Relationship. *Psychology Today.*

5. PositivePsychology.com. (2019). Emotional Intelligence Frameworks, Charts, Diagrams & Graphs.

6. McLeod, S. A. (2023). Carl Rogers Person-Centred Therapy And Core Conditions. *Simply Psychology.*

7. Cooper, M., & McLeod, J. (2011). Person-centered therapy: A pluralistic perspective. *Person-Centered and Experiential Psychotherapies, 10*(3), 210-223.

8. Brown, R. (2000). Social Identity Theory: Past achievements, current problems and future challenges. *European Journal of Social Psychology, 30*(6), 745-778.

9. Tajfel, H., & Turner, J. C. (1979). An integrative theory of intergroup conflict. In W. G. Austin & S. Worchel (Eds.), *The social psychology of intergroup relations* (pp. 33-47). Monterey, CA: Brooks/Cole.

10. Ellemers, N., & Haslam, S.A. (2011). Social Identity Theory. In P. van Lange, A. Kruglanski, & T. Higgins (Eds.), *Handbook of theories of social psychology* (pp. 379-398). London: Sage.

11. Ryan, R. M., & Deci, E. L. (2017). Self-Determination Theory: Basic psychological needs in motivation, development, and wellness. *Guilford Press.*

12. Ryan, R. M., & Deci, E. L. (2000). Self-Determination Theory and the facilitation of intrinsic motivation, social development, and well-being. *American Psychologist, 55*(1), 68–78.

13. Niemiec, C. P., & Ryan, R. M. (2009). Autonomy, competence, and relatedness in the classroom: Applying Self-Determination Theory to educational practice.

14. Greene, K., Derlega, V. J., & Mathews, A. (2006). Self-disclosure in personal relationships. In A. L. Vangelisti & D. Perlman (Eds.), *The Cambridge Handbook of Personal Relationships* (pp. 409-427). Cambridge: Cambridge University Press.

15. Altman, I., & Taylor, D. A. (1973). *Social penetration: The development of interpersonal relationships.* New York: Holt, Rinehart, & Winston.

16. Csikszentmihalyi, M. (2013). Flow: The psychology of optimal experience. *New York, NY: Random House.*

17. Nakamura, J., & Csikszentmihalyi, M. (2009). Flow theory and research. In C. R. Snyder & S. J. Lopez (Eds.), *Handbook of positive psychology* (pp. 195-206).

18. Koehn, S., Morris, T., & Watt, A. P. (2013). Flow state in self-paced and externally-paced performance contexts: An examination of the flow model. *Psychology of Sport & Exercise, 14*(6), 787-795.

19. Rankin, C. H., Abrams, T., Barry, R. J., et al. (2009). Habituation revisited: an updated and revised description of the behavioral characteristics of Habituation. *Neurobiology of Learning and Memory, 92*(2), 135-138.

20. Schmid, S., Wilson, D. A., & Rankin, C. H. (2015). Habituation mechanisms and their importance for cognitive function. *Frontiers in Integrative Neuroscience, 8.*

21. Rehman, I., Mahabadi, N., Sanvictores, T., & Rehman, C. (2017). Classical Conditioning. In *StatPearls*. StatPearls Publishing.

22. Operant Conditioning: Reinforcement and Punishment. (n.d.). In *Saylor Academy.*

23. O'Donnell, J. M. (1985). *The origins of behaviorism: American psychology 1870-1920.* New York: New York University Press.

Playful Teasing:

25. Eckert, J., Winkler, S. L., & Cartmill, E. A. (2020). Just kidding: the evolutionary roots of playful teasing. *Biology Letters, 16*(9), 20200370.

24. Kruger, J., Gordon, C. L., & Kuban, J. (2006). Intentions in teasing: when "just kidding" just isn't good enough. *Journal of Personality and Social Psychology, 90*(3), 412-425.

25. Poulin-Dubois, D., Brooker, I., & Chow, V. (2009). The developmental origins of naive psychology in infancy. *Advances in Child Development and Behavior, 37*, 55-104.

26. Keltner, D., Tracy, J. L., Sauter, D., Cordaro, D., & McNeil, G. (2016). Expression of emotion. In L. Feldman Barrett, M. Lewis, & J. M. Haviland-Jones (Eds.), *Handbook of emotions* (4th ed., pp. 467-482). New York, NY: Guilford Press.

27. Reddy, V. (1991). Playing with others' expectations: Teasing and mucking about in the first year. In A. Whiten (Ed.), *Natural theories of mind: Evolution, development and simulation of everyday mindreading* (pp. 143-158). Cambridge, MA: Basil Blackwell.

28. Scott-Phillips, T. C., Blancke, S., & Heintz, C. (2018). Four misunderstandings about cultural attraction. *Evolutionary Anthropology: Issues, News, and Reviews, 27*(4), 162-173.

29. Reddy, V. (2008). *How infants know minds*. Harvard University Press.

30. Keltner, D., Capps, L., Kring, A., Young, R. C., & Heerey, E. A. (2001). Just teasing: A conceptual analysis and empirical review. *Psychological Bulletin, 127*(2), 229-248.

31. Reddy, V., & Mireault, G. (2015). Teasing and clowning in infants. *Current Biology, 25*(1), 20-24.

32. Zosh JM, Hirsh-Pasek K, Hopkins EJ, Jensen H, Liu C, Neale D, Solis SL, Whitebread D. (2018). Accessing the Inaccessible: Redefining Play as a Spectrum. *Front Psychol, 9*, 1124.

33. Emmons, S. L. A. (2000). A disarming laughter: The role of humor in tribal cultures. An examination of humor in contemporary Native American literature and art.

34. Dunbar, R. I. M. (2022). Laughter and its role in the evolution of human social bonding. *Philosophical Transactions of the Royal Society B: Biological Sciences, 377*(1863), 20210176.

35. Li, N. P., Griskevicius, V., Durante, K. M., Jonason, P. K., Pasisz, D. J., & Aumer, K. (2009). An Evolutionary Perspective on Humor: Sexual Selection or Interest Indication? *Personality and Social Psychology Bulletin, 35*(7), 923–936.

36. Alexander, R. D. (2022). Evolution and Humor. In *Human Social Evolution: The Foundational Works of Richard D. Alexander.* Oxford University Press.

37. Kramer CK, Leitao CB. (2023). Laughter as medicine: A systematic review and meta-analysis of interventional studies evaluating the impact of spontaneous laughter on cortisol levels. *PLoS One, 18*(5):e0286260.

38. Sridharan K, Sivaramakrishnan G. (2016). Therapeutic clowns in pediatrics: a systematic review and meta-analysis of randomized controlled trials. *Eur J Pediatr, 175*(10):1353-1360.

39. Cai, C., Yu, L., Rong, L., & Zhong, H. (2014). Effectiveness of humor intervention for patients with schizophrenia: A randomized controlled trial. *Journal of Psychiatric Research, 59*, 174-178.

40. Gray, A. W., Parkinson, B., & Dunbar, R. I. (2015). Laughter's influence on the intimacy of self-disclosure. *Human Nature, 26*(1), 28-43.

41. Proyer, R. T. (2014). Playfulness over the lifespan and its relation to happiness: Results of an online survey. *Zeitschrift für Gerontologie und Geriatrie, 47*(6), 508-512.

42. Aune, K. S., & Wong, N. C. (2002). Antecedents and consequences of adult play in romantic relationships. *Personal Relationships, 9*(3), 279-286.

43. Proyer, R. T., Ruch, W., & Buschor, C. (2013). Testing strengths-based interventions: A preliminary study on the effectiveness of a program targeting curiosity, humor, and playfulness. *Frontiers in Psychology, 4*, 810.

44. Hall, J. A. (2015). Sexual selection and humor in courtship: A case for warmth and extroversion. *Evolutionary Psychology, 13*(3), 147470491501300314.

45. Yip, J. A., & Martin, R. A. (2006). Sense of humor, emotional intelligence, and social competence. *Journal of Research in Personality, 40*(6), 1202-1208.

46. Cann, A., Norman, M. A., Welbourne, J. L., & Calhoun, L. G. (2008). Attachment styles, conflict styles and humour styles: Interrelationships and associations with relationship satisfaction. *European Journal of Personality, 22*(2), 131-146.

47. Fraley, B., & Aron, A. (2004). The effect of a shared humorous experience on closeness in initial encounters. *Personal Relationships, 11*(1), 61–78.

48. Kuiper, N. A., & Martin, R. A. (1998). Laughter and stress in daily life: Relation to positive and negative affect. *Motel Research in Personality, 32*(2), 178-189.

49. DiDonato, T. E., & Jakubiak, B. K. (2016). Strategically funny: Romantic motives affect humor style in relationship initiation. *European Journal of Psychology, 12*(3), 390-405.

50. Dyck, K. T., & Holtzman, S. (2013). Understanding humor styles and well-being: The importance of social relationships and gender. *Personality and Individual Differences, 55*(1), 53-58.

51. Keltner, D., Young, R. C., Heerey, E. A., Oemig, C., & Monarch, N. D. (1998). Teasing in hierarchical and intimate relations. *Journal of Personality and Social Psychology, 75*(5), 1231–1247.

52. De Koning, E., & Weiss, R. L. (2002). The Relational Humor Inventory: Functions of humor in close relationships. *American Journal of Family Therapy, 30*(1), 1-18.

Intellectual Connection

53. Byrne, R. W., & Bates, L. A. (2007). Sociality, evolution, and cognition. *Current Biology, 17*(16), R714-R723.

54. Breuer, T., Ndoundou-Hockemba, M., & Fishlock, V. (2005). First observation of tool use in wild gorillas. *PLoS Biology, 3*(11), e380. https://journals.plos.org/plosbiology/article?id=10.1371/journal.pbio.0030380

55. Byrne, R. W. (2016). Evolving insight. Oxford: Oxford University Press.

56. Byrne, R. W., & Corp, N. (2004). Neocortex size predicts deception rate in primates. *Proceedings of the Royal Society B: Biological Sciences, 271*(1549), 1693-1699. https://royalsocietypublishing.org/doi/10.1098/rspb.2004.2780

57. Byrne, R. W., & Whiten, A. (Eds.) (1988). Machiavellian intelligence: Social expertise and the evolution of intellect in monkeys, apes, and humans. Oxford: Clarendon Press.

58. Anderson, S. A., Marín, O., Horn, C., Jennings, K., & Rubenstein, J. L. (2001). Distinct cortical migrations from the medial and lateral ganglionic eminences. *Development, 128*(3), 353-363.

59. Rakic, P. (1995). A small step for the cell, a giant leap for mankind: A hypothesis of neocortical expansion during evolution. *Trends in Neurosciences, 18*(9), 383-388.

60. Dunbar, R. I. M. (1998). The social brain hypothesis. *Evolutionary Anthropology: Issues, News, and Reviews, 6*(5), 178-190.

61. Miller, G. (2000). The Mating Mind: How Sexual Choice Shaped the Evolution of Human Nature. Doubleday & Co.

62. Miller, G. (2019). Virtue Signaling: Essays on Darwinian Politics & Free Speech. Cambrian Moon.

63. Rizzolatti, G., Fadiga, L., Gallese, V., & Fogassi, L. (1996). Premotor cortex and the recognition of motor actions. *Cognitive Brain Research, 3*(2), 131-141.

64. Gallese, V., Fadiga, L., Fogassi, L., & Rizzolatti, G. (1996). Action recognition in the premotor cortex. *Brain, 119*(2), 593-609.

65. Iacoboni, M., & Dapretto, M. (2006). The mirror neuron system and the consequences of its dysfunction. *Nature Reviews Neuroscience, 7*(12), 942-951.

66. Rizzolatti, G., & Craighero, L. (2004). The mirror-neuron system. *Annual Review of Neuroscience, 27*, 169-192.

67. Rizzolatti, G., & Sinigaglia, C. (2010). The functional role of the parieto-frontal mirror circuit: interpretations and misinterpretations. *Nature Reviews Neuroscience, 11*(4), 264-274.

68. Hasson, U., Nir, Y., Levy, I., Fuhrmann, G., & Malach, R. (2004). Intersubject synchronization of cortical activity during natural vision. *Science, 303*(5664), 1634-1640.

69. Stephens, G. J., Silbert, L. J., & Hasson, U. (2010). Speaker-listener neural coupling underlies successful communication. *Proceedings of the National Academy of Sciences, 107*(32), 14425-14430.

70. Hasson, U., Ghazanfar, A. A., Galantucci, B., Garrod, S., & Keysers, C. (2012). Brain-to-brain coupling: a mechanism for creating and sharing a social world. *Trends in Cognitive Sciences, 16*(2), 114-121.

71. Gottman, J. M., & Gottman, J. S. (2017). The Natural Principles of Love. *Journal of Family Theory & Review, 9*(1), 7-26.

72. Feldman, R. (2007). Parent–infant synchrony: biological foundations and developmental outcomes. *Current Directions in Psychological Science, 16*(6), 340-345.

73. Pemment, J. (2021). The Intellectual Complexities of Loving. *Psychology Today*.

74. McDow, Candis (2023). Intellectual Attraction: When Minds Connect.

75. RelationTips HQ. (2023). How to Cultivate Intellectual Intimacy and Authentic Connections.

76. Hasselmo, M. E. (2006). The role of acetylcholine in learning and memory. *Current Opinion in Neurobiology, 16*(6), 710-715.

77. Meneses, A. (2013). 5-HT systems: emergent targets for memory formation and memory alterations. *Rev Neurosci, 24*(6), 629-64.

78. Meneses, A. (2012). Serotonin and emotion, learning and memory. *PubMed*.

79. Serena Camuso, S., & La Rosa, P. (2022). Pleiotropic effects of BDNF on the cerebellum and hippocampus: Implications for neurodevelopmental disorders. *Neurobiology of Disease, 163,* 105606.

80. Bathina, S., & Das, U. N. (2015). Brain-derived neurotrophic factor and its clinical implications. *Archives of Medical Science: AMS, 11*(6), 1164–1178.

81. Arias-Carrión, O., & Pöppel, E. (2013). Dopamine, learning, and reward-seeking behavior. *Acta Neurobiologiae Experimentalis.*

82. Juárez Olguín, H., et al. (2016). The role of dopamine and its dysfunction as a consequence of oxidative stress. *Oxidative Medicine and Cellular Longevity.*

83. De Haan, H. J. (2010). Origins and import of reinforcing self-stimulation of the brain.

84. Kasanova, Z., Ceccarini, J., Frank, M. J., et al. (n.d.). Striatal dopaminergic modulation of reinforcement learning predicts reward-oriented behavior in daily life.

85. Baik, J.-H. (2020). Stress and the dopaminergic reward system. *Experimental & Molecular Medicine.*

86. Buckholtz, J. W., Treadway, M. T., Cowan, R. L., et al. (2010). Mesolimbic dopamine reward system hypersensitivity in individuals with psychopathic traits.

87. Teicher, M. H., Samson, J. A., Anderson, C. M., & Ohashi, K. (2016). The effects of childhood maltreatment on brain structure, function and connectivity.

88. Arias-Carrión, O., et al. (2010). Dopaminergic reward system: a short integrative review. *International Archives of Medicine.*

89. Lembke, A. (2021). Dopamine nation: Finding balance in the age of indulgence. *Dutton, an imprint of Penguin Random House LLC.*

90. Wilson, G. D., & Cousins, J. M. (2003). Partner similarity and relationship satisfaction: Development of a compatibility quotient.

91. Joel, S., & Eastwick, P. (2020). Massive new study on predictors of relationship satisfaction.

92. Leist, A. K., & Müller, D. (2013). Humor types show different patterns of self-regulation, self-esteem, and well-being. *Journal of Happiness Studies, 14,* 551-569.

93. Rodkey, K. L., & Rodkey, E. N. (2020). Family, friends, and faith-communities: Intellectual community and the benefits of unofficial networks for marginalized scientists. *History of Psychology, 23*(4), 289.

94. Thriveworks. (2023). Fostering emotional intimacy: Expert guidance.

95. Bem, D. J. (1967). Self-perception: An alternative interpretation of cognitive dissonance phenomena. *Psychological Review, 74*(3), 183.

96. Sternberg, R. J. (2000). *Practical intelligence in everyday life.* Cambridge University Press.

97. Tupper, K. W. (2002). Entheogens and existential intelligence: The use of plant teachers as cognitive tools. *Canadian Journal of Education/Revue Canadienne de l'Éducation*, 499-516.

98. Cavas, B., & Cavas, P. (2020). Multiple intelligences theory—Howard Gardner. In *Science Education in Theory and Practice: An Introductory Guide to Learning Theory* (pp. 405-418).

99. Abdulwahid, K. S. (2021). Social factor effects on linguistic performance, emotional and spiritual intelligence. *International Journal of Islamic Educational Psychology, 2*(1), 15-35.

Creative Expression

100. Furnham, A., Batey, M., Anand, K., & Manfield, J. (2008). Personality, hypomania, intelligence and creativity. *Personality and Individual Differences, 44*(5), 1060-1069.

101. Silvia, P. J., & Beaty, R. E. (2012). Making creative metaphors: The importance of fluid intelligence for creative thought. *Intelligence, 40*(4), 343-351.

102. The Smithsonian Institution's Human Origins Program. (2024). Early stone age tools.

103. Piperno, M., & others. (2012). The origin of tool use and the evolution of social space in Palaeolithic times. In A. Berthelet & J. Chavaillon (Eds.), *The Use of Tools by Human and Non-human Primates* (Symposia of the Fyssen Foundation). Oxford Academic.

104. Kuhn, S. L., & Clark, A. E. (2014). Stone tool technology. In V. Cummings, P. Jordan, & M. Zvelebil (Eds.), *The Oxford Handbook of the Archaeology and Anthropology of Hunter-Gatherers* (Oxford Academic).

105. American Museum of Natural History. (2021, April 21). Creativity and community: How modern humans overcame the Neanderthals. *ScienceDaily.*

106. Nature.com. Evolution of genetic networks for human creativity. *Molecular Psychiatry.*

107. Science News. (2022). Ancient Homo sapiens were more culturally creative than once thought.

108. AIATSIS Collection. (2021). C15: WARLPIRI.

109. ANCIENT AUSTRALIANS - LibGuides at Swan Valley Anglican Community School.

110. NTS Radio. (2020, October 7). Enter the portal: Australian Indigenous love songs.

111. JSTOR. (2024). Yuendumu and the Warlpiri: Early history.

112. The Ulwazi Programme. (2022). Zulu courting customs.

113. BEING AFRICAN. (2021). Music & dance in Zulu culture.

114. Wikipedia contributors. (2024). History of the concept of creativity. In *Wikipedia*.

115. Stanford Encyclopedia of Philosophy. (2003). Episteme and techne.

116. Bryn Mawr Classical Review. (2017). Creation and the function of art: Technē, poiesis, and the problem of aesthetics. *Bloomsbury Studies in Continental Philosophy*.

117. Idea to Value. (2021, April 26). The 1950 speech that started creativity research.

118. Guilford, J. P. (1950). Creativity. *American Psychologist, 5*(9), 444–454.

119. Chong, A., Tolomeo, S., Xiong, Y., Angeles, D., Cheung, M., Becker, B., Lai, P. S., Lei, Z., Malavasi, F., Tang, Q., Chew, S. H., & Ebstein, R. P. (2021). Blending oxytocin and dopamine with everyday creativity. *Scientific Reports, 11*(1), 16185.

120. Schnitzer, G., Holttum, S., & Huet, V. (2021). A systematic literature review of the impact of art therapy upon post-traumatic stress disorder. *International Journal of Art Therapy, 26*(4), 147-160.

121. Pizarro, J. (2004). The efficacy of art and writing therapy: Increasing positive mental health outcomes and participant retention after exposure to traumatic experience. *Art Therapy, 21*(1), 5-12.

122. Beauregard, C. (2014). Effects of classroom-based creative expression programmes on children's well-being. *The Arts in Psychotherapy, 41*(3), 269-277.

123. O'Neill, A. A. (2023). Therapy, art, friendship, and flourishing in illness: A mixed methods pilot randomised controlled trial of an art therapy group intervention for paediatric patients with chronic illnesses (Doctoral dissertation, University of Dublin).

124. Bryant, F. B., & Veroff, J. (2017). Savoring: A new model of positive experience. *Psychology Press*.

125. Hinz, L. D. (2019). Expressive therapies continuum: A framework for using art in therapy. *Routledge*.

126. Fancourt, D., & Finn, S. (2019). What is the evidence on the role of the arts in improving health and well-being? A scoping review. World Health Organization. Regional Office for Europe.

127. Campbell, K., & Kaufman, J. (2017). Do you pursue your heart or your art? Creativity, personality, and love. *Journal of Family Issues, 38*(3), 287-311.

128. Carswell, K. L., Finkel, E. J., & Kumashiro, M. (2019). Creativity and romantic passion. *Journal of Personality and Social Psychology, 116*(6), 919–941.

129. Hendrick, C., & Hendrick, S. S. (1988). Lovers wear rose-colored glasses. *Journal of Social and Personal Relationships, 5*(2), 161-183.

130. Hendrick, C., & Hendrick, S. S. (2006). Styles of romantic love. In R. J. Sternberg & K. Weis (Eds.), *The new psychology of love* (pp. 149-170).

131. Coholic, D. (2010). *Arts activities for children and young people in need: Helping children to develop mindfulness, spiritual awareness and self-esteem.* Jessica Kingsley Publishers.

132. Stalp, M. C. (2006). Negotiating time and space for serious leisure: Quilting in the modern US home. *Journal of Leisure Research, 38*(1), 104-132.

133. Ivcevic, Z., & Hoffmann, J. D. (2019). Emotions and creativity: From process to person and product. In J. C. Kaufman & R. S. Sternberg (Eds.), *Cambridge Handbook of Creativity* (pp. 273-295).

134. Ivcevic, Z. (2023). What is the role of emotions in creativity? - Fifteen Eighty Four | Cambridge University Press. *Cambridge Blog.*

135. Amabile, T. M. (1998). How to kill creativity (Vol. 87). Harvard Business School Publishing.

136. Bryant, F. B., & Veroff, J. (2017). *Savoring: A new model of positive experience.* Psychology Press.

137. Griskevicius, V., Cialdini, R. B., & Kenrick, D. T. (2006). Peacocks, Picasso, and parental investment: The effects of romantic motives on creativity. *Journal of Personality and Social Psychology, 91*(1), 63.

138. Regan, P. C., Levin, L., Sprecher, S., Christopher, F. S., & Gate, R. (2000). Partner preferences: What characteristics do men and women desire in their short-term sexual and long-term romantic partners? *Journal of Psychology & Human Sexuality, 12*(3), 1-21.

Culinary Sharing

139. Jaeggi, A. V., & Gurven, M. (2013). Reciprocity explains food sharing in humans and other primates independent of Kin Selection and tolerated

scrounging: A phylogenetic meta-analysis. *Proceedings of the Royal Society B: Biological Sciences, 280*(1768), 20131615.

140. Jaeggi, A. V., & van Schaik, C. P. (2011). The evolution of food sharing in primates. *Behavioral Ecology and Sociobiology, 65*(11), 2125-2140.

141. Wilson, M. L., Kahlenberg, S. M., Wells, M., & Wrangham, R. W. (2012). Ecological and social factors affect the occurrence and outcomes of intergroup encounters in chimpanzees. *Animal Behaviour, 83*(1), 277-291.

142. Gurven, M. (2004). To give and to give not: The behavioral ecology of human food transfers. *Behavioral and Brain Sciences, 27*(4), 543-583.

143. Kaplan, H., & Gurven, M. (2005). The natural history of human food sharing and cooperation: A review and a new multi-individual approach to the negotiation of norms. In H. Gintis, S. Bowles, R. Boyd, & E. Fehr (Eds.), *Moral Sentiments and Material Interests: The Foundations of Cooperation in Economic Life* (pp. 75-113).

144. Gintis, H., Smith, E. A., & Bowles, S. (2001). Costly signaling and cooperation. *Journal of Theoretical Biology, 213*(1), 103-119.

145. Hawkes, K., O'Connell, J. F., & Blurton Jones, N. G. (2001). Hadza meat sharing. *Evolution and Human Behavior, 22*(2), 113-142.

146. Mintz, S. W., & Du Bois, C. M. (2002). The anthropology of food and eating. *Annual Review of Anthropology, 31*, 99-119.

147. Wiessner, P. (2002). The vines of complexity: Egalitarian structures and the institutionalization of inequality among the Enga. *Current Anthropology, 43*(2), 233-269.

148. Fiese, B. H., Foley, K. P., & Spagnola, M. (2006). Routine and ritual elements in family mealtimes: Contexts for child well-being and family identity. *New Directions for Child and Adolescent Development, 2006*(111), 67-89.

149. Larson, R. W., Branscomb, K. R., & Wiley, A. R. (2006). Forms and functions of family mealtimes: Multidisciplinary perspectives. *New Directions for Child and Adolescent Development, 2006*(111), 1-15.

150. Musick, K., & Meier, A. (2012). Assessing causality and persistence in associations between family dinners and adolescent well-being. *Journal of Marriage and Family, 74*(3), 476-493.

151. Sobal, J., & Nelson, M. K. (2003). Commensal eating patterns: A community study. *Appetite, 41*(2), 181-190.

152. DeVault, M. L. (1991). *Feeding the family: The social organization of caring as gendered work*. University of Chicago Press.

153. Locher, J. L., Yoels, W. C., Maurer, D., & van Ells, J. (2005). Comfort foods: An exploratory journey into the social and emotional significance of food. *Food and Foodways, 13*(4), 273-297.

154. Herz, R. S. (2016). The role of odor-evoked memory in psychological and physiological health. *Brain Sciences, 6*(3), 22.

155. Kiecolt-Glaser, J. K., & Newton, T. L. (2001). Marriage and health: His and hers. *Psychological Bulletin, 127*(4), 472-503.

156. Meier, U., & Gressner, A. M. (2004). Endocrine regulation of energy metabolism: Review of pathobiochemical and clinical chemical aspects of leptin, ghrelin, adiponectin, and resistin. *Clinical Chemistry, 50*(9), 1511-1525.

157. MacCormack, J. K., & Muscatell, K. A. (2019). The metabolic mind: A role for leptin and ghrelin in affect and social cognition. *Social and Personality Psychology Compass, 13*(9), Article e12496.

158. Myers, A. (2021). Serotonin & The Gut: The Gut-Brain Axis.

159. Jenkins, T. A., Nguyen, J. C., Polglaze, K. E., & Bertrand, P. P. (2016). Influence of Tryptophan and Serotonin on Mood and Cognition with a Possible Role of the Gut-Brain Axis. *Nutrients, 8*(1), 56.

160. Ke, S., Guimond, A. J., Tworoger, S. S., Huang, T., Chan, A. T., Liu, Y. Y., & Kubzansky, L. D. (2023). Gut feelings: Associations of emotions and emotion regulation with the gut microbiome in women.

161. Zadeh, M. H. (2023). The link between hormone imbalances and smell and taste disorders.

162. Moments Log. (2023). Food and Connection: The Bonding Power of Cooking and Sharing Meals.

163. Appetite For Change. (2024). Social Eating: How Sharing Meals Builds Connection.

164. AckySHINE. (2023). The Intimacy of Food: Nurturing Connection Through Shared Meals and Culinary Adventures.

165. McCarthy, B. W., & McCarthy, E. (2011). *Discovering your couple sexual style: Sharing desire, pleasure, and satisfaction.* Routledge.

166. Baisil, S. (2023, June 11). Cooking across cultures: Strengthening bonds through shared culinary experiences. *Parentzo.*

167. Julier, A. P. (2013). *Eating together: Food, friendship and inequality.* University of Illinois Press.

168. Villares, J. M., & Segovia, M. G. (2006). The family meal: Somewhat more than eating together. *Acta Pediatrica Espanola, 64*(11), 554.

169. Katz, R. (2012). Passing the salt: How eating together creates community.

170. Kremmer, D., Anderson, A. S., & Marshall, D. W. (1998). Living together and eating together: Changes in food choice and eating habits during the transition from single to married/cohabiting. *The Sociological Review, 46*(1), 48-72.

171. Trofholz, A. C., Tate, A. D., Draxten, M. L., Neumark-Sztainer, D., & Berge, J. M. (2018). What's being served for dinner? An exploratory investigation of the associations between the healthfulness of family meals and child dietary intake. *Journal of the Academy of Nutrition and Dietetics, 118*(1), 75-82.

172. Conner, M., & Armitage, C. J. (2002). The social psychology of food. *Open University Press.*

173. Fischler, C. (1988). Food, self and identity. *Social Science Information, 27*(2), 275-292.

174. DeVault, M. L. (1991). *Feeding the family: The social organization of caring as gendered work.* University of Chicago Press.

175. Counihan, C., & Van Esterik, P. (Eds.). (1997). *Food and culture: A reader.* Routledge.

Kind Contributions

176. Boehm, C. (1999). *Hierarchy in the forest: The evolution of egalitarian behavior.* Harvard University Press.

177. Hill, K. (2002). Altruistic cooperation during foraging by the Ache, and the evolved human predisposition to cooperate. *Human Nature, 13*(1), 105-128.

178. Smith, E. A., & Bird, R. L. (2000). Turtle hunting and tombstone opening: Public generosity as costly signaling. *Evolution and Human Behavior, 21*(4), 245-261.

179. Gurven, M., & Hill, K. (2009). Why do men hunt? A reevaluation of "man the hunter" and the sexual division of labor. *Current Anthropology, 50*(1), 51-74.

180. Dyble, M., Salali, G. D., Chaudhary, N., Page, A., Smith, D., Thompson, J., ... & Mace, R. (2015). Sex equality can explain the unique social structure of hunter-gatherer bands. *Science, 348*(6236), 796-798.

181. Henrich, J., & Gil-White, F. J. (2001). The evolution of prestige: Freely conferred deference as a mechanism for enhancing the benefits of cultural transmission. *Evolution and Human Behavior, 22*(3), 165-196.

182. Wiessner, P. (2014). Embers of society: Firelight talk among the Ju/'hoansi Bushmen. *Proceedings of the National Academy of Sciences, 111*(39), 14027-14035.

183. Lee, R. B., & DeVore, I. (Eds.). (1968). *Man the Hunter: The First Intensive Survey of a Single, Crucial Stage of Human Development—Man's Once Universal Hunting Way of Life*. Chicago: Aldine.

184. Lee, R. B. (1979). *The !Kung San: Men, Women, and Work in a Foraging Society*. Cambridge: Cambridge University Press.

185. Lee, R. B., & DeVore, I. (Eds.). (1976). *Kalahari Hunter-Gatherers: Studies of the !Kung San and Their Neighbors*. Cambridge, MA: Harvard University Press.

186. Wilson, E. O., Nowak, M. A., & Tarnita, C. E. (2010). The evolution of eusociality. *Nature, 466*(7310), 1057-1062.

187. Foster, K. R., Wenseleers, T., & Ratnieks, F. L. W. (2006). Kin Selection is the key to Altruism. *Trends in Ecology & Evolution, 21*(2), 57-60.

188. Tomasello, M., Melis, A. P., Tennie, C., Wyman, E., & Herrmann, E. (2012). Two key steps in the evolution of human cooperation: The interdependence hypothesis. *Current Anthropology, 53*(6), 673-692.

189. Platt, M. L., & Seyfarth, R. M. (2012). The social brain. *Nature Neuroscience, 15*(12), 1726-1729.

190. Marsh, A. A. (2016). Neural, cognitive, and evolutionary foundations of human Altruism. *Wiley Interdisciplinary Reviews: Cognitive Science, 7*(1), 59-71.

191. de Waal, F. B. (2008). Putting the Altruism back into Altruism: the evolution of empathy. *Annual Review of Psychology, 59*, 279-300.

192. Buck, R. (2011). Communicative genes in the evolution of empathy and Altruism. *Behavioral Genetics, 41*(6), 876-888.

193. Preston, S. D. (2013). The origins of Altruism in offspring care. *Psychological Bulletin, 139*(6), 1305-1341.

194. Yamamoto, S. (2017). Primate empathy: Three factors and their combinations for empathy-related phenomena. *Wiley Interdisciplinary Reviews: Cognitive Science, 8*(3), e1431.

195. Rhoads, S. A., O'Connell, K., Berluti, K., Ploe, M. L., Elizabeth, H. S., Amormino, P., Li, J. L., Dutton, M. A., VanMeter, A. S., & Marsh, A. A. (2023). Neural responses underlying extraordinary altruists' generosity for socially distant others. *PNAS Nexus, 2*(7), pgad199.

196. (2020). Reciprocal Altruism Theory: Selfish Selflessness. Shortform Books.

197. (2020). A History of Modern Philanthropy.

198. SOFII. (2011). Philanthropy in ancient times: Some early examples from the Mediterranean.

199. Encyclopaedia Britannica. (2024). *Philanthropy | Definition, History, & Facts.*

200. Bremner, R. H. (1988). *American Philanthropy.* University of Chicago Press.

201. Dossey, L. (2018). The helper's high. *Explore, 14*(6), 393-399.

202. PubMed. (2017). Altruistic behavior: Mapping responses in the brain. *PubMed.*

203. Baumgartner, T., Knoch, D., Hotz, P., Eisenegger, C., & Fehr, E. (2011). Dorsolateral and ventromedial prefrontal cortex orchestrate normative choice. *Nature Neuroscience, 14*(11), 1468-1474.

204. Christov-Moore, L., & Iacoboni, M. (2016). Self-other resonance, its control and prosocial inclinations: Brain-behavior relationships. *Human Brain Mapping, 37*(4), 1544-1558.

205. Mathur, V., Harada, T., Lipke, T., & Chiao, J. (2010). Neural basis of extraordinary empathy and altruistic motivation. *NeuroImage, 51*(4), 1468-1475.

206. Moll, J., Krueger, F., Zahn, R., Pardini, M., de Oliveira-Souza, R., & Grafman, J. (2006). Human fronto-mesolimbic networks guide decisions about charitable donation. *Proceedings of the National Academy of Sciences, 103*(42), 15623-15628.

207. Post, S. G. (2005). Altruism, happiness, and health: it's good to be good. *International Journal of Behavioral Medicine, 12*(2), 66-77.

208. Rowland, L., & Curry, O. S. (2018). A range of kindness activities boost happiness. *Journal of Social Psychology, 158*(3), 313-330.

209. Suttie, J. (2021, February 17). How Kindness Fits Into a Happy Life. *Greater Good Magazine.*

210. Dixon, A. (2011, September 6). Kindness Makes You Happy... and Happiness Makes You.... *Greater Good Magazine.*

211. American Psychological Association. (2020). When doing good boosts health, well-being.

212. Martin, M. W. (1994). Virtuous giving: Philanthropy, voluntary service, and caring. Indiana University Press.

213. Dees, J. G. (2012). A tale of two cultures: Charity, problem solving, and the future of social entrepreneurship. *Journal of Business Ethics, 111*, 321-334.

214. Jaffe, D. T., & Lane, S. H. (2004). Sustaining a family dynasty: Key issues facing complex multigenerational business-and investment-owning families. *Family Business Review, 17*(1), 81-98.

215. Gillis-Paulgaard, S. (2016, December 6). The important role communications plays in fundraising campaigns. *Take Roots.*

216. Rockefeller Philanthropy Advisors. (2023). *Giving as a Couple.*

217. National Center for Family Philanthropy. (2021, May 16). *Legacy in Family Philanthropy: A Modern Framework.*

218. Legacy. (2023). *Charitable Giving Decisions Made By U.S. Couples.*

219. Putnam Consulting Group. (2023). *Clarifying Your Philanthropic Legacy: A Guide for Families and Foundation Leaders.*

220. Philanthropy Associates, LLC. (2021). *Couples & Families.*

221. Laskey, D. (2016). Marrying Philanthropy: When Couples Choose to Give Rather than Get. *Non Profit News* | Nonprofit Quarterly.

222. Foundation Source. (2024). Balancing Collective and Individual Interests in Family Philanthropy.

223. Aperio Philanthropy. (2019). How to make time for relationships.

224. Giving Compass. (2021, August 19). Navigating Philanthropy as a Nextgen Donor.

225. National Center for Family Philanthropy (NCFP). (n.d.). *Navigating Family Philanthropy*: Choosing Your Social Impact Strategies.

Adventurous Bonding

226. Smithsonian Institution's Human Origins Program. (2022, June 29). *Terra Amata Shelter*

227. Britannica. (n.d.). *Terra Amata* | archaeological site in southern France.

228. de Lumley, H. (2007). *La Grande Histoire des premiers hommes européens*. Paris: Odile Jacob.

229. Villa, P. (1983). *Terra Amata and the Middle Pleistocene archaeological record of southern France.* Berkeley: University of California Press.

230. Rosenbaum, S., Vigilant, L., Kuzawa, C. W., & Stoinski, T. S. (2018). Caring for infants is associated with increased reproductive success for male mountain gorillas. Scientific reports, 8(1), 15223.

231. JSTOR. (2018). *Maternal influences on primate social development.*

232. Fashing, P. J. (2001). Male and female strategies during intergroup encounters in guerezas (Colobus guereza): evidence for resource defense

mediated through males and a comparison with other primates. Behavioral Ecology and Sociobiology, 50, 219-230.

233. Leivers, S., & Simmons, L. W. (2014). Human sperm competition: playing a defensive strategy. *Advances in the Study of Behavior*, 46, 1-44.

234. Henderson, K. A., Bialeschki, M. D., Shaw, S. M., & Freysinger, V. J. (1989). A leisure of one's own: A feminist perspective on women's leisure. *Venture Publishing*.

235. Cole, E., Rothblum, E. D., & Tallman, E. M. (2014). Wilderness therapy for women: The power of adventure. Routledge.

236. Little, D. E. (2002). Women and adventure recreation: Reconstructing leisure constraints and adventure experiences to negotiate continuing participation. *Journal of Leisure Research*, 34(2), 157-177.

237. Buss, D. M. (2005). The handbook of evolutionary psychology. John Wiley & Sons.

238. Kenrick, D. T., Griskevicius, V., Neuberg, S. L., & Schaller, M. (2010). Renovating the pyramid of needs: Contemporary extensions built upon ancient foundations. *Perspectives on Psychological Science*, 5(3), 292-314.

239. Shen, A. (2016). Bad Girls throughout History: 100 Remarkable Women Who Changed the World. Chronicle Books.

240. Engle, B. S. (1942). the Amazons in ancient Greece. The Psychoanalytic Quarterly, 11(4), 512-554.

241. Howell, G. (2010). Gertrude Bell: Queen of the desert, shaper of nations. Farrar, Straus and Giroux.

242. Hughes, J. D. (1990). Artemis: Goddess of conservation. Forest and conservation history, 34(4), 191-197.

243. Boniface, M. (2006). The meaning of adventurous activities for 'women in the outdoors'. *Journal of Adventure Education & Outdoor Learning*, 6(1), 9-24.

244. Arnould, J., & Venayre, S. (2015). *The History and Philosophy of Adventure*. Public Books.

245. Bennett, R. M. (2022). OUTDOOR-ADVENTURE-PLAY INTERVENTIONS (OAPIS): A FOREST OF FACTORS.

246. Morrison, S. M. (2023). *Overcoming Infertility Together: Expanding the Theory of Resilience and Relational Load* (Doctoral dissertation, University of Missouri-Columbia).

247. Levoy, G. Psychology Today. (2021). Adrenaline Makes the Heart Grow Fonder.

248. Dufnet. (2023). Exploring the Intersection of Adrenaline and Love.

249. McKendree University. (2011). The Effects of Adrenaline on Arousal and Attraction.

250. Science in the News. (2017). *Love, Actually*: The science behind lust, attraction, and companionship.

251. White, G. L., Fishbein, S., & Rutsein, J. (1981). Passionate love and the misattribution of arousal. *Journal of Personality and Social Psychology*, 41(1), 56.

252. Hyman, I. E., Jr. (2010). Is This Love Or Too Much Caffeine? Misattributions of Arousal Strengthen Relationships. *Psychology Today*.

253. Neurodivergent Insights. (2023). Unmasking Emotions: The Science of Misattribution in Social Psychology.

254. Practical Psychology. (2023). Misattribution of Arousal (Definition + Examples)

255. Wu, J. *Psychology Today.* (2020). The Power of Oxytocin.

256. Khajehei, M., & Behroozpour, E. (2018). Endorphins, oxytocin, sexuality and romantic relationships: An understudied area. *World Journal of Obstetrics and Gynecology,* 7(2), 17-23.

257. Purdy, E. (2018, January 4). 20 *Natural Ways to Increase GABA and Serotonin to Help Your Anxiety.*

258. Cutler, A. J., Mattingly, G. W., & Maletic, V. (2023). Understanding the mechanism of action and clinical effects of neuroactive steroids and GABAergic compounds in major depressive disorder. *Translational psychiatry,* 13(1), 228.

259. Zuckerman, M. (2006). Biosocial bases of sensation seeking. *Biology of personality and individual differences,* 37-59.

260. Cognitive Neuroscience Society. (2013, August 1). How Testosterone Affects Risk-Taking in Adolescent Boys and Girls.

261. Vermeersch, H., T'Sjoen, G., Kaufman, J. M., & Vincke, J. (2008). The role of testosterone in aggressive and non-aggressive risk-taking in adolescent boys. *Hormones and behavior,* 53(3), 463–471.

262. Rehbein, E., Kogler, L., Hornung, J., Morawetz, C., Bayer, J., Krylova, M., Sundström-Poromaa, I., & Derntl, B. (2021). Estradiol administration modulates neural emotion regulation. *Psychoneuroendocrinology,* 134, 105425. Advance online publication.

263. Sharma, R., Cameron, A., Fang, Z., Ismail, N., & Smith, A. (2021). The regulatory roles of progesterone and estradiol on emotion processing in women. *Cognitive, affective & behavioral neuroscience,* 21(5), 1026–1038

264. Sagebrush Counseling. (2024). Exploring the Science Behind Adventure's Impact on Relationships.

265. Abrams, Z. (2023, May 11). The science of why friendships keep us healthy

266. Clough, P., Houge Mackenzie, S., Mallabon, L., & Brymer, E. (2016). Adventurous physical activity environments: a mainstream intervention for mental health. *Sports Medicine, 46*, 963-968.

267. Pomfret, G., & Varley, P. (2019). Families at leisure outdoors: well-being through adventure. *Leisure studies*, 38(4), 494-508.

268. Brymer, E., & Schweitzer, R. (2013). Extreme sports are good for your health: A phenomenological understanding of fear and anxiety in extreme sport. *Journal of Health Psychology,* 18(4), 477-487.

269. Buckley, R. (2018). Adventure Therapy: Theory, Research, and Practice. *Routledge.*

270. Posten, A. (2021). The Importance of Mental and Physical Fitness Prep - *Adventure 101.*

271. Terrapin Adventures. (2017). The Mental and Physical Benefits of Outdoor Adventures for Adults.

272. Pashley, T. (2019). Physical, Social, Emotional and Intellectual Benefits of Outdoor Recreation.

273. Warrell, M. (2013). Stop Playing Safe: Rethink Risk, Unlock the Power of Courage, Achieve Outstanding Success. *John Wiley & Sons.*

274. Barton, B. (2006). Safety, risk and adventure in outdoor activities. *Safety, Risk and Adventure in Outdoor Activities,* 1-200.

Spiritual Bonding

275. Wightman, G. J. (2014). The origins of religion in the Paleolithic. rowman & littlefield.

276. Renfrew, C., Morley, I., & Boyd, M. (Eds.). (2015). *Ritual, Play and Belief in Evolution and Early Human Societies.*

277. Bellah, R. N. (2011). Religion in human evolution: From the Paleolithic to the Axial Age. Harvard University Press.

278. Gowlett, J., Gamble, C., & Dunbar, R. (2012). Human evolution and the archaeology of the social brain. *Current Anthropology,* 53(6), 693-722.

279. Renfrew, C., Morley, I., & Boyd, M. (Eds.). (2015). Ritual, Play, and Belief in Early Human Societies. *School of Anthropology & Museum Ethnography.*

280. Karandashev, V. (2015). The Cultural Evolution of Human Bonding - *The Diversity of Love.*

281. Torrey, E. Fuller, 'Ancestors and Agriculture: A Spiritual Self', Evolving Brains, Emerging Gods: Early Humans and the Origins of Religion (New York, NY, 2017; online edn, Columbia Scholarship Online, 24 Jan. 2019),

282. Sheldrake, P (2019). A Brief History of Spirituality: From Ancient Traditions to Modern Practices. All Divinity.

283. Cartwright, M. (2018). Ancient Greek Religion. World History Encyclopedia.

284. Mahoney, A. (2013). The spirituality of us: Relational spirituality in the context of family relationships.

285. Kellert, S. R., & Farnham, T. (Eds.). (2013*). The good in nature and humanity*: connecting science, religion, and spirituality with the natural world. Island Press.

286. Starr, C. G. (1991). A history of the ancient world. Oxford University Press, USA.

287. Thornton, B. S. (2018). Eros: the myth of ancient Greek sexuality. *Routledge.*

288. Basham, A. L. (1991). The origins and development of classical Hinduism. Oxford University Press, USA.

289. Sheldrake, P. (2012). Spirituality: A very short introduction. OUP Oxford.

290. Trainor, K. (Ed.). (2004). Buddhism: The illustrated guide. *Oxford University Press, USA.*

291. Feuerstein, G. (2003). The deeper dimension of yoga: Theory and practice. Shambhala Publications.

292. Ryan Z. Cortazar. Harvard Gazette. (2007, April 26). Scholar: Cave paintings show religious sophistication.

293. Britannica. (2023). Cave art | Definition, Characteristics, Images, & Facts.

294. Wikipedia. (2024). Paleolithic religion.

295. Teasdale, W. (2001). The mystic heart: Discovering a universal spirituality in the world's religions. New World Library.

296. De Michelis, E. (2005). A history of modern yoga: Patanjali and western esotericism. A&C Black.

297. Altglas, V. (2014). From yoga to kabbalah: Religious exoticism and the logics of bricolage. *Oxford University Press, USA.*

298. Ferngren, G. B. (2014). Medicine and religion: A historical introduction. JHU Press.

299. Clark, R. (2003). The sacred magic of ancient Egypt: The spiritual practice restored. Llewellyn Worldwide.

300. Eltorai, I. M. (2019). A Spotlight on the History of Ancient Egyptian Medicine. CRC Press.

301. Kaeuper, R. W. (2009). Holy Warriors: The Religious Ideology of Chivalry. University of Pennsylvania Press.

302. Bumke, J. (1991). Courtly culture: Literature and society in the high middle ages. *Univ of California Press.*

303. Boase, R. (1977). The origin and meaning of courtly love: a critical study of European scholarship. *Manchester University Press.*

304. Oord, T. J. (2010). Defining love: A philosophical, scientific, and theological engagement. Brazos Press.

305. Lazăr, M. (2015). Islam: Faith and Practice. *AnALize: Revista de studii feministe,* (4 (18)), 7-30.

306. Lavee, Y., & Katz, R. (2003). The family in Israel: Between tradition and modernity. *Marriage & Family Review,* 35(1-2), 193-217.

307. Lesthaeghe, R., & Neidert, L. (2006). The second demographic transition in the United States: Exception or textbook example? *Population and Development Review,* 32(4), 669-698.

308. Wang, W., & Parker, K. C. (2014). Record share of Americans have never married: As values, economics and gender patterns change. Washington DC: Pew Research Center, Social & Demographic Trends Project.

309. Esteve, A., Lesthaeghe, R., & López-Gay, A. (2012). The Latin American cohabitation boom, 1970–2007. *Population and Development Review,* 38(1), 55-81.

310. McAloney, K. (2013). Inter-faith relationships in Great-Britain: Prevalence and implications for psychological well-being. *Mental Health, Religion, & Culture,* 16(7), 686-694.

311. Pew Research Center. (2016, October 26). One in five adults were raised in interfaith homes: A closer look at religious mixing in American families.

312. Yahya, S., & Boag, S. (2014). "My family would crucify me!": The perceived influence of social pressure on cross-cultural and interfaith dating and marriage. *Sexuality and Culture,* 18, 759-772.

313. Murphy, C. (2015, June 2). Interfaith marriage is common in U.S., particularly among the recently wed. Pew Research Center.

314. Edwards, S. (2018). Religion and culture intertwined. *In JCC Connexions,* Vol. 8, No. 4. NASPA - Student Affairs Administrators in Higher Education.

315. Connell, E. G. (2012). Soulmates: A phenomenological study of women who believe they knew their romantic partner in a previous lifetime. Alliant International University.

316. Richardson, R. D. (1995). Emerson: The mind on fire. University of California Press.

317. Gura, P. F. (2007). American Transcendentalism: A History. Hill and Wang.

318. Emerson, R. W. (2009). *Nature and Other Essays.* Dover Publications.

319. Keltner, D., & Haidt, J. (2003). Approaching awe, a moral, spiritual, and aesthetic emotion. *Cognition and Emotion,* 17(2), 297-314.

320. Fredrickson, B. L., & Joiner, T. (2002). Positive emotions trigger upward spirals toward emotional well-being. *Psychological Science,* 13(2), 172-175.

321. Kabat-Zinn, J. (1994). Wherever you go, there you are: Mindfulness meditation in everyday life. Hyperion.

322. Davidson, R. J., & Lutz, A. (2008). Buddha's Brain: Neuroplasticity and Meditation. *IEEE Signal Processing Magazine,* 25(1), 176-174.

323. Walsh, R., & Shapiro, S. L. (2006). The meeting of meditative disciplines and Western psychology: A mutually enriching dialogue. *American Psychologist,* 61(3), 227-239.

324. Laski, M. (1961). Ecstasy in secular and religious experiences. *J.P. Tarcher.*

325. Newberg, A., & Waldman, M. R. (2009). How God changes your brain: Breakthrough findings from a leading neuroscientist. *Ballantine Books.*

326. Carter, C. S. (1998). Neuroendocrine perspectives on social attachment and love. *Psychoneuroendocrinology,* 23(8), 779-818.

327. Uvnäs-Moberg, K., Handlin, L., & Petersson, M. (2015). Oxytocin linked to social interaction. In Choleris, E., Pfaff, D. W., & Kavaliers, M. (Eds.), Oxytocin, vasopressin and related peptides in the regulation of behavior. Cambridge University Press.

328. Zak, P. J. (2012). The moral molecule: The source of love and prosperity. Dutton

329. Stevens, J. (1990). John Denver: Rocky Mountain High. Cherry Lane Music.

330. Partably. (2020). The Default Mode Network: The Hidden Key to a Calmer, Happier, Content You.

331. Hasson, U., Yang, E., Vallines, I., Heeger, D. J., & Rubin, N. (2008). A hierarchy of temporal receptive windows in human cortex. *Journal of Neuroscience, 28*(10), 2539-2550.

332. Greicius, M. D., Supekar, K., Menon, V., & Dougherty, R. F. (2009). Resting-state functional connectivity reflects structural connectivity in the default mode network. *Cerebral Cortex, 19*(1), 72-78.

333. Mindworks Staff. (2024). *Meditation for Healing the Autonomic Nervous System (ANS)*. Mindworks.

334. Bratman, G. N., Daily, G. C., Levy, B. J., & Gross, J. J. (2015). The benefits of nature experience: Improved affect and cognition. *Landscape and Urban Planning, 138*, 41-50.

335. Klisanin, D. (2022). Rewild Yourself with Mindfulness Meditation in Nature. *Psychology Today.*

336. Mahoney, A. (2010). Religion in families 1999–2009: A relational spirituality framework. *Journal of Marriage and Family, 72*(4), 805-827.

337. Fincham, F. D., Stanley, S. M., & Beach, S. R. (2007). Spiritual behaviors and relationship satisfaction: A critical analysis of the role of prayer. *Journal of Social and Clinical Psychology, 26*(7), 760-775.

338. Goodman, M. A., & Dollahite, D. C. (2006). How religious couples perceive the influence of God in their marriage. *Review of Religious Research, 48*(2), 141-155.

339. Larson, L. E., & Goltz, J. W. (1989). Religious participation and marital commitment. *Review of Religious Research, 30*(4), 387-400.

340. Dollahite, D. C., & Lambert, N. M. (2007). Forsaking all others: How religious involvement promotes marital fidelity in Christian, Jewish, and Muslim couples. *Review of Religious Research, 48*(3), 290-307.

341. Wilcox, W. B., & Wolfinger, N. H. (2008). Then comes marriage? Religion, race, and marriage in urban America. *Social Science Research, 37*(2), 471-489.

342. Goldsmith, B. (2023). Why Compassion Is So Important for a Romantic Relationship.

343. Müller, N. (2020, November 25). Cultivating Peace: Buddhist-Inspired Approaches to Conflict Resolution. *Buddhistdoor Global.*

344. Buddhistdoor Global. (2020, March 20). Buddhism and Conflict Resolution.

345. Kobe, R. (2023). From the Heart. Richmond Kobe.

346. Abdul Cader, A. (2017). Islamic principles of conflict management: A model for human resource management. *International Journal of Cross Cultural Management,* 17(3), 345-363.

347. Shah, K. H. Relevance of Non-violence In The Modern World with Special Reference To Jainism.

348. Chinna Natesan, N., Keeffe, M. J., & Darling, J. R. (2009). Enhancement of global business practices: lessons from the Hindu Bhagavad Gita. *European Business Review,* 21(2), 128-143.

349. McCullough, M. E., Bono, G., & Root, L. M. (2005). *Religion and forgiveness. Handbook of the psychology of religion and spirituality,* 394-411.

350. Kippenberg, H. (2002). Discovering Religious History in the Modern Age. Princeton University Press.

351. Glasson, T. (2012). Mastering Christianity: Missionary Anglicanism and Slavery in the Atlantic World.

352. Sirota, B. S. (2014). The Christian Monitors: The Church of England and the Age of Benevolence, 1680-1730. Yale University Press.

353. Flood, G. (2002). The importance of religion: Meaning and action in our strange world. Oxford, UK: Blackwell Publishers.

354. Taylor, C. (2007). A secular age. Cambridge, MA: Harvard University Press.

355. The Biblical Truth. (2023, February 27). Practical wisdom for modern believers: Applying Paul's teachings to everyday life.

356. Thich Nhat Hanh. (1998). The heart of the Buddha's teaching: Transforming suffering into peace, joy, and liberation. Berkeley, CA: Parallax Press.

357. Eck, D. L. (2001). A new religious America: How a "Christian country" has become the world's most religiously diverse nation. San Francisco, CA: HarperSanFrancisco.

358. Barnes, L. L., Plotnikoff, G. A., Fox, K., & Pendleton, S. (2000). Spirituality, religion, and pediatrics: Intersecting worlds of healing. *Pediatrics,* 106(Supplement_3), 899-908.

359. De Waal, F. B., & De Waal, F. B. M. (1990). Peacemaking among primates. Harvard University Press.

Physical Presence

360. De Waal, F. B., & Lanting, F. (2023). Bonobo: The forgotten ape. Univ of California Press.

361. Jablonski, N. G. (2020). Social and affective touch in primates and its role in the evolution of social cohesion. *Neuroscience, 448*, 188-204.

362. Dunbar, R. I. (2010). The social role of touch in humans and primates: Behavioral function and neurobiological mechanisms. *Neuroscience and Biobehavioral Reviews, 34*(2), 260-268.

363. Grandi, L. C. (2016). From sweeping to the caress: Similarities and discrepancies between human and non-human primates' pleasant touch. Frontiers in Psychology, 7, 1371.

364. Simpson, E. A., Maylott, S. E., Lazo, R. J., Leonard, K. A., Kaburu, S. S. K., Suomi, S. J., Paukner, A., & Ferrari, P. F. (2019). Social touch alters newborn monkey behavior. *Infant Behavior and Development, 57*, 101368.

365. Harlow, H. F. (1958). The nature of love. *American Psychologist, 13*(12), 673-685.

366. Harlow, H. F., & Zimmermann, R. R. (1959). Affectional responses in the infant monkey. *Science, 130*(3373), 421-432.

367. Rutter, M. (1979). Maternal deprivation, 1972-1978: New findings, new concepts, new approaches. *Child Development*, 50(2), 283-305.

368. Schaffer, H. R., & Emerson, P. E. (1964). The development of social attachments in infancy. Monographs of the Society for Research in Child Development, 29(3), 1-77.

369. Nelson, C. A. (2007). A neurobiological perspective on early human deprivation. *Child Development Perspectives, 1*(1), 13-18.

370. Feldman, R. (2016). The neurobiology of mammalian parenting and the biosocial context of human caregiving. Hormones and behavior, 77, 3-17.

371. Couture, B. N. (2016). A Subjective Experience of Maternal Attachment With Premature Infants Through Skin-to-Skin Contact (Doctoral dissertation, The Chicago School of Professional Psychology).

372. Field, T. (2014). Touch. MIT press.

373. Zeanah, C. H., Nelson, C. A., Fox, N. A., & Smyke, A. T. (2012). A randomized clinical trial of foster care as an intervention for early institutionalization: Long-term improvements in white matter microstructure. *JAMA Pediatrics*, 166(3), 211-219.

374. Gibbons, C. H. (2019). Basics of autonomic nervous system function. Handbook of clinical neurology, 160, 407-418.

375. Emmons, R. A. (2007). Thanks!: How the new science of gratitude can make you happier. Houghton Mifflin Harcourt.

376. Rakel, D. (2018). The compassionate connection: The healing power of empathy and mindful listening. WW Norton & Company.

377. Sorokowski, P., Kowal, M., Sternberg, R. J., Aavik, T., Akello, G., Alhabah-ba, M. M., ... & Sorokowska, A. (2023). Modernization, collectivism, and gender equality predict love experiences in 45 countries. *Scientific reports,* 13(1), 773.

378. Nummenmaa, L., Tuominen, L., Dunbar, R., Hirvonen, J., Manninen, S., Arponen, E., Machin, A., Hari, R., Jääskeläinen, I. P., & Sams, M. (2016). Social touch modulates endogenous μ-opioid system activity in humans. *NeuroImage,* 138, 242

379. Barnett, R., & Rivers, C. (2009). Same difference: How gender myths are hurting our relationships, our children, and our jobs. *Hachette UK.*

380. Fisher, H. (2016). Anatomy of love: A natural history of mating, marriage, and why we stray (completely revised and updated with a new introduction). WW Norton & Company.

381. Jakubiak, B. K., & Feeney, B. C. (2017). Affectionate touch to promote relational, psychological, and physical well-being in adulthood: A theoretical model and review of the research. Personality and Social Psychology Review, 21(3), 228-252.

382. Gardner, A., & West, S. A. (2014). Inclusive Fitness: 50 years on. Philosophical Transactions of the Royal Society B: *Biological Sciences,* 369(1642), 20130356.

383. Schmidt, R. A., & Voss, B. L. (2005). *Archaeologies of sexuality. Routledge.*

384. Jacobs, S. E., Thomas, W., & Lang, S. (Eds.). (1997). Two-spirit people: Native American gender identity, sexuality, and spirituality. University of Illinois Press.

385. Roughgarden, J. (2013). Evolution's rainbow: Diversity, gender, and sexuality in nature and people. Univ of California Press.

386. Christov-Moore, L., Simpson, E. A., Coudé, G., Grigaityte, K., Iacoboni, M., & Ferrari, P. F. (2014). Empathy: Gender effects in brain and behavior. *Neuroscience & biobehavioral reviews,* 46, 604-627.

387. Lehmiller, J. (2020). The Power of Touch: Physical Affection is Important in Relationships, but Some People Need More Than Others.

388. Ben-Ze'ev, A. (n.d.). Why a Lover's Touch Is So Powerful. Psychology Today.

389. Brown, G. (2018). Why Physical Touch Is So Important in Relationships.

390. Thompson, J. L. (2024). The Power of Physical Touch and Affection: A Key to Emotional Well-Being.

391. Botnick, V. (n.d.). How to Balance Dependence and Independence in a Relationship.

392. Kendrick, D. (n.d.). Finding the Balance Between Dependence and Independence in Relationships. Dan Kendrick Counseling Longmont.

Inspirational Support

393. Raglin, J. S. (2001). Factors in exercise adherence: Influence of spouse participation. *Quest,* 53(3), 356-361.

394. Maziriri, E. T., Nyagadza, B., Maramura, T. C., & Mapuranga, M. (2022). "Like mom and dad": using narrative analysis to understand how couplepreneurs stimulate their kids' entrepreneurial mindset. Journal of Entrepreneurship in Emerging Economies, (ahead-of-print).

395. Brock, T. (2010). Young adults and higher education: Barriers and breakthroughs to success. The future of children, 109-132.

396. G&G Fitness Equipment. (n.d.). Fit to be in love: a couples workout plan.

397. Klem, M. L., Wing, R. R., McGuire, M. T., Seagle, H. M., & Hill, J. O. (1997). A descriptive study of individuals successful at long-term maintenance of substantial weight loss. *American Journal of Clinical Nutrition*, 66(2), 239-246.

398. 3Catenacci, V. A., Odgen, L., Phelan, S., Thomas, J. G., Hill, J., Wing, R. R., & Wyatt, H. (2014). Dietary habits and weight maintenance success in high versus low exercisers in the National Weight Control Registry. *Journal of Physical Activity and Health,* 11(8), 1540-1548

399. Klem, M. L., Wing, R. R., McGuire, M. T., Seagle, H. M., & Hill, J. O. (1998). Psychological symptoms in individuals successful at long-term maintenance of weight loss. *Health Psychology*, 17(4), 336-345.

400. King, S. (2000). On writing: A memoir of the craft. Simon and Schuster.

401. Andrews, L. (2024, February 19). What the National Weight Control Registry Tells Us About Weight Loss. *Food and Health Communications*.

402. Townsend, L. (2022) Nine masterworks that almost never happened. PBS.

403. Whiten, A. (2000). Primate culture and social learning. *Cognitive Science*, 24(3), 477-508.

404. Want, S. C., & Harris, P. L. (2002). How do children ape? Applying concepts from the study of non-human primates to the developmental study of 'imitation'in children. *Developmental Science*, 5(1), 1-14.

405. Van Overwalle, F. (2009). Social cognition and the brain: a meta-analysis. *Human brain mapping,* 30(3), 829-858.

406. Adolphs, R. (2009). The social brain: neural basis of social knowledge. *Annual review of psychology,* 60, 693-716.

407. Hari, R., & Kujala, M. V. (2009). Brain basis of human social interaction: from concepts to brain imaging. *Physiological reviews,* 89(2), 453-479.

408. Young, L., & Koenigs, M. (2007). Investigating emotion in moral cognition: a review of evidence from functional neuroimaging and neuropsychology. *British Medical Bulletin,* 84, 69-79.

409. Hathaway, B. (2013). Research in the News: Evolution of thought: new thinking on how the human brain developed.

410. Wood, J. N. (2003). Social cognition and the prefrontal cortex. *Behavioural and Cognitive Neuroscience Reviews,* 2(2), 97-114.

411. Wiessner, P. (2014). Cooperation and the evolution of hunter-gatherer storytelling. *Nature Communications,* 5, 5101.

412. Darling, L. T. (2013). A history of social justice and political power in the Middle East: The circle of justice from Mesopotamia to globalization. Routledge.

413. Kovacs, M. G. (1989). The epic of Gilgamesh. Stanford University Press.

414. Dalley, S. (Ed.). (1998). Myths from Mesopotamia: creation, the flood, Gilgamesh, and others. Oxford University Press, USA.

415. Tigay, J. H. (2002). The evolution of the Gilgamesh epic. Bolchazy-Carducci Publishers.

416. Woods, P. R., & Lamond, D. A. (2011). What would Confucius do?–Confucian ethics and self-regulation in management. *Journal of Business Ethics,* 102, 669-683.

417. Lambert, A. (2022). Friendship in the Confucian Tradition. The Routledge Handbook of Philosophy of Friendship.

418. Gandhi, M., & SCHEDULE, T. (2014). Mahatma Gandhi. Columbia.

419. Mandela, N. (1990). Nelson Mandela: the struggle is my life: his speeches and writings brought together with historical documents and accounts of Mandela in prison by fellow-prisoners. Popular Prakashan.

420. Mandela, N. (2008). Long walk to freedom: The autobiography of Nelson Mandela. Hachette UK.

421. McCarty, L. T. (2009). Coretta Scott King: A Biography. Bloomsbury Publishing USA.

422. King, C. S. (2020). Coretta Scott King: An Unyielding Voice for Change.

423. Oakes, E. H. (2007). Encyclopedia of world scientists. Infobase Publishing.

424. House, J. S., Umberson, D., & Landis, K. R. (1988). Structures and processes of social support. *Annual review of sociology,* 14(1), 293-318.

425. Shumaker, S. A., & Brownell, A. (1984). Toward a theory of social support: Closing conceptual gaps. *Journal of social issues,* 40(4), 11-36.

426. Darley, J. M., & Latané, B. (1968). Bystander intervention in emergencies: diffusion of responsibility. *Journal of personality and social psychology,* 8(4p1), 377.

427. Latané, B. (1981). The psychology of social impact. American psychologist, 36(4), 343.

428. Lieberman, M. D. (2013). Social: Why our brains are wired to connect. OUP Oxford.

429. Ashar, Y. K., Andrews-Hanna, J. R., Dimidjian, S., & Wager, T. D. (2016). Toward a neuroscience of compassion. *Positive neuroscience,* 125-142.

430. Atzil, S., Hendler, T., & Feldman, R. (2014). The brain basis of social synchrony. *Social cognitive and affective neuroscience,* 9(8), 1193-1202.

431. House, J. S. (1981). Work stress and social support. Addison-Wesley.

432. Thorsteinsson, E. B., & James, J. (1999). A meta-analysis of the effects of experimental manipulations of social support during laboratory stress. *Psychology & Health,* 14(5), 869-886.

433. Watson, D., Clark, L. A., & Tellegen, A. (1988). Development and validation of brief measures of positive and negative affect: The PANAS scales. *Journal of Personality and Social Psychology,* 54(6), 1063-1070.

434. Closa Leon, T., Nouwen, A., & Sheffield, D. (2007). Social support and individual variability in patterns of haemodynamic reactivity and recovery. *Journal of Health Psychology,* 12(3), 475-487.

435. Snydersmith, M. A., & Cacioppo, J. T. (1992). Parsing complex social factors to determine component effects: I. Autonomic activity and reactivity as a function of human association. *Journal of Social and Clinical Psychology,* 11(3), 215-228.

436. Sullivan, K. T., & Davila, J. (Eds.). (2010). Support processes in intimate relationships. Oxford University Press.

437. Ellsworth, P. C., & Smith, C. A. (1988). From appraisal to emotion: Differences among unpleasant feelings. *Motivation and Emotion,* 12(3), 271-302.

438. Taibbi, R. (2018). Active vs. passive partners: How to stop the power struggle. Psychology Today.

439. Feldman, R. (2012). Oxytocin and social affiliation in humans. *Hormones and behavior,* 61(3), 380-391.

440. Li, S. C. (2003). Biocultural orchestration of developmental plasticity across levels: the interplay of biology and culture in shaping the mind and behavior across the life span. *Psychological bulletin,* 129(2), 171.

441. Staudinger, U. M. (2020). The positive plasticity of adult development: Potential for the 21st century. *American Psychologist*, 75(4), 540.

442. Mattson, M. P. (2015). Lifelong brain health is a lifelong challenge: from evolutionary principles to empirical evidence. *Ageing research reviews*, 20, 37-45.

443. Immordino-Yang, M. H., Darling-Hammond, L., & Krone, C. R. (2019). Nurturing nature: How brain development is inherently social and emotional, and what this means for education. *Educational Psychologist*, 54(3), 185-204.

444. Allman, J. M., Hakeem, A., Erwin, J. M., Nimchinsky, E., & Hof, P. (2001). The anterior cingulate cortex. The evolution of an interface between emotion and cognition. *Annals of the New York Academy of Sciences*, 935, 107-117.

445. Dixon, M. L., Thiruchselvam, R., Todd, R., & Christoff, K. (2017). Emotion and the prefrontal cortex: An integrative review. *Psychological bulletin*, 143(10), 1033.

446. Bastian, B., Jetten, J., Hornsey, M. J., & Leknes, S. (2014). The positive consequences of pain: A biopsychosocial approach. *Personality and Social Psychology Review*, 18(3), 256-279.

447. Poston, B. (2009). Maslow's hierarchy of needs. *The surgical technologist*, 41(8), 347-353.

448. Lucas, B. J., & Nordgren, L. F. (2020). The creative cliff illusion. *Proceedings of the National Academy of Sciences*, 117(33), 19830-19836.

449. Tonsing, K., Zimet, G. D., & Tse, S. (2012). Assessing social support among South Asians: The multidimensional scale of perceived social support. *Asian journal of psychiatry*, 5(2), 164-168.

450. Grant, A. M., & Parker, S. K. (2009). 7 redesigning work design theories: the rise of relational and proactive perspectives. The Academy of Management Annals, 3(1), 317-375.

451. Bruwer, B., Emsley, R., Kidd, M., Lochner, C., & Seedat, S. (2008). Psychometric properties of the Multidimensional Scale of Perceived Social Support in youth. *Comprehensive psychiatry*, 49(2), 195-201.

452. Jackson, B., Gucciardi, D. F., Lonsdale, C., Whipp, P. R., & Dimmock, J. A. (2014). "I think they believe in me": The predictive effects of teammate-and classmate-focused relation-inferred self-efficacy in sport and physical activity settings. *Journal of Sport and Exercise Psychology*, 36(5), 486-505.

453. Pitzer, J., & Skinner, E. (2017). Predictors of changes in students' motivational resilience over the school year: The roles of teacher support,

self-appraisals, and emotional reactivity. *International Journal of Behavioral Development,* 41(1), 15-29.

454. Fitzsimons, G. M., & Finkel, E. J. (2010). Interpersonal influences on self-regulation. *Current Directions in Psychological Science,* 19, 101-105.

455. Brunstein, J. C., Dangelmayer, G., & Schultheiss, O. C. (1996). Personal goals and social support in close relationships: Effects on relationship mood and marital satisfaction. *Journal of Personality and Social Psychology,* 71, 1006–1019.

456. Feeney, B. C., & Collins, N. L. (2014). A new look at social support: A theoretical perspective on thriving through relationships. Personality and Social Psychology Bulletin.

457. Oettingen, G. (2014). Rethinking positive thinking: Inside the new science of motivation. New York: Penguin Group.

458. Chartrand, T. L., Dalton, A., & Fitzsimons, G. J. (2007). Relationship reactance: When priming significant others triggers opposing goals. *Journal of Experimental Social Psychology,* 43, 719–726.

459. Gleason, M. E. J., Iida, M., Bolger, N., & Shrout, P. E. (2003). Daily supportive equity in close relationships. *Personality and Social Psychology Bulletin,* 29, 1036-1045

460. Tawwab, N. G. (2021). Set Boundaries, Find Peace: A Guide to Reclaiming Yourself. TarcherPerigee.

Caring Companionship

461. Kahn Jr, P. H., & Kellert, S. R. (Eds.). (2002). Children and nature: Psychological, sociocultural, and evolutionary investigations. MIT press.

462. Richerson, P., Baldini, R., Bell, A. V., Demps, K., Frost, K., Hillis, V., ... & Zefferman, M. (2016). Cultural group selection plays an essential role in explaining human cooperation: A sketch of the evidence. *Behavioral and Brain Sciences,* 39, e30.

463. Riedman, M. L. (1982). The evolution of alloparental care and adoption in mammals and birds. *The Quarterly review of biology,* 57(4), 405-435.

464. Page, A. E., Thomas, M. G., Smith, D., Dyble, M., Viguier, S., Chaudhary, N., ... & Migliano, A. B. (2019). Testing adaptive hypotheses of alloparenting in Agta foragers. *Nature human behaviour,* 3(11), 1154-1163.

465. Abraham, E., & Feldman, R. (2018). The neurobiology of human allomaternal care; implications for fathering, coparenting, and children's social development. *Physiology & behavior,* 193, 25-34.

466. Ahern, T. H., & Young, L. J. (2009). The impact of early life family structure on adult social attachment, alloparental behavior, and the neuropeptide

systems regulating affiliative behaviors in the monogamous prairie vole (Microtus ochrogaster). *Frontiers in behavioral neuroscience, 3,* 748.

467. Hrdy, S. B. (2011). Mothers and others: The evolutionary origins of mutual understanding. Harvard University Press.

468. Sear, R., & Mace, R. (2008). Who keeps children alive? A review of the effects of kin on child survival. *Evolution and Human Behavior, 29*(1), 1-18.

469. Clark, M. S., & Mils, J. (1993). The difference between communal and exchange relationships: What it is and is not. *Personality and social psychology bulletin, 19*(6), 684-691.

470. Clark, M. S., Fitness, J., & Brissette, I. (2001). Understanding people's perceptions of relationships is crucial to understanding their emotional lives. *Blackwell handbook of social psychology: Interpersonal processes, 2,* 253-278.

471. Sterelny, K. (2012). The evolved apprentice. MIT press.

472. Marlowe, F. W. (2005). Hunter-gatherers and human evolution. *Evolutionary Anthropology: Issues, News, and Reviews: Issues, News, and Reviews, 14*(2), 54-67.

473. History of Gift-Giving: From Cavemen to Gen Z. (2021, September 10). Dundle Magazine.

474. Wise, E. (2009). An" Odor of Sanctity": The Iconography, Magic, and Ritual of Egyptian Incense. *Studia Antiqua, 7*(1), 8.

475. Traunecker, C. (2001). The gods of Egypt. Cornell University Press.

476. Kyle, D. G. (1996). Gifts and Glory. Worshipping Athena: Panathenaia And Parthenon, 106.

477. Lapatin, K. (2015). Luxus: the sumptuous arts of Greece and Rome. Getty Publications.

478. Deubel, T. (2020). Gift-Giving as Social Capital: Changing Customs of Ṣaḥrāwi Women's Gift Exchange in Laayoune. *Hesperis Tamuda, 55,* 305-21.

479. Ruby, R. H., & Brown, J. A. (1981). Indians of the Pacific Northwest: A history (Vol. 158). University of Oklahoma Press.

480. Goldenweiser, A. (1940). Culture of the indian tribes of the Pacific Northwest. *Oregon Historical Quarterly, 41*(2), 137-146.

481. Lystra, K. (1992). Searching the heart: Women, men, and romantic love in nineteenth-century America. *Oxford University Press.*

482. Cherlin, A. J. (2010). The marriage-go-round: The state of marriage and the family in America today. *Vintage.*

483. Volsche, S. (2022) Introduction to Evolution & Human Behavior: Human Cooperation and Resource Sharing. Boise State University.

484. Lawler, E. J., Thye, S. R., & Yoon, J. (2009). *Social commitments in a depersonalized world. Russell Sage Foundation.*

485. John, N. A. (2013). The social logics of sharing. *The communication review*, 16(3), 113-131.

486. Pfaff, D. W. (2015). The altruistic brain: How we are naturally good. Oxford University Press, USA.

487. Dulewicz, V., & Higgs, M. (2000). Emotional intelligence–A review and evaluation study. *Journal of managerial Psychology*, 15(4), 341-372.

488. Bradberry, T., & Greaves, J. (2006). The emotional intelligence quick book: Everything you need to know to put your EQ to work. Simon and Schuster.

489. Munley, P. H. (1975). Erik Erikson's theory of Psychosocial Development and vocational behavior. *Journal of Counseling Psychology*, 22(4), 314.

490. Berman, J. Z., Barasch, A., Levine, E. E., & Small, D. A. (2018). Impediments to Effective Altruism: The Role of Subjective Preferences in Charitable Giving. *Psychological Science*, 29(5), 834.

491. Social Sci LibreTexts. (2021, June 18). Erik Erikson – Theory of Psychosocial Development.

492. Parincu, Z. (2023). Emotional Support: Definition, Examples, and Theories.

493. Positive Parenting. (2014, April 22). Sharing Responsibilities.

494. University of Missouri-Columbia. (2013, April 8). Marriages benefit when fathers share household, parenting responsibilities. ScienceDaily.

495. Eco Karen. (2023, September 28). The Role of Financial Security in Relationships.

496. Elle Blonde. (2023). 6 Important Reasons Financial Security In Relationships Affects Decisions & Expectations

497. GLASSCOCK, A. P. (2023). GIVING GIFTS AND MAKING FRIENDS. *Oxford Studies in Ancient Philosophy, Volume* 62, 22, 261.

498. Gottman, J. M., & Silver, N. (1999). The Seven Principles for Making Marriage Work. New York, NY: Crown Publishers.

499. Gottman, J. M., & Levenson, R. W. (2002). A two-factor model for predicting when a couple will divorce: Exploratory analyses using 14-year longitudinal data. Family Process, 41(1), 83-96.

500. Driver, J. L., & Gottman, J. M. (2004). Daily marital interactions and positive affect during marital conflict among newlywed couples. Family Process, 43(3), 301-314.

501. Perel, E., & Miller, M. A. (2023). When Transitioning Between Stages of a Relationship, Practice Adaptability. Esther Perel's Blog.

502. Roggero, V. (2023). The Role Of Flexibility In Healthy Relationships.

503. Cochran, M., & Walker, S. K. (2006). Parenting and personal social networks. In Parenting (pp. 251-290). Routledge.

504. Komter, A., & Vollebergh, W. (1997). Gift Giving and the Emotional Significance of Family and Friends. *Journal of Marriage and Family*, 59(3), 747–757. https://doi.org/10.2307/353958

Empathetic Conversation

505. Tomasello, M. (2010). Origins of human communication. MIT press.

506. Tomasello, M., Carpenter, M., Call, J., Behne, T., & Moll, H. (2005). Understanding and sharing intentions: The origins of cultural cognition. *Behavioral and brain sciences,* 28(5), 675-691.

507. Fuentes, A. (2017). The creative spark: How imagination made humans exceptional. Penguin.

508. Chilton, P. A., & Kopytowska, M. W. (Eds.). (2018). Religion, language, and the human mind. Oxford University Press.

509. Hubbard, B. M. (2015). Conscious evolution: Awakening the power of our social potential. New World Library.

510. Howe, D. (2012). Empathy: What it is and why it matters. Bloomsbury Publishing.

511. Friederici, A. D. (2017). Language in our brain: The origins of a uniquely human capacity. MIT Press.

512. Kemmerer, D. (2022). Cognitive neuroscience of language. Routledge.

513. Di Cesare, G., Marchi, M., Errante, A., Fasano, F., & Rizzolatti, G. (2018). Mirroring the social aspects of speech and actions: the role of the insula. *Cerebral Cortex,* 28(4), 1348-1357.

514. Tomasello, M. (2009). Why we cooperate. MIT press.

515. Grinde, B. (2009). An evolutionary perspective on the importance of community relations for quality of life. *TheScientificWorldJOURNAL,* 9, 588-605.

516. Partanen, E., Kujala, T., Näätänen, R., Liitola, A., Sambeth, A., & Huotilainen, M. (2013). Learning-induced neural plasticity of speech processing

before birth. *Proceedings of the National Academy of Sciences*, 110(37), 15145-15150.

517. Brazelton, T. B. (2013). Learning to listen: A life caring for children. Da Capo Press.

518. Grusec, J. E. (1994). Social Learning Theory and developmental psychology: The legacies of Robert R. Sears and Albert Bandura.

519. Bandura, A. (1969). Social-learning theory of identificatory processes. *Handbook of socialization theory and research*, 213, 262.

520. Groeschel, S., Vollmer, B., King, M. D., & Connelly, A. (2010). Developmental changes in cerebral grey and white matter volume from infancy to adulthood. *International Journal of Developmental Neuroscience*, 28(6), 481-489.

521. Mills, K. L., Goddings, A. L., Clasen, L. S., Giedd, J. N., & Blakemore, S. J. (2014). The developmental mismatch in structural brain maturation during adolescence. Developmental Neuroscience, 36(3-4), 147-160.

522. Hoff, E. (2006). How social contexts support and shape language development. Developmental Review, 26(1), 55-88.

523. McFarland, D. H. (2001). Respiratory markers of conversational interaction. Journal of Speech, Language, and Hearing Research, 44(1), 128–143.

524. Kret, M. E. (2015). Pupil-mimicry conditions trust in partners: Moderation by oxytocin and group membership. Proceedings of the Royal Society B: Biological Sciences, 282(1801), 20142213.

525. Hasson, U., Ghazanfar, A. A., Galantucci, B., Garrod, S., & Keysers, C. (2012). Brain-to-brain coupling: a mechanism for creating and sharing a social world. Trends in Cognitive Sciences, 16(2), 114-121.

526. Hoemann, K., Gendron, M., & Barrett, L. F. (2018). Emotion words, emotion concepts, and emotional development in children: A constructionist hypothesis. *Developmental Psychology*, 54(9), 1834-1849.

527. Zaki, J., & Ochsner, K. (2012). The neuroscience of empathy: progress, pitfalls and promise. *Nature Neuroscience*, 15(5), 675-680.

528. Barker, E. T., & Christensen, J. P. (2013). Homer: A Beginner's Guide. Simon and Schuster.

529. Kahler, E. (2017). The inward turn of narrative (Vol. 211). Princeton University Press.

530. M'Baye, B. (2010). The Trickster Comes West: Pan-African Influence in Early Black Diasporan Narratives. Univ. Press of Mississippi.

531. Novia, L., & Vidya, A. The Art of Intercultural Communication: Tips and Techniques for Bridging the Gap. Ananta Vidya.

532. Schütte, H., & Ciarlante, D. (2016). Consumer behaviour in Asia. Springer.

533. Debes, R. (2015). From einfühlung to empathy. *Sympathy: A history*, 286-322.

534. Lanzoni, S. (2018). Empathy: A history. Yale University Press.

535. Staemmler, F. M. (2012). Empathy in psychotherapy: How therapists and clients understand each other. Springer Publishing Company.

536. Sharma, A., Lin, I. W., Miner, A. S., Atkins, D. C., & Althoff, T. (2023). Human–AI collaboration enables more empathic conversations in text-based peer-to-peer mental health support. *Nature Machine Intelligence*, 5(1), 46-57.

537. Luxton, D. D. (2014). Recommendations for the ethical use and design of artificial intelligent care providers. *Artificial intelligence in medicine*, 62(1), 1-10.

538. Seligman, M. E. (2002). Authentic happiness: Using the new positive psychology to realize your potential for lasting fulfillment. Simon and Schuster.

539. Seligman, M. E. (2012). Positive psychology in practice. John Wiley & Sons.

540. Campeau, N. (2019). Boost your Heart Energy: Experience Increased Energy by Harnessing the Power of your Heart (Vol. 2). Rebiere.

541. Banks, A., & Hirschman, L. A. (2015). Four ways to click: Rewire your brain for stronger, more rewarding relationships. Penguin.

542. Decety, J., & Fotopoulou, A. (2015). Why empathy has a beneficial impact on others in medicine: unifying theories. *Frontiers in behavioral neuroscience*, 8, 457.

543. Taylor, S. E. (2006). Tend and befriend: Biobehavioral bases of affiliation under stress. *Current directions in psychological science*, 15(6), 273-277.

544. Gottman, J. M. (2013). Marital interaction: Experimental investigations. Elsevier.

545. Gottman, J. M., Murray, J. D., Swanson, C. C., Tyson, R., & Swanson, K. R. (2005). The mathematics of marriage: Dynamic nonlinear models. mit press.

546. Miller, G. E., Cohen, S., & Ritchey, A. K. (2002). Chronic psychological stress and the regulation of pro-inflammatory cytokines: a glucocorticoid-resistance model. Health psychology, 21(6), 531.

547. Upthegrove, R., Manzanares-Teson, N., & Barnes, N. M. (2014). Cytokine function in medication-naive first episode psychosis: a systematic review and meta-analysis. *Schizophrenia research*, 155(1-3), 101-108.

548. Shonkoff, J. P., Garner, A. S., Committee on Psychosocial Aspects of Child and Family Health, Committee on Early Childhood, Adoption, and Dependent Care, and Section on Developmental and Behavioral Pediatrics, Siegel, B. S., Dobbins, M. I., Earls, M. F., ... & Wood, D. L. (2012). The lifelong effects of early childhood adversity and toxic stress. *Pediatrics*, 129(1), e232-e246.

549. Karatsoreos, I. N., & McEwen, B. S. (2013). Annual research review: The neurobiology and physiology of resilience and adaptation across the life course. Journal of Child Psychology and Psychiatry, 54(4), 337-347.

550. Xu, X., Zhang, Y., Li, S., Liu, Q., & Yang, N. (2020). Effects of Patients' Perceptions of Physician-Patient Relational Empathy on an Inflammation Marker in Patients with Crohn's Disease: The Intermediary Roles of Anxiety, Self-Efficacy, and Sleep Quality. Psychotherapy Research and Behavioral Management, 13, 141-150.

551. Petruso, F., Giff, A. E., Milano, B. A., De Rossi, M. M., & Saccaro, L. F. (2023). Inflammation and emotion regulation: a narrative review of evidence and mechanisms in emotion dysregulation disorders. *Neuronal Signal*, 7(4), NS20220077.

552. Segerstrom, S. C., & Miller, G. E. (2004). Psychological stress and the human immune system: A meta-analytic study of 30 years of inquiry. Psychological Bulletin, 130(4), 601-630.

553. Chapman, B. P., Fiscella, K., Kawachi, I., Duberstein, P. R., & Muennig, P. (2013). Emotion suppression and mortality risk over a 12-year follow-up. *Journal of Psychosomatic Research*, 75(4), 381-385.

554. Tabert, M. H., Borod, J. C., Tang, C. Y., Lange, G., Wei, T. C., Johnson, R., ... & Buchsbaum, M. S. (2001). Differential amygdala activation during emotional decision and recognition memory tasks using unpleasant words: an fMRI study. *Neuropsychologia*, 39(6), 556-573.

555. Davidson, R. J. (2004). Well–being and affective style: neural substrates and biobehavioural correlates. Philosophical Transactions of the Royal Society of London. *Series B: Biological Sciences*, 359(1449), 1395-1411.

556. Ruff, C. C., & Fehr, E. (2014). The neurobiology of rewards and values in social decision making. *Nature Reviews Neuroscience*, 15(8), 549-562.

557. Fehr, E., & Camerer, C. F. (2007). Social neuroeconomics: the neural circuitry of social preferences. *Trends in cognitive sciences*, 11(10), 419-427.

558. Blood, A. J., Iosifescu, D. V., Makris, N., Perlis, R. H., Kennedy, D. N., Dougherty, D. D., ... & Phenotype Genotype Project on Addiction and Mood Disorders. (2010). Microstructural abnormalities in subcortical reward circuitry of subjects with major depressive disorder. *PloS one*, 5(11), e13945.

559. Cramer, D., & Jowett, S. (2010). Perceived empathy, accurate empathy and relationship satisfaction in heterosexual couples. Journal of Social and Personal Relationships, 27, 327–349.

560. Feshbach, N. D., & Feshbach, S. (2009). Empathy and education. In J. Decety & W. Ickes (Eds.), The social neuroscience of empathy (pp. 85-97). MIT Press.

561. Mirivel, J. C. (2021). The Art of Positive Communication: Theory and Practice. Oxford University Press.

562. Ulmer, R. R. (2017). Effective Crisis Communication: Moving from Crisis to Opportunity. SAGE Publications

563. Pexman, P., Reggin, L., & Lee, K. (2019). Addressing the challenge of verbal irony: Getting serious about sarcasm training. *Languages,* 4(2), 23.

564. Vicente, A., & Falkum, I. L. (2023). Accounting for the preference for literal meanings in autism spectrum conditions. *Mind & Language*, 38(1), 119-140.

565. Kreisman, J. J., & Straus, H. (2021). I Hate You--Don't Leave Me:: Understanding the Borderline Personality. Penguin.

566. Bateman, A. W., & Krawitz, R. (2013). Borderline personality disorder: An evidence-based guide for generalist mental health professionals. Oxford University Press, USA.

567. Martinez, R. (2021, May 31). Avoiding assumptions = improved communication! Heredia Therapy Group.

568. McClure, K. (2023). ADHD and communication: 10 essential tips for success.

569. Lobel D. (2022). How to communicate with a loved one with BPD.

570. BrainLine. (2012). Tips for communicating with people with TBI and PTSD

571. Orloff, J. (2019). The Importance of Self-Care for Sensitive People.

572. Bailey, J. (2023). Balancing Empathy and Self-Care.

573. Stanton, A. L., & Low, C. A. (2012). Expressing emotions in stressful contexts: Benefits, moderators, and mechanisms. Current directions in psychological science, 21(2), 124-128.

574. Robinson, L., Segal, J., Ph.D., & Smith, M. (2023). Effective Communication

575. Pink. (2018). When: The Scientific Secrets of Perfect Timing. Riverhead Books. "Experiencing and Expressing Emotion." University of Illinois Counseling Center.

Reinventing Dating and Friendship Apps

576. Finkel, E. J., Eastwick, P. W., & Karney, B. R. (2012). Online Dating: A Critical Analysis From the Perspective of Psychological Science. Psychological Science in the Public Interest, 13(1), 3-66.

577. Lang, C. (2016). Platform Gratifications: Tinder vs. Match. com. West Virginia University.

578. Miller, D. (2011). Tales from facebook. Polity.

579. Rosenfeld, M. J., & Thomas, R. J. (2012). Searching for a Mate: The Rise of the Internet as a Social Intermediary. *American Sociological Review*, 7

580. Anderson, M., Vogels, E. A., & Turner, E. (2020). The Virtues and Downsides of Online Dating. Pew Research Center.

581. Gatter, K., & Hodkinson, K. (2016). On the Differences Between Tinder Versus Online Dating Agencies: Questioning a Myth. An Exploratory Study.

582. Schwartz, B. (2004). The paradox of choice: Why more is less. New York.

583. Hoffman, R. (2018). Dating and Mating in a Techno-Driven World: Understanding How Technology Is Helping and Hurting Relationships. Bloomsbury Publishing USA.

584. Brown, A. (2020). Nearly half of US adults say dating has gotten harder for most people in the last 10 years. Washington, DC: Pew Research Center.

585. Johnson, K., Vilceanu, M. O., & Pontes, M. C. (2017). Use of online dating websites and dating apps: Findings and implications for LGB populations. Journal of Marketing Development and Competitiveness, 11(3), 60-66.

586. Gama Filho, J., & Hopkins, M. (2018). Filling the Void: Investigating the Impact of The Digital Society on Generation Z's Relationships.

587. Pronk, T. M., & Denissen, J. J. (2020). A rejection mind-set: Choice overload in online dating. *Social Psychological and Personality Science*, 11(3), 388-396.

588. Pessoa, L., Thompson, E., & Noë, A. (1998). Finding out about filling-in: A guide to perceptual completion for visual science and the philosophy of perception. *Behavioral and brain sciences,* 21(6), 723-748.

589. Phenomenology, G., Wertheimer, Ψ. M., Köhler, W., Koffka, K., Lewin, K., Perls, F. F., & Perls, L. (2022). 15 Gestalt Psychology. History and Systems of Psychology, 301.

590. Todorovic, D. (2008). Gestalt Principles. *Scholarpedia*, 3(12), 5345.

591. Churchland, P. S., & Sejnowski, T. J. (1992). The computational brain. MIT press.

592. Ramachandran, V. S., & Gregory, R. L. (1991). Perceptual filling in of artificially induced scotomas in human vision. *Nature,* 350(6320), 699-702.

593. Friston, K., & Kiebel, S. (2009). Predictive Coding under the free-energy principle. Philosophical transactions of the Royal Society B: Biological sciences, 364(1521), 1211-1221.

594. Kilner, J. M., Friston, K. J., & Frith, C. D. (2007). Predictive Coding: an account of the mirror neuron system. *Cognitive processing,* 8, 159-166.

595. Binstock, R. H., George, L. K., Cutler, S. J., Hendricks, J., & Schulz, J. H. (Eds.). (2011). Handbook of aging and the social sciences. Elsevier.

596. Bahemia, N. To swipe or not to swipe: the decision-making process behind online dating.

597. Williams, A. (2024). Not My Type: Automating Sexual Racism in Online Dating. Stanford University Press.

598. Braziel, S. (2015). Why Swipe Right? An ethnographic exploration of how college students use Tinder.

599. Mendes Morais Rodrigues Carvalho, J. C. (2022). Relating Dating Platforms and Social Anxiety.

600. Cummings, K. (2011). Nonverbal communication and first impressions (Doctoral dissertation, Kent State University).

601. Thomson, A. (2015) Psychology: First Impressions. Princeton Alumni.

602. Willis, J., & Todorov, A. (2006). First Impressions: Making Up Your Mind After a 100-Ms Exposure to a Face. *Psychological Science,* 17(7), 592-598.

603. Lawrence, C. R. (1987). The id, the ego, and equal protection: Reckoning with unconscious racism. *Stanford Law Review*, 317-388.

604. Gale, E. Swiping Left on Empathy: Gamification and Commodification of the (Inter) face. Ethics in Design and Communication, 28.

605. Howard, A., & Borenstein, J. (2018). The ugly truth about ourselves and our robot creations: the problem of bias and social inequity. Science and engineering ethics, 24, 1521-1536.

606. Rovnak, M. (2023). Strategies to identify and mitigate unconscious biases in algorithmic hiring/Author Matus Rovnak.

607. Flowers, J. C. (2019). Rethinking algorithmic bias through phenomenology and pragmatism. Computer ethics-philosophical enquiry (CEPE) proceedings, 2019(1), 14.

608. Buolamwini, J. A. (2017). Gender shades: intersectional phenotypic and demographic evaluation of face datasets and gender classifiers (Doctoral dissertation, Massachusetts Institute of Technology).

609. Manyika, J., Silberg, J., & Presten, B. (2019). What Do We Do About the Biases in AI. Harvard Business Review.

610. D'ignazio, C., & Klein, L. F. (2023). Data feminism. MIT press.

611. Hassenzahl, M., Heidecker, S., Eckoldt, K., Diefenbach, S., & Hillmann, U. (2012). All you need is love: Current strategies of mediating intimate relationships through technology. ACM Transactions on Computer-Human Interaction (TOCHI), 19(4), 1-19.

612. Guerrero, L. K., Andersen, P. A., & Afifi, W. A. (2017). Close encounters: Communication in relationships. Sage Publications.

613. Baumer, S. (2013). Social media, human connectivity and psychological well-being. The Sage Handbook of Digital Technology Research, London, 71-87.

614. Twenge, J. M., Martin, G. N., & Campbell, W. K. (2018). Decreases in psychological well-being among American adolescents after 2012 and links to screen time during the rise of smartphone technology. *Emotion,* 18(6), 765.

615. Twenge, J. M., & Campbell, W. K. (2003). "Isn't it fun to get the respect that we're going to deserve?" Narcissism, social rejection, and aggression. Personality and Social Psychology Bulletin, 29(2), 261-272.

616. Cigna, U. S. (2018). Loneliness Index. New Cigna Study Reveals Loneliness at Epidemic Levels in America.'May, 1.

617. Smith, M. L., Chen, E., Lau, C. A., Davis, D., Simmons, J. W., & Merianos, A. L. (2023). Effectiveness of chronic disease self-management education (CDSME) programs to reduce loneliness. *Chronic Illness,* 19(3), 646-664.

618. Ueda, P., Mercer, C. H., Ghaznavi, C., & Herbenick, D. (2020). Trends in frequency of sexual activity and number of sexual partners among adults aged 18 to 44 years in the US, 2000-2018. JAMA network open, 3(6), e203833-e203833.

619. Bozon, M., & Kontula, O. (2022). Sexual initiation and gender in Europe: A cross-cultural analysis of trends in the twentieth century. In Sexual behaviour and HIV/AIDS in Europe (pp. 37-67). Routledge.

620. Stolte, A. (2023). The Structural and Social Determinants of Intergenerational Health Inequities: How State Policy Contexts and Discrimination Shape Birth Outcomes (Doctoral dissertation, Duke University).

621. National Center for Health Statistics. (2023). Births: Final data for 2022. National Vital Statistics Reports, 72(1). Hyattsville, MD: National Center for Health Statistics.

622. McMurtry, A. (2022, June 15). Births in Spain drop to lowest level on record.

623. Wordlometer. (2023). Population Trends

624. Reuters. (2023, October 26). Births in Italy heading for new record low in 2023 - stats office.

625. Kovacs, B., Caplan, N., Grob, S., & King, M. (2021). Social networks and loneliness during the COVID-19 pandemic. *Socius*, 7, 2378023120985254.

626. Holt-Lunstad, J. (2022). Social connection as a public health issue: The evidence and a systemic framework for prioritizing the "social" in social determinants of health. *Annual Review of Public Health*, 43, 193-213.

627. Jeste, D. V., Lee, E. E., & Cacioppo, S. (2020). Battling the modern behavioral epidemic of loneliness: suggestions for research and interventions. *JAMA psychiatry*, 77(6), 553-554.

628. Androutsopoulos, J. (2021). Polymedia in interaction. Pragmatics and Society, 12(5), 707-724.

629. Częstochowska, J., Gligorić, K., Peyrard, M., Mentha, Y., Bień, M., Grütter, A., ... & West, R. (2022, May). On the context-free ambiguity of emoji. In Proceedings of the International AAAI Conference on Web and Social Media (Vol. 16, pp. 1388-1392).

630. Cruz-Moya, O., & Sánchez-Moya, A. (2021). A discursive examination of the use of emoji in WhatsApp groups: a cross-generational study. A discursive examination of the use of emoji in WhatsApp groups: a cross-generational study, 45-65.

631. Franco, C. L., & Fugate, J. M. (2020). Emoji face renderings: Exploring the role emoji platform differences have on emotional interpretation. *Journal of Nonverbal Behavior*, 44(2), 301-328.

632. Dainas, A. R., & Herring, S. C. (2021). Interpreting emoji pragmatics. Approaches to internet pragmatics: Theory and practice, 107-144.

633. Lieberman, A., & Schroeder, J. (2020). Two social lives: How differences between online and offline interaction influence social outcomes. Current opinion in psychology, 31, 16-21.

634. Osler, L. (2024). Taking empathy online. Inquiry, 67(1), 302-329.

635. Pancani, L., Aureli, N., & Riva, P. (2022). Relationship dissolution strategies: Comparing the psychological consequences of ghosting, orbiting, and rejection. Cyberpsychology: *Journal of Psychosocial Research on Cyberspace*, 16(2).

636. Mahdavifar, S. (2020). The relationship between rejection sensitivity of online dating app users' mental well-being and self-esteem (Bachelor's thesis, University of Twente).

637. Gionet, A. (2023) How Many Swipes Does It Take to Find a Significant Other?

638. Harper, B. (2024) Tinder Statistics in 2024

639. Lenton-Brym, A. P., Santiago, V. A., Fredborg, B. K., & Antony, M. M. (2021). Associations between social anxiety, depression, and use of mobile dating applications. *Cyberpsychology, Behavior, and Social Networking*, 24(2), 86-93.

640. Pitcho-Prelorentzos, S., Heckel, C., & Ring, L. (2020). Predictors of social anxiety among online dating users. *Computers in Human Behavior*, 110, 106381.

641. Goodman, E. (2020) Your Anxiety Beast and You: A Compassionate Guide to Living in an Increasingly Anxious World

642. D'Cost, K. (2014) Catfishing: The Truth About Deception Online.

643. Stouffer, C. (2024). Romance scams in 2024: What you need to know + online dating scam statistics

644. FBI (2019) 2019 Internet Crime Report Released

645. Reinicke, C. (2022) Online daters lost a record $547 million to scams in 2021. How to stay safe, according to Nev Schulman from MTV's 'Catfish'

646. Beldo, S. (2016) What percentage of online dating profiles are fake?

647. Castillo, L. (2023). Fake Online Dating Profiles Statistics [Fresh Research]

648. O'Driscoll, A. (2023) 15+ dating and romance scam statistics – singles beware!

649. Stathis, J. (2022). What Is Catfishing? 7 Signs to Watch Out For

650. Koebert, J. (2023). Catfish Capitals: These Are the Places You're Most Likely To Fall Victim to a Catfishing Scam

651. The Federal Trade Commission (2023). Romance scammers' favorite lies exposed

652. Boxall, H., Napier, S., Teunissen, C., & Brown, R. (2022). The sexual exploitation of Australian children on dating apps and websites. Trends and Issues in Crime and Criminal Justice [electronic resource], (658), 1-14.

653. Hatchel, T., Torgal, C., El Sheikh, A. J., Robinson, L. E., Valido, A., & Espelage, D. L. (2021). LGBTQ youth and digital media: Online risks. In Child and Adolescent Online Risk Exposure (pp. 303-325). Academic Press.

654. Marciano, A., & Antebi-Gruszka, N. (2022). Offline and online discrimination and mental distress among lesbian, gay, and bisexual individuals:

the moderating effect of LGBTQ facebook use. Media Psychology, 25(1), 27-50.

655. Godbout-Kinney, K. (2020). AI and sex robots: an examination of the technologization of sexuality.

656. Gawdat, M. (2021). Scary smart: the future of Artificial Intelligence and how you can save our world. Pan Macmillan.

657. Suleyman, M. (2023). The coming wave: technology, power, and the twenty-first century's greatest dilemma. Crown.

Made in the USA
Columbia, SC
28 July 2024

a4313954-dfd9-4d48-b63d-c79fd05c5c29R01